Richard and Bookey Peek are professional safari guides. After an idyllic childhood in the Bvumba Mountains and 10 years spent travelling the world, Bookey became a lawyer, a profession she was only too happy to leave for a life in the bush. She was a winner of the prestigious Africa Geographic Travel Writer of the Year competition in 2003. Her other books include *All the Way Home: Stories from an African Wildlife Sanctuary* and *Wild Honey*.

Richard Peek was born in Zimbabwe and raised on a farm in Mashonaland. He spent 14 years in the Department of National Parks and Wildlife Management as a game ranger and then as an ecologist, after obtaining a degree in zoology. He later became curator of mammals at the National Museum of Natural History. Winner of two Agfa photographic awards, Richard has published his work in magazines, calendars, travel brochures and major publications such as the *Handbook of Birds of the World* and the more recently published *Handbook of Mammals of the World*. His documentary, *Honey Badger: Raising Hell*, has been distributed internationally by National Geographic Television

Beyond the Wild Wood

Bookey Peek
with Richard Peek

First published in the United Kingdom in 2011 by Max Press,
Little Books Ltd, 73 Campden Hill Towers, 112 Notting Hill Gate,
London W11 3QP.

ISBN: 9781906251482

Printed and bound by CPI Group (UK) Ltd, Croydon, CR0 4YY

For our brood –
Nicki, Nige and David, with all our love

'And beyond the wild wood again?' Mole asked. 'Where it's all blue and dim, and you can see what may be the hills or the smoke of towns, or just clouds?'

'Beyond the wild wood comes the wide world,' said the Rat. 'And that's something that doesn't matter to you or me. I've never been there and I'm never going, nor you either, if you've got any sense at all!'

The Wind in the Willows – Kenneth Grahame

Contents

Chapter One – Waiting For Abigail

If my doctor had a dollar for every time he'd prescribed Prozac since the year 2000, he'd be living on the Côte d'Azur. At least that's what he tells me – and he's on the stuff himself.

But that's life in Zimbabwe: the uncertainty and sheer craziness of it all drives you to drink, drugs or plain despair, depending on your economic status. And it explains why I was standing in a small dark shop in Johannesburg in January 2007, waiting for Abigail.

'Sorry, she's running a bit late,' said the girl behind the counter. A massive power failure had put most of the city, including the traffic lights, out of commission, and there was chaos on the roads.

'That's all right,' I told her. 'I'm used to it; it makes me feel at home.'

Dreamy New Age music played as I wandered around the shop in the candlelight, trying not to bump into tightly packed glass shelves, on which dozens of statues of Jesus and Mary rubbed shoulders with Hindu deities and tubby, smiling figurines of Buddha. I ducked around the sparkling strings of crystals hanging from the ceiling, and ended up at the book section where I found one called *Communicating with Animals*. It looked rather promising.

Ten minutes later, a loud tinkling of wind chimes at the door announced the hurried arrival of an attractive girl in her mid-thirties, wearing black pants and a floral blouse. She looked like my son David's kindergarten teacher: a husband in finance, perhaps, two kids, a Labrador and a swimming pool in the backyard. That sort of thing. Definitely not someone versed in the Dark Arts who was about to look into my soul, as my old school friend Lee likes to put it.

I've always laughed at Lee's fondness for fortune-tellers; I didn't think devout Catholics were supposed to dabble in the supernatural, but she'd told me astonishing stories about Abigail's abilities and that's why I was here – searching for an answer to the one question that had haunted us for months.

Abigail apologised for her lateness and led me to a small room at the back of the shop, where a joss stick sent up a curling ribbon of smoke, filling the air with the scent of lemon grass. She closed the door and we sat, facing each other across a wooden table, with a candle flickering between us. She held a pack of tarot cards, and gave me a blank foolscap pad and a pen so that I could make notes. I was glad of the

2

dark because I'd taken a lot of trouble with my disguise: a long-sleeved shirt covered the scars inflicted by our honey badger at play. I kept my hands under the table to hide the dirt under my nails, which never quite disappears, no matter how much I scrub. Lipstick, mascara, earrings – I reckoned I looked like any other Johannesburg lady on the wrong side of 50. As long as I didn't smile too much and crease up my eyes with what I like to call laughter lines (but what are more to do with years of exposure to the sun).

Two people were carrying on a loud conversation in the hairdressing salon on the other side of the wall. It was annoying and it spoiled the atmosphere, but at least they were not listening to us.

Abigail began to shuffle her cards. I unclenched my hands and spread my fingers on my lap, consciously trying to relax so communication could flow freely between us.

'I see a bed,' she said, looking up at me, 'and a feeling of powerlessness.'

Which was the perfect description of the absolute inertia that had affected me all through the Christmas holidays: dealing with two losses, and a new level of uncertainty. Some drink, some smoke to forget their troubles. I just go to sleep.

'But you always manage to put on a happy face for your son, your only child. You worry about him, but you don't have to. He's a level-headed boy and he's going to do well for himself when he grows up. Abigail picked up a card. 'For some reason, though, he seems to travel at lot.'

She looked puzzled and I decided to move things along.

'That's right, he's at boarding school.'

Abigail smiled. 'So's my son. But this school isn't in a town. I'm seeing a road leading into the mountains and lots of trees. And some old buildings.'

3

My fingers began to tingle. David's school was in the lower Drakensberg range: an area of montane forest and vast plantations of exotic trees. The office buildings were all that remained of an old hotel, the first one to be built on the mountain.

Abigail went on to talk about my father's death a couple of months before, and she described his difficulties in breathing, the pain through his whole body.

'He's with you,' she said. 'And you'll know when he's close. You'll have a feeling of calmness, even though he may not have been a very calm person in life.'

Oh yes. Dad, aged 65, planting a punch on the jaw of a brawling young soldier who had refused to leave the bar at the Park Lane Hotel in Harare. He broke his hand, but said it was worth it.

'You live amongst a lot of buildings, some quite high. I keep seeing a kitchen. And clutter, lots of clutter.'

Good God, now this was getting a bit personal. If she meant the office, well, that was mostly my husband, Rich's fault: the stacks of black tin trunks full of his slides; the camera equipment, wires and gadgets, ancient and modern; the dusty boxes and the piles of paper. Or had she seen the tablecloth in the dining room smeared with marmalade from the squirrel's breakfast, or the mysterious soup ladle without a handle which has been lying next to the defunct telephone for the last couple of years – close to the skull of the young leopard killed by an adult male in the Pundamuka Valley? Let's hope she couldn't see inside our pantry or our deep freeze, with its sausages, cheese and frozen puff adders.

The question was out before I could stop myself. 'How does your family feel about living with a psychic? Doesn't it make life a bit uncomfortable for them?'

'Oh, I don't do it at home,' said Abigail, but I didn't quite believe her.

The mere possibility of detection would quash any chance of her husband having an affair with his secretary, and what hope for her kids, pretending to have done their homework?

'There's that kitchen again,' said Abigail, bringing me back to the present. 'I think you must work from home.'

No problem there. The kitchen and the buildings around it are part of our safari lodge in the Matobo Hills, once popular with foreign tourists until the land invasions that began in 2000 frightened them away. Since then the lodge has been empty – to the considerable relief of my antisocial family.

Warm and getting warmer, but just how far could Abigail go?

'Birds!' she exclaimed. 'Why do they keep coming up? It's like that bird sanctuary at Dullstroom. Do you know it?'

I didn't.

She closed her eyes. 'And a beautiful view, plenty of trees and grass. And hills, lots of hills!'

I shouldn't have wasted my time with the long-sleeved shirt and the earrings. Abigail was looking far beyond my physical presence and right into my mind, just as Lee had told me she would. Otherwise, how could she know about the tumbling hills of stone that surround us? Did the cards tell her how lovely it is in winter with its tawny grasses and leaves of russet and gold, when the bare rocks rise up against cloudless blue skies; or how it is in the summer rains, run through with streams and rocky pools and filled with dancing shadows and secret places? We'd been away for three days, and I was already feeling homesick.

'That's Stone Hills, our wildlife sanctuary!' I blurted out.

'That land, and the animals on it are your passion,' said

5

Abigail, as if she hadn't heard me.

She was silent for a moment, shuffling the cards. Then she looked up and straight at me.

'That's what worries you. The fear that you might lose your land.'

I stared back at her. A woman I'd never met, who hadn't been told my name or a single thing about me, somehow knew exactly what was burning a hole in my head.

Farm invasions had begun in 2000, but we'd been living with the threat of eviction ever since the Land Acquisition Act had been passed soon after we bought Stone Hills 13 years before. First to go were the richly productive farms up north, in Mashonaland – producing tobacco, flowers for export, and wheat – in an orgy of violence, murder and looting. Then the madness spread throughout the country. Confined to their houses by militant war veterans ('wovvets'), some farmers managed to stick it out for a while, but they had to sit back and watch their crops die, to be replaced by thatched huts and patches of tattered mealies.

Months became years, and the invasions continued, till only a handful of farms were left untouched. Stone Hills had been one of them, and although many cattle farmers in our district had lost some land, they, too, were still in their homes – lying low, desperate for anonymity.

But the threats never let up, and just before Christmas every year, as predictably as the arrival of a sweating Santa and the jolly strains of 'Jingle Bells' in the Meikles department store in Bulawayo, there would be an announcement that *all* white farmers were to be evicted by a certain date. It didn't happen.

Then, on the 19th of May 2006, a notice appeared in the newspaper, which came to the attention of a friend as he sat in his office having morning tea. Stone Hills, along with a number of other farms, had been nationalised, but that was the only notification we were ever to receive. Soon afterwards, farmers were given yet another ultimatum: stop operations by a certain date and leave the land 90 days thereafter, or face the consequences – a fine or two years imprisonment. Although some farmers were forcibly evicted, the rest of us just carried on, doggedly, heads down, like pack donkeys that have been beaten so often they no longer feel the whip.

For years, Zimbabweans have had a touching belief that a responsible body we called 'the Rest of the World' would come to our rescue. Only recently has the realisation hit home that there is no such entity nor has there ever been – only individual countries preoccupied with their own problems, to which Zimbabwe is no more than an insignificant irritation. And the media follows the exploits of our megalomaniac leaders in the same way as they write about the excesses of celebrities like Paris Hilton – it makes good copy.

Seven bulging files marked 'Land' are piled up inside our safe. I know I should organise them properly but I haven't got the energy. And anyway, what difference would it make? Endless documents, hundreds of letters to supposedly influential people – they all basically say the same thing. We are not a farm, we are a tourist facility and a wildlife rehabilitation and research centre. Both tourism and wildlife are crucial to Zimbabwe's economy. If we are forced to vacate, both the property and the animals will be destroyed, just as they have been all over the country. Phone calls, letters, trips to Harare, meetings – they've all been a waste of time, money and paper.

'We've got a few more minutes,' said Abigail softly. 'Do you have any questions for me?'

Only one, and I had a feeling that she could answer it.

'Are we going to lose Stone Hills?'

She flicked slowly through her cards, and shook her head.

'No, I don't see immediate loss, but to keep the land, you're going to have to outwit these people. Play them at their own game. Look, one day you will have to leave, the pressure will be too great, but not now.'

That was good enough for me. Stone Hills had a stay of execution, maybe even a reprieve. One day didn't mean tomorrow. It could be in 10 or 20 years' time – provided we kept our wits about us. I bought the book on communicating with animals and danced out of that door into the dazzling neon lights of the shopping centre. Johannesburg was back in business, and so were we.

Chapter Two – A Pesky Varmint

As usual, Badger is bothering something down a hole, I wrote in my diary. Suddenly, a head appears and out comes 15 foot of python – a lot more than he expected. He scuttles backwards, seeking refuge between Rich's legs. Rich also goes into reverse but he keeps filming – it's the biggest snake he has ever seen, with a girth as thick as his thigh. It stops, head raised, and Badger immediately approaches, cautiously at first, but then more and more confidently when it doesn't react. Our cub's head is far smaller than his opponent's, but he's eyeballing it, cocky as a bantamweight boxer.

'*Badger!*' *Rich whispers urgently, terrified for him, but not wanting to break his concentration. Naturally, Badge ignores him.*

He takes a sniff at the python's tail in preparation for his first bite of a substantial breakfast. And the snake begins to hiss. Not in the way of a bicycle puncture, or even a Toyota tyre, but a slow, blood-chilling whoo-oosh-sh! like the pressure release of a steam train. It goes on for minutes before the snake stops and drags in its breath with another interminable hiss.

After his initial surprise, Badger refuses to be intimidated. The python's head is higher than his and he stretches up to it, his nose no more than 50 centimetres away. Badge has come a very long way since we adopted him as a helpless cub, but it looks as though, this time, he's issuing the last challenge of his short life ...

People used to envy the serenity of our lives. 'Stone Hills is special,' wrote one enraptured guest. 'It has the most rare and precious commodity of all: a near magical sense of peace and stillness.'

The best way to experience this is simply to wander amongst the hills – something I do every evening, and an event that used to be preceded by a few minutes of pleasurable contemplation. Should I climb a koppie or stroll about in the trees on the other side of the river? The Egyptian geese had eight chicks on the dam yesterday – perhaps I should go and check if the marauding fish eagle is around and if so, how many chicks are left. In the end, my destination was never a conscious decision; a place sort of swam into my mind and off I went, never knowing what I might find along the way.

For all its wild beauty, the Matobo Hills is a friendly place. Of course, there's always a chance one might step on a puff adder or meet a wounded leopard, but these are unlikely occurrences, and the joy in my serendipitous wandering was well worth any minor risk. In any case, if I was accompanied by someone like Poombi the warthog or Nandi the Labrador, or indeed any other reasonable type of animal, they'd give me advance warning of any danger.

And then along came a honey badger, touted as the most fearless animal in the world: one to whom Trouble and Danger are the very stuff of life. He is totally unreasonable. He hates peace and quiet – he's a one-man street gang, the Mafia Boss, the executioner waiting at the scaffold with a great grin on his face. Trouble? Bring it on. I'm ready.

It wasn't always like that. Badger's mother was killed by a hunter in Zimbabwe's south-east lowveld as she was carrying him through the bush one night. The safari operator kept him at home for a few weeks before sending him down to us in a small cardboard box. He was so thin and weak that he could barely stand. Fearless? As an infant Badge fled from bees, and he was terrified of the dragonflies that zipped over his head at the river. But not for long.

'Males have quite exceptionally large testes in proportion to their size,' reports Jonathan Kingdon. Or to put it more bluntly, Badgers have Balls and gallons of testosterone, as their enemies, including some ill-advised lions and leopards, have discovered to their cost. By the time he was a year old, our cub was actively looking for, and invariably finding, trouble or (as he preferred to call it) good clean fun.

The South African defence forces call one of their armoured troop carriers (or is it a minesweeper?) the 'ratel' – the Afrikaans name for the honey badger – which refers to the rattling roar, worthy of a lion, that they produce if suitably aroused.

He is built for punishment. Pound for pound, the badger is reckoned to be the toughest animal in Africa – and he couldn't be too far from the top on a global scale. A thick skull and dense bones make him pretty well bombproof – as we discovered when our cub was kicked in the head by a giraffe when he was six months old. And then there's his skin that fits him like a loose rubber wetsuit, so he can twist and turn in it, making it easy to latch onto some part of his attacker's anatomy. Furthermore, it's thick, particularly on the neck, so this is the place that the badger presents first in a skirmish.

Getting to grips with a badger is well-nigh impossible, as he's not only flexible, but also completely double-jointed. If you grab him behind the head, as you would to subdue a cat or a dog, he'll simply stretch up his front legs and claw your hands away with his feet.

He has one final defence for those who haven't already learned their lesson, and it's enough to make the most determined attacker cross-eyed. He turns tail and bombards them with the truly foul concoction stored in his anal glands; the last and most devastating weapon in his arsenal.

Let me tell you, mothering a carnivore is no joke, especially if like me, you can fool yourself that the bunch of thugs with tight shorts and bulging biceps attempting to kill each other on the rugby field, are actually enjoying a jolly nice game. But for all the bravado, the young badger was still a mummy's boy. Soon after sunrise, Scout Jabulani Khanye would give him breakfast in his enclosure outside our bedroom window, while Rich collected his camera equipment. Then, having shut all the windows, I would peer through a chink in the curtains as they opened the gate and let him out. The next few moments were crucial. If Badge had already decided on a plan of action, he would take off at a trot with his minders in hot pursuit, possibly making a slight diversion to the garage to see if he could find anything worth stealing. Or (and this was the worst case scenario) he would start patrolling around the house, scratching at the doors and demanding that Mummy come too. And that, for me, meant incarceration in a hot stuffy bedroom for as long as it took for Rich and Khanye to change his mind.

Only when Badger had crossed the river and I heard the 'all clear' on the radio could I emerge and get on with feeding the other animals. And there was no point in responding – if he heard my voice, Badge would come galloping back to the house to find me. Instead, I used a morse code, tapping with my nail on the radio handset to confirm that I had received the message.

Since his tummy was full, serious hunting was unnecessary, so mornings were devoted to badgering and bothering, mostly at the expense of the local warthogs.

Warthogs need their sleep. Our warthog, Poombi, another unforgettable character who came to us as an orphan and later lived wild on the farm, would curl up in her box with two woollen blankets on winter nights, and sometimes emerge only late the next morning, especially when it was wet and cold. It's even nicer for a sounder of hogs, usually consisting of a mother and her offspring. They all climb into bed together in the depths of an abandoned antbear hole, working up a terrific fug of pigglety warmth and comfort.

Badger couldn't leave warthogs alone. You could almost see him gleefully rubbing his paws together as he tiptoed up to an occupied den before the sun was up, occasionally glancing over his shoulder, bright-eyed, to make sure we were watching. Having once been flattened by enraged pig, he'd learned to approach on tiptoe from behind, very slowly and quietly. And then, when he was at the lip of the hole, he'd push a tiny bit of soil into it from above – and wait. If there was no response, he'd do it again, sending more soil raining down into the entrance. And more ... till finally the terrified pigs, convinced that a leopard was lying in wait for them, would burst out into the open.

When the warthogs got wise to this, Badge became even bolder. If they didn't respond to his initial baiting from above, he would nip around to the entrance of the hole and start shovelling mountains of soil directly onto their heads. Then when he heard the hogs rumbling into action, he'd make a quick sideways leap to safety, leaving unwary onlookers in the firing line.

After that, he'd run after them, tail up, looking very chipper. Rich has a sequence in his film *Honey Badger: Raising Hell* where Cassidy (as in Hopalong, the piglet with the gammy leg) turned in mid-flight, took a swing at Badger with his head and lifted him clean off his feet. Off went Cassidy, and after a second or two to catch his breath, off went Badge, back on his tail again.

I have no doubt that if we'd taken him bungee jumping, Badger would have opted to do it blindfolded, minus the elastic.

One chilly evening, he evicted an old warthog boar, who had plugged his hole with dry grass.

'Oh dear,' said Khanye, looking at the trail of scattered chaff, 'he's left his blankets behind.'

We could only hope that the old chap hadn't met a leopard as he charged headlong into the darkness.

The trouble was that Badge was determined to include us

in every facet of his life. He never really understood why we wouldn't dig for frogs with him or climb trees, and why I didn't share his delight in decapitated mice or three-legged tortoises. Often, when he was in the middle of digging, he'd come over and give us a quick bite on the foot, clearly exasperated with his useless family.

Until Colleen and Keith Begg, world authorities on the honey badger, began their 12-year study in both the Kalahari and northern Mozambique, using radio collars and telemetry, almost nothing was known about badgers. To start with, they are mainly nocturnal, and then they are so secretive that sightings are rare. Over the years, the Beggs collected extensive information, but as they were dealing with totally wild badgers, their observations were almost always made from a vehicle. As far as we knew at the time, we were the only people who were able to accompany a badger on foot as he made the perilous journey from dependent cub to, we hoped, a measure of self-reliance in his own world. We never once considered keeping him in a cage. Badger was born wild and that is where he belonged.

A cub will stay with his mother for up to two years, if she doesn't boot him out prior to that when she's ready to mate again. He has an enormous amount of learning to do in that time, and we were all concerned that without maternal guidance, Badge might never be able to achieve real independence.

Nature versus nurture, instinct versus learning – call it what you will – it's hard enough to weigh their relative significance in human beings, let alone in one little orphaned badger cub. Somehow, though, in his first year, Badger seemed to be instinctively aware of some of his shortcomings. To our surprise, when we first offered him a honeycomb, he turned away, wrinkling up his nose in disgust. Only months later did he plunder his own stingless mopane beehive, graduating over time to African beehives and learning to deal with their aggrieved occupants. Was he perhaps aware in those early days that his body was not yet ready to cope with their stings?

Honey badgers and certainly some mongooses, appear to possess a high tolerance to toxins – which is just as well, as scorpions and dangerous snakes are some of their favourite foods. But how does this occur? Does resistance build up slowly, through a process of envenomation, as the badger cub progresses over time from mildly poisonous toads to the 'big numbers', like black mambas and puff adders? Or does he have an inbuilt immunity to all those toxins from birth? No one really knows, and if finding out necessitates experiments like the one conducted many years ago in South Africa, I hope we never do.

In it, two captive honey badgers were each injected with enough black mamba venom to kill an ox, but apparently, after only an hour, both animals were back on their feet and ready to roll.

Dangerous snakes are only too common on Stone Hills, and it was important that Badge learned respect at an early age. So when he was a few months old, and we discovered a mildly venomous herald snake in the bedroom, we arranged an introduction. After bumbling about for a while, Badger tripped over the snake, which responded most unfairly by biting him on the nose.

The lesson stuck – for a while. He tracked up a harmless beaked blind snake some months later, and jumped away when it feigned aggression, finally managing to put it out of action with a bite behind the head. Very impressive, but then, typically, Badger started to get cocky. More tuition was required.

Rich found a metre-long python crossing the road, which was ideal for the job. Not surprisingly, the snake disagreed, and before Rich could get a good grip on the back of its neck, it managed to sink its needle-tipped teeth into a vein in his hand, leading to much bloodletting and cursing.

Rich released the python in an open area, then called to Badge, who came in at a run, saw the python and skidded to a halt. Oops! Now *here* was something interesting. He sank down and approached slowly and deliberately, totally focused on the snake, which lay there, quite still, watching him. Inch by inch, Badger crept towards it. Then he stretched out his neck and gave its tail a good loud sniff, which was just what the snake had been waiting for. It whipped around, struck at him, and Badge leapt out of its way. But he had no intention of giving up: this was just the sort of challenge he relished. Having circled the snake a couple of times, he went in more assertively from the front. *Whack*! The snake uncoiled so fast it was a blur and bit poor Badge on the end of the nose. Again. His eyes closed at the moment of impact, his face screwed up, and then suddenly he was tumbling head over heels, backwards, as fast as he could. And he kept going, rolling and somersaulting like a circus clown, but all the while with his eyes fixed on that dreadful creature.

Distraction, confusion, embarrassment? Whatever the reason for the performance, we were helpless with laughter. In Rich's film, the scene was originally put to the strains of the Blue Danube waltz, its closing notes fading out as Badger reached the edge of the clearing and trotted away.

Soon afterwards, when the memory of his sore nose was still fresh, Badge met another python. But this time, he had a very good look from a safe distance, and left it well alone.

The encounter with the monster snake I described at the beginning of this chapter happened when he was two years old. Having issued his challenge, our little pugilist then did something utterly remarkable. He set to work clearing the area around the snake, pulling branches right away from it, so that he could move in and out unhindered. But Rich wasn't prepared to wait for the next bout. He walked away, calling, and finally Badger followed. Luckily, he'd had one significant advantage in the encounter. The python had been sloughing, and its eyes were glassy and partially blinded by an opaque ocular scale.

Badge went straight back to the same spot the next day but his opponent was gone. Sometime later, he located it down another hole, lured it out, and once again began taunting it. But now the python could see, and Khanye managed to call him away before it managed to exact its revenge on that pesky varmint.

Our cub showed a lot more sense when it came to scorpions, one of his best-loved snacks – once he'd learned the technique of first biting off their tails.

Scorpions, like spiders, are arachnids, having eight legs instead of the insects' six. And spiders are captivating. They are explorers, engineers, inventors, mimics, and often great lovers too. Intending travellers climb up to a suitable launching pad, lift their bottoms, and pay out enough silk to catch the breeze. Then off they float, usually no further than the nearest bush, but sometimes up to around 5 kilometres above the earth, and huge distances across land and sea. It's no wonder that these tiny creatures, attached to their gossamer parachutes, are some of the first colonisers to arrive on newly formed volcanic islands.

As for engineering – *Nephila* spins the largest web of all her kind, a great golden orb with strands that are more elastic than nylon and stronger than steel. And for innovation, how about the bolas spider, who hunts by twirling a gluey glob on the end of a line till it connects and sticks to her prey? Or the little spider who lies in ambush cunningly (but not very tastefully) disguised as a glistening blob of bird poo?

As for love, one species of tiny crab spider woos his lady with a tender stroking and tapping of her abdomen. Okay, he's trying to persuade her not to eat him, but what a charming approach?

I'm afraid that scorpions just don't measure up. Certainly, they have the distinction of having been around, much in the same form as they are today, 200 million years *before* the dinosaurs. And they are far more conscientious parents than the spiders. The trouble is that they simply lack style – and they can pack a sting that can leave you in agony for days, as I discovered when I accidentally pinched a golden green striking scorpion between finger and thumb in bed one night.

There was no doubt about whodunnit: the golden greens often scurry around the house in the rainy season, and none of our other regular visitors inflict that level of instantaneous agony, so while I was jumping up and down in the bathroom, Rich searched the bed for the culprit – who was not to be found. The extraordinary thing was that the pain didn't merely concentrate in my thumb; I could actually feel it travelling right up my arm and then lodging itself in my chest, as I told Rich, giving him a running commentary between anguished yelps. To my surprise, he didn't seem unduly concerned. In fact, he was gazing at me through his glasses with a kind of clinical interest, like a researcher watching the results of one of his experiments. Of course, I knew as well as he did that there wouldn't be any long-term effects from the venom of the golden green, but I *was* expecting a bit more sympathy. At any rate, we were back in bed half an hour later where I lay moaning softly (and bravely) while nursing my index finger.

'Shit!' There was a sudden eruption under the blankets, and Rich leapt out of bed. 'The bloody thing's stung me under the arm!'

I'm not saying I was pleased (of course I wasn't) but it was rather funny to see him grinding his teeth and the way his face twitched as the venom got to work. It goes without saying that he didn't utter a sound, not even a whimper – at least not while I was watching him. He wouldn't have dared.

The most common species of scorpion in these parts, like the nasty but comparatively innocuous little golden green, have slender tails and large powerful pincers with which to capture their prey, and Badger quickly learned to dispatch them. Then came the day when he encountered *Parabuthus raudus*, the first one ever seen on Stone Hills and hopefully the last. With its telltale slender pincers and thick-spiked tail packed with poison, it belongs to one of the most dangerous families of scorpions on earth.

Khanye took a large step backwards, and even Badger hesitated. Then, instead of his usual technique of first biting off the tail, he began to scratch at the scorpion's body, presumably to disperse the poison. Only when he had totally immobilised it, did he bite off the tail and settle down to enjoy his meal. An hour or so later, he dug up a golden green and quickly dispatched it with the usual grab, bite and swallow. Perhaps he was alerted to the higher level of toxins in the *Parabuthus* by its different smell – we know that a badger's scenting abilities are phenomenal. But what this did show us was that Badge's innate reactions were highly developed. He didn't need his mother to show him what an evil fellow the *Parabuthus* was: he knew it, instinctively, and figured out how to deal with it himself.

Depending on the time of the year, our morning walks ended at around 8am, when the sun was bright and well over the hills, and it was then that Badger changed from warrior to wimp. His tail dropped low, the swashbuckling swagger became a skulk. Adventures forgotten, he would scuttle off to a suitable koppie and spend the day holed up amongst the rocks till we came to fetch him in the late afternoon. We never knew what he got up to during the day. Once he had established himself in a secure place, he might well have emerged every now and then to harass the local dassies, or to play. Often when we arrived in the evenings, we would find him rolling about with a stick, or some other treasure, twiddling it between those amazingly dexterous paws.

Always a keen collector, Badger had created his own little stockpile of treasures in a deep hole in the rocks on Grain Bin Koppie, and that's where he had taken Rich's shoe the day he cunningly levered it off while Rich was fiddling with his camera equipment. Months later, Rich followed him to his secret playpen surrounded by rocks, and found a hoard of plastic bottles, bits of old tin, a glove and the shoe, mucky and slightly mangled, but not much tattier than it had been at the time of the theft. Still, for some reason, they were Rich's favourite pair, and he was determined to get the stolen shoe back. Immediately sensing his interest, Badger pounced on the shoe.

'Bring it to me!' Rich commanded him sternly. Badge obeyed, dragging it between his legs and then lay in front of Rich, clasping it to his chest and inviting him to play. The idea was to distract him so you could snatch it away when he loosened his grip. So Rich picked up a stick and waved it in front of his nose. Badge lunged towards it, then dropped into his Lost Shoe Shuffle, humping along after the stick, but still hugging his prize. Patience was required; he was quite prepared to play these games for hours, especially if it meant keeping you occupied for as long as possible. Finally, Rich saw his chance. A go-away bird called overhead, and as Badge looked up, Rich grabbed his shoe and swung it up into the air. Badge danced around him, crying 'Foul!' and tried to climb up his leg. While Khanye distracted him by pretending to steal the glove, Rich wedged the shoe tightly in the fork of a high tree, for lack of a better idea. And then they tried to continue with their walk.

'Come on, Badge!' they called, but he was already halfway up the tree. And once the prize was safely back in the cave, along with all his other treasures, he joined them. Needless to say, Rich never saw his shoe again. The interesting thing was that Badge could sense exactly how much something meant to us, and the more valuable he thought it was, the harder it was to retrieve it.

There's a lovely story in Eugene Linden's book *The Octopus and the Orangutan* about a zookeeper who accidentally dropped a $50 bill in Koundo the gorilla's cage. Trying not to appear too desperate, he offered the gorilla a can of peaches in exchange. But these were quite a treat, and they alerted Koundo that he had possession of something rather valuable. So instead of handing over the bill, he tore a tiny piece off it and thrust it through the bars, presumably hoping to improve the offer. Now very agitated, the keeper rushed off and came back with a veritable cornucopia of edibles that he laid out enticingly in front of the gorilla. Koundo contemplated this feast for a moment, and then made up his mind. He ate the $50 bill.

Leaving Badge in the mornings was relatively simple for Rich or Khanye. Once he had chosen his hideout, Badge would jump onto a rock and start his wrinkle-squeak routine, an imploring little whine with his face scrunched up. Then he would get his bit of apple, and while he was munching on it, Rich and Khanye would sneak quietly away.

But there were often days when I had to do the morning walks alone, and that was when Badge made life very difficult. However much he was enjoying his apple, the moment he noticed that I was trying to sneak away, he'd drop it and come tearing after me. And then I had to call on the services of Badger's bogeyman. As soon as I had an idea where Badge was headed, I would radio Head Scout Mafira to give him our position. I often used the radio when we were out, and normally Badger took no notice at all, but come the moment when I called: 'Mafira, Mafira, do you read?' Badge would grab hold of my foot with both legs and begin to whine. And he would sit there, crying, with a heartrending expression on his face – until the bogeyman arrived and said, in a very deep, stern voice: 'Okay, Badger, time for bed,' whereupon he would turn tail and slink into the shelter of the rocks, and I would start walking home with Mafira behind me – in my footsteps, leaving a scent trail that Badge wouldn't dare to follow.

Thank heavens for the radio. Although often signal would be lost when we were in the hills, I knew that by getting some height I could probably contact home if there was a problem.

It also came into good use in a totally unexpected way.

It was 9pm on a summer evening; we'd been in town all day and Khanye was out walking with Badge. They'd normally be back at around eight, so I gave him a call on the radio.

'Everything okay, Khanye?'

'Badger won't come home,' he replied. 'He's digging for sand frogs on the Mathole River.'

'Have you tried leaving him to see if he'll follow?'

'Lots of times. But he's not interested.'

I didn't really feel like a long walk, but if I didn't go, he could be out all night.

'Okay, Khanye. I'm on my way.'

The idea came to me at the garden gate. I went back into the house and called Khanye again.

'Take the radio to Badge and put it by his ear. I'll talk to him and let's see what he does.'

'Okay,' said Khanye, a few moments later, 'I've got him.'

'Badgee! I called in my most loving, come-hither voice. 'Come home, Badgie boy, come back to Mummy! Supper!'

I repeated this a couple of times. It was a long shot. I had enough trouble calling my son away from some absorbing task, let alone a nocturnal honey badger stuffing his face with frogs.

Then we heard Khanye laughing. 'He heard you and now he's running home!'

And 15 minutes later, they arrived, Badge on the front step with Khanye 10 minutes behind him, both panting.

Badge threw himself into my lap wriggling with delight.

He wrapped himself around an arm and started to wrestle with it, but before he could really get stuck in, I picked him up and took him to his house for supper and bed.

Rich shook his head. 'My God,' he said. 'Will this little animal ever cease to amaze us?'

Chapter Three – Lost And Found

The wintry afternoon of the 8th of June begins like any other. At 4.30pm, after a cup of tea, I put a two-way radio, watch, binoculars and a beanie into my backpack, and sling an awkward contraption resembling a large TV aerial over my shoulder. Then, having bid Rich goodbye, I head into the bush – alone.

With the aerial bumping uncomfortably against my side, I strike out at a brisk walk for Digit Rocks, some 3 kilometres down the track. After that, I have no idea where I'll go. All being well, I'll be home in time for dinner, at around 8pm, but it may turn out to be much later than that.

The local people gave traditional names to some of the larger koppies, others we have named ourselves, like Digit with its four deformed fingers sticking up from a fist of granite. I scramble up it as far as I can and stand out on a rock surveying the swaying grasslands of the Pundamuka Valley, as they slope gently into the jumble of rugged koppies the scouts call the White Hills. It's 5pm; the shadows are already lengthening over the mixed herd of wildebeest and zebra grazing peacefully below me. At sunset, they'll make their way into the lee of the hills for warmth and protection from the wind.

I press the orange button on the receiver strapped to the aerial and it crackles and hisses at me like an untuned radio. Holding it above my head, with the two crossbars parallel to the ground, I slowly swing it around in a circle. With direct line of sight, you can pick up a signal some 2.5 kilometres away, but in this broken, hilly country, the range is erratic and often much less. I start behind me: south towards the boundary with neighbouring farm Good Luck; then swinging across the tops of the koppies, with Three Streams beyond; over the white quartz ridge, into the valley of the proteas and along the edge of the White Hills. Nothing heard. That dot in the sky is one of the Verreaux's eagles, returning to its chick that hatched a week ago in their eyrie halfway up a sheer cliff face. I follow it for a moment, move slowly north and stop. And listen. Could that have been a tiny peep above the static? I slide the aerial back a couple of inches, and yes, there it is again. The faintest of signals tells me that Mr Badger, having spent the day at Digit Rocks, where Rich left him at 7.30am, has taken himself deep into the hills. And if I want to join him before dark, I'd better get going.

A few months before, Badge would always be waiting in the same place that we left him but, at a year old, he's far more

27

independent. Sometimes he'll wait for us; other times, like this afternoon, he'll disappear off on his own. And without the use of telemetry, it would be impossible to find him. Young honey badgers suffer from the delusion that they are invincible; they survive only because they have their mother's protection for up to two years, and sometimes, if they can wangle it, even longer. So, reluctantly, when Badger was six months old, we called on Gerard Stevenage, our vet, to insert a transmitter with two batteries encased in a special wax, into his stomach cavity. We wouldn't have been brave enough to make such a decision without some expert advice. Keith and Colleen Begg, the Badger experts, had visited Stone Hills a couple of months previously to meet our cub. During their four years in the Central Kalahari, they successfully fitted over 50 transmitters to badgers large and small, none of whom showed any signs of discomfort or rejection. The batteries had a life of around 22 months, which would allow us to see Badge through his most vulnerable time.

I cross the track at the foot of Digit and head down the valley through tussocks of rattling dry grass to the Pundamuka River, in the direction of the signal. Absently snapping off a few brittle stems, I'm suddenly overpowered by a stench of sour sweat. A shaggy brown hyaena has also passed this way, leaving messages for his mates by pasting the grass with secretions from his anal gland. I believe that on average he leaves one of these nauseating communiqués every 380 metres, so although we very rarely see them, they give us constant updates on their movements. I try rubbing my hand in the dirt, but it doesn't help and, in any case, it's also on my clothes, so I'm going to smell until I get home and can scrub it off.

Besides a few rock pools, all the streams and waterways

that meander through the hills are dry in the winter months. Crossing the riverbed, I step into the hardened spoor of a giraffe and that of a couple of impala sunk into the baked, black mud. Once I'm on higher ground, the aerial picks up a faint signal about a kilometre away in the direction of some massive boulders rising above the trees. Countless of these cascading stone castles, each with its own unique character, are scattered amongst the woodlands and wide, windswept valleys of the Matobo Hills. Lying in deep shadow, there's something faintly sinister about this one, in contrast to other friendlier places nearby – like the soaring cliff face where the Verreaux's eagles have nested for hundreds, maybe thousands, of years. Standing at its summit, you feel as though you could fling out your arms and, like the eagle, go sailing away forever over the endless miles of broken granite hills that seem to stretch out forever below you.

A well-trodden game path snakes around the koppie to its sunny side, and I follow it to the foot of a towering wall of rock we call the Monolith. In my early wanderings on the farm, I found rock paintings at the base of the Monolith, but I can't remember what they were and I need to make a note of them. We try to record every one we find, although in many cases all that is left is a line or two of the original painting. It won't take long. I know their exact location: at eye level, superimposed on the band of limey white deposit that runs down the rock. There are two antelope in red ochre, goofy-looking creatures, resembling tsessebe, but hornless, with heads far too large for the body, and long, shapeless legs. I know them well – they pop up all over the farm amongst thousands of other perfectly executed images – a kind of Stone Age graffiti that must have infuriated the true artists. But there are other, mysterious paintings too: a long sinuous outline with two arms that might almost be a human body in repose – or perhaps a fallen tree with small branches growing from it – and clusters of wriggly lines that look like a handful of snakes. These images are new to me, so I settle down and sketch them out in my notebook. I love to think of the Bushmen sitting here, thousands of years ago, gazing out over this same, timeless landscape, and listening to the piping whistles of the red-winged starlings as they swoop down onto the tops of the koppies to catch the fading warmth of the day.

I put the notebook into my backpack and pull out a watch. It's 5.45pm, later than I thought, and the sun is already on its final rapid dive to the horizon. There is no signal from the errant Badge amongst these tightly clustered hills, so I must make a decision: either to go back by road, which will be safe but boring, or to make directly for home on Dibe – our largest koppie, unmistakably silhouetted on the horizon, with the two stone tortoises lumbering up its southern flank. It'll be around 4 kilometres of rough going, but it's a clear evening and if I keep fixing my position by familiar stars, I should be home in a couple of hours. I get back onto the path and it leads me between the rocks and down into the heart of the hills.

There is no wilder place on the farm: the Matabele army fought for months from amongst the maze of koppies and caves in the Matobo during the 1896 Rebellion against the British colonists. It was impossible to rout them out, but in the end hunger and the need to treat their wounded forced them from their stronghold to parley with Cecil John Rhodes.

The aerial keeps catching in the bushes and sliding off my shoulder. If Khanye was here, he'd hang it around his neck, but that's even more uncomfortable. And anyway, he's on holiday for six weeks and I'm on Badger patrol alone, so there's no one to help me with the damn thing.

Shadows are creeping through the valleys, and now the tops of the tallest rocks are caught in a blaze of light, setting fire to the vivid reds, greens and acid yellows of the lichen.

As the path gets steeper, the far horizon disappears and I'm confronted by a dense wall of koppies. From somewhere in the grass comes the manic chorus: 'I'll drink your beer! I'll drink your beer!' – a covey of Shelley's francolin bidding each other goodnight. There's no time for mountain climbing, so I duck into a gloomy tunnel of trees in the gap between two hills. It's a gentle ascent, but littered with boulders, fallen branches and twisted roots. And when I finally reach the top, the ground drops away to more hills, now a solid black silhouette against a darkening sky, fingered with crimson. None of them look familiar but then again, every koppie changes depending on where you are. The two tortoises that define Dibe from the east, for instance, are replaced by the head of a scowling old man with a jutting jaw on its western side.

I switch on the receiver and slowly swing the aerial around. Still nothing. Over I go, and straight into a thicket of woolly-leafed bushes with rigid interlacing branches that close around me like the bars of a cage. Their name – *Ililangwe* – means 'where the leopard sleeps', and though it's a wise choice for that secretive cat, right now it's the worst place for me. Almost immediately, my eyes start to run, my throat is burning and I'm sneezing violently every couple of minutes from the clouds of fine hairs released by their leaves. Reedy whistles of alarm, and the light clatter of hooves on rock announce the rapid departure of a couple of klipspringer. So much for a peaceful walk in the hills: every animal for miles around will have heard me sneezing and cursing.

Fifteen minutes later, I've at last fought my way out of the

31

thicket. My arms and legs are scratched and bleeding, and I'm standing in a small clearing, blowing my nose. Above me, hangs the new moon, a mere sliver of silver, as tender as a baby's thumbnail. The stars are brilliant overhead, and I can see the Southern Cross low on the horizon at my left shoulder, so I know I'm still heading in the right direction. The wind races through the trees at the tops of the koppies setting up a roar like a distant sea. I pull the beanie out of the backpack, jam it down over my ears, and fit the head torch over it. It starts to flicker – stupidly I've forgotten to change the batteries even though I knew they were getting low on last night's walk. But they'll last, provided I'm not out too long. I press the light on the watch face – 7.15pm – three quarters of an hour till dinner. If Badge hasn't found food for himself, he'll probably be home before I am.

From behind me, somewhere in the White Hills, a leopard calls into the chilly, star-studded night – a rhythmic, rasping cough. How many times do we pass them unawares, staring down at us from the top of a koppie, or melting into the woodland's dappled sunlight? I'm not afraid; unless it is cornered or injured, a leopard won't harm me. But I feel a rush of excitement: a primitive response to a predator by an unarmed human – a helpless creature with defective hearing, eyesight and smell. In the daytime, we believe ourselves to be the careless masters of all we survey, but only in the darkness, when our position is lost, can we truly measure ourselves against the natural world, and know how badly we are wanting.

My torch picks up a game trail. If I follow it downhill it should lead to water, perhaps a familiar river. In any case, it's better than blundering through the bush. For a couple of hundred yards, I stride along quite confidently, until it suddenly narrows, then peters out and is lost in the long grass.

I've made the wrong decision – there's no easy route home – so I'd better radio Rich to tell him that I'm going to be late for dinner. Turning to slip off my backpack, I stumble and crash heavily into a pile of rocks, taking my full weight on my right knee. Pain rips through it, and for a moment, I think the knee might be smashed, so I roll into a sitting position and start rubbing it furiously: however sore it is, massaging always seems to help. I've fallen over a rustic grave; there are many of them on Stone Hills, but it's the only one I've examined so closely. Squeezing my eyes shut, I will the pain to go away.

A silver-stemmed *Commiphora* tree grows in front of the low headstone, a memorial planted there perhaps for a mother by her family. If this had been a man, there would be a much larger and more impressive stone, and another placed at the foot of the grave. But though no one has visited it for years, this woman is not forgotten. A year or so after her death, her family would have held the *umbuyiso* ceremony, calling her spirit back to the home, and asking her to remain with them forever as their adviser and protector.

Lying on my back, I blow puffs of icy smoke at the stars, and try to bring my breathing under control. This is our second winter with Badger, and in my many nights of following him, I'm gradually learning to recognise some of the constellations. I make up names for some of the ones I don't know – there's the small oval that looks like an egg, and the long, undulating line lying to the north in the shape of an easy chair. As I scan the sky, it suddenly strikes me that the Southern Cross is not where it should be.

Using the rocks for support, I push myself up, and gingerly put my right foot on the ground. Nothing broken, thank God, though the knee still hurts like hell. Once I'm standing on the path, the cross should be at my left shoulder. But it's not, it's on my right. I let out a groan. I've been so sure that I was heading straight for home, but somewhere I've deviated, which means turning around and plunging back into the darkness of the hills. For the first time, I feel a slight flutter of panic. It's not that I mind spending the night in the bush – it would be quite exciting to sleep in a cave, out of the wind – but Rich would worry, and, even worse, imagine how ridiculous I would look to everyone else. Mafira wouldn't comment, but I could imagine his little smile of sympathy. Poor Mrs Peek, lost in her own backyard. No, not lost, I tell myself sternly, just temporarily disorientated. It's a small matter of climbing to the top of the next hill and seeing the lights of home glowing in the darkness. Except that climbing is now out of the question. If only Badger was with me; he'd know exactly where he was.

The trees tower over me, koppies loom suddenly out of the darkness – and I can't help thinking about little Eunis Shone, lost and alone in this bewildering place in the early 1920s. The family was living on Wilfred's Hope, the next-door farm, and Eunis became separated from her friends while searching for wild fruits in the veld, something the children used to do every afternoon. Everybody joined in a massive search that lasted for three days, but finally it was her father who found her, curled up asleep in the grass, somewhere on Stone Hills. Members of her family said she spoke of seeing a 'big spotted kitty' amongst the koppies. Traumatised and suffering from exposure, she later developed complications that affected her heart, and she died the following year, aged only four. She is buried on Wilfred's Hope.

It's 7.45pm and the sputtering beam of the head torch is getting dimmer. I twiddle the knob of the radio to make sure it's on our internal channel 3: 'Rich, Rich, come in.' Silence. And a few, long minutes later – 'Rich, come in – do you read me?' Clearly, he doesn't – the koppies are blocking the signal – and in a way, I'm rather relieved: he'd only ask where I am and how long I'll be, and I can't answer either question.

Hands bunched in my pockets, I limp along as fast as I can, heading straight into the wind that cuts through the valley, flaying the long grass and stinging my cheeks.

I don't hear Badge galloping through the grass; I don't even see him until he bursts out of the night and skids to a halt, covering my feet with foaming saliva. There is only one way to greet a badger. I sit down, far quicker than I intended, grimacing at the sharp spike of pain in my knee, and he falls squirming with joy into my lap, mouthing my hands, his breath coming in tortured squeaks and rattles. Somewhere, far back in the hills, he has picked up my scent and followed it, maybe for miles, stopping for nothing. I hold him tight and kiss the top of his head. Lost? Of course not. I've been doing a bit of exploring, that's all, and now we're heading home for supper, together, the Badger and I. Suddenly, everything looks familiar again, the wind has a friendly sound, the trees have shrunk to their usual size. I take a bottle of water from the backpack, and pour some into my cupped hands, Badger drinks it, handful after handful, with a desperate thirst.

He lies, almost inert, for 10 minutes or so, head over my leg and still puffing, but then I feel a paw sliding surreptitiously into the side of my shoe, and the slightest wiggle of claws. This is Badger's favourite game – if I stand up now, he'll hook the shoe off my foot and run away with it. And the more desperate I become, barefoot and wonky-kneed, the more determined he will be to keep it. I slip my hand over his paw and gently remove it. He whines: this is not fair.

'Come on, Badge, let's go home for supper!' (this last word said with the special breathless intonation I've used since he was a baby – inducing, I hope, a vision of his tin plate brimming with juicy red meat).

I push him off my lap, stand up and hobble off. After a few steps he collapses again with a loud sigh, so I turn my back on him – something, I've been told, that dogs absolutely hate. Desperate to regain your attention, they will immediately try to get back into favour by doing as you ask.

Another 10 minutes pass, I'm still waiting and it's now 8.15pm. I turn around to find Badge lying on his back with his paws in the air. He hasn't moved. In desperation, I do exactly what he wants: pick him up and stagger down the path for a few back-wrenching yards with 10 kilograms of comatose mustelid flopped in my arms.

'That's enough!' I dump him back on the ground. 'I'm off,' (though I wasn't sure where), 'and you can do what you like.'

This time, he knows I mean it: within minutes, he brushes past my leg and takes the lead at a springy trot. Then he's off down a path, tail fluffed out and held aloft, and it's all I can do to keep him in the fast-fading light of my torch. But Badger knows my limitations and when he takes a sudden detour after an interesting smell or gets too far ahead, all I have to do is to call his name, or make our prt-prt-prt contact call, and he'll be back to find me.

A hiss from the radio – 'Bookey, Bookey – come in.'

I stop for a moment to pull it out of its case, and press the respond button.

'Hi darling, we're here.'

'Is everything okay? I tried calling a couple of times earlier, but couldn't raise you.'

'We were behind the hills. Badger only joined me a little while ago, but we're on our way home.'

'Don't be too long. Dinner's on the table.'

'Okay. See you in a few minutes.'

I hope.

We've now arrived at the base of a koppie so large I'm hoping it's Dunu; if it is, the house will be on the other side – another 10 or 15 minutes' walk. My knee is aching, but I hardly notice it. Badger trots through the woodland, and suddenly stops and sniffs at an antbear hole with a pile of freshly dug soil at its entrance.

If he decides to investigate, he'll be busy for hours.

'No, Badge! Come on, supper!'

At that moment, thank God, a plate of food appeals more to him than harassing some unfortunate antbear or warthog. So on we go, and, as we round the side of the koppie and emerge from the trees, there they are at last: a string of lights twinkling across the other side of the valley on the slopes of Dibe Hill – the mother ship riding the swell of the dark ocean. Safe haven for the hunter, and home for his adoring, but utterly hopeless mother.

Chapter Four – Home In The Hills

In our house, it's always five past three
Late for lunch
And early for tea.

The other clock stands at twenty-four minutes to five,
But that wouldn't rhyme so well.

Along with the push-button telephone, four tortoise shells
and the rusty old horseshoe that adorn the enormous granite
mantelpiece over the fireplace, the clocks have become purely

ornamental – a reminder of the distant past when time had some importance in our lives. These days, my only deadline is dictated by my stomach; I insist on being back from the evening Badger-walk for Badger's dinner and mine at around 8pm. Naturally, Badge would like to stay out all night. But having disembowelled a minibus, and torn the foam rubber tractor seat to shreds, his next challenge will surely be the lodge and the chalets, all of which offer plenty of fun and destructive opportunities for a young fellow with time on his hands.

I reach up through the open kitchen window for Badger's tin plate of food (even he can't destroy that), and he dances around my feet until we reach the gate of his enclosure. If I want to keep all my fingers, I must somehow fling the plate, frisbee-like, onto the flat top of his stone house without losing it on the other side. Badge pounces on it with a growl, and I duck back through the gate and bolt it behind me. I have to be quick: if he has found plenty to eat on his walk, he'll try to escape – and then no amount of bribery will bring him back again.

From the back garden, I can see Rich's head in the lighted window of the office, and for a few moments, standing there in the darkness, I feel as though I'm a stranger, looking in on someone else's life. Who is this bearded man bent over his computer, headphones stuck to his ears, hair standing on end? What is he doing in this lonely house amongst the hills? I have the same feeling when I climb high into the rocks on Dibe Hill, looking down over the thatched roofs of the house and lodge, and the rising smoke from the kitchen boiler – seeing it all as the starlings do when they fly up there to roost. And if I were that stranger, I'd be envious of the people I saw, living the life that I had always dreamed of.

Now that Badge is safely incarcerated, I can open the doors

and let Nandi, our 10-year-old black Labrador and erstwhile Badger companion, out of the house. Last time they met, and just for a laugh, Badge locked his jaws around her throat, while Nandi stood quite still, her eyes pleading for deliverance. Now she takes her daily walks separately and in peace.

Our back veranda leads directly into the dining room, which is actually a raised extension of the lounge. When we are having breakfast, we lean out of the window and hand pieces of toast to Mary the bushbuck, who at 14, is the same age as David. Two stone-clad flower boxes flank the three steps down to the lounge. Last year, the remaining maidenhair fern was eaten by a dassie, and since, in my life, there's no contest between dassies and decor, the beds remain empty, save for the red toads, who like to keep moist in winter by burying themselves in the soil.

Not long ago, a little clay Bushman sat next to the fern, picking a thorn out of his foot, until a friend, visiting from Johannesburg, blew the cobwebs off him for a closer look.

'He's beautiful!' she exclaimed. 'How can you treat him so badly?'

Truth is, I found his company rather dull, so he was duly cleaned up, bubble-wrapped, and transported to Sandton, where I met him some months later, perched smugly on a mahogany table under a David Shepherd painting of a Cape buffalo. I heard my friend crooning to him, when she thought I was out of earshot: 'Don't worry, little Bushman, you're safe with me now. *I'll* take care of you!'

I was glad she didn't see the scattering of dormouse droppings that fell out my clothes when I unpacked my bag.

In an ideal world, my house would be an open shelter, where animals could wander in and out at will – but winter nights in Matobo can fall well below zero, so we needed something more substantial. Rich compromised by designing a house that is light, airy and cool; warmed in winter by a central granite-clad fireplace soaring 18 metres through a pyramid of thick golden thatch. The house, like the land, is dominated by stone – cut from ancient rocks, tempered by weather and stained with the myriad hues of the lichen that cling to it.

The only disadvantage of such a high roof is that the birds, who come inside by accident, head straight up into the beams, and we have to shut ourselves in the office until they feel brave enough to come down and fly away. The tomb bats have worked out a better strategy. They arrive in the summer months to roost and breed under the eaves of the house, and have learned to slip in and out through the window behind the bedroom curtains in search of insects attracted by the lights.

With the sliding doors opening onto the front veranda, and the French windows at the back, there is almost always a breeze through the house in summer. And except for a couple of rugs, the floor is bare; its square clay tiles stained with the deep reds and ochres of earthenware pots.

But there is no escaping those leaden winter days, especially in July, when the south-east wind comes roaring up the vlei and batters at the glass. Then we shake the scorpions out of the socks and the beanies and the big jackets, and wear them all day, inside the house and out. That's the time when the kudu, eland and giraffe arrive at the garden fence in the late afternoon asking for their daily ration of game cubes, and Mary the bushbuck waits under the dining room window for her bowl of hot tea with milk and one sugar. Sometimes we have a fire at night, but only if the starlings, barn owls or purple rollers aren't nesting in the chimney.

We shivered all through the winter of 2000 for a different

reason. Earlier that year, almost all the Matabeleland farmers, including ourselves, vacated their land for weeks after the killing of Martin Olds near Bulawayo – one in a number of murders of white farmers. David and I went to Australia to stay with my parents till elections were over, but Rich returned to Stone Hills after a few days. He kept a small bag packed for a speedy escape should he be targeted, and he mapped out a cross-country route over the border into Botswana, some 40 kilometres away. He hid the maps in the chimney.

The most important items in our lounge are the books on natural history, all of which are colour-coded, indexed and meticulously arranged by Rich in seven glass-fronted bookshelves. The furniture is purely functional. Our lounge suite started to fall apart after Poombi, our warthog, moved in, and Badger's early attempts at digging speeded up the process of disintegration. On a visit to Kenya, I bought two Masai shukas in a gaudy African tartan – one blue and one red. They've brightened up the room, and do a good job of covering the holes in the seats.

No matter how inviting your surroundings, a house can so easily become a comfortable trap. I'm quite content to dream at my desk in our bedroom, watching the comings and goings at the bird bath below the window, and the shifting patterns of light and shadows on the two stone towers of Hongwe Tengana, rising up in the east like the turrets of a castle. But Badger has cured us of any temptation to vegetate: his daily morning and afternoon excursions are compulsory. In a sense, we are also trapped into his routine, but we are his willing prisoners. In fact, there is nothing in the world we would rather do than accompany our honey badger on his journey back to the wild. And he has provided us with another convincing excuse to disengage ourselves from the world outside – a process that has been going on ever since we moved to Stone Hills in 1989.

It was different when we lived in town and the highlight of our limited social calendar was dinner at Winchester House – the gracious old home of our English friends, Richard and Marion Trotter. Those were the days of leisured conversations, laughter and plans; a time we can hardly remember, when there was food on the shelves of the supermarkets – sugar, oil, bread, flour – basics everyone could afford.

Those were the days when Marion's maid, Winnie, answered the telephone with the same intonation and beautifully modulated accent as hers – causing some consternation when I once addressed her as 'you silly old cow'. 'Could you repeat that, madam?' said Winnie.

Winchester House was built in 1896 by a Colonel Napier, making it one of the oldest buildings in Bulawayo. Fruit bats roosted in the enormous jacarandas in the garden, brilliant bougainvilleas spilled from the green tin roof and over the garden walls, and as you walked in through the front door, the wooden floors creaked under your feet and the air was redolent with the scent of freshly cut roses.

A portrait of Henry V presided over dinner, looking rather stern on the eve of the Battle of Agincourt, and if we were lucky, old Solomon Ncube, long-time cook for a wealthy Johannesburg family, would come limping out of the kitchen bearing cordon bleu dishes on gleaming silver platters.

But all that ended 20 years ago. The Trotters have long since returned to England, and if the gang of car thieves who hijacked Winchester House are still throwing dinner parties, we're not on the guest list.

Nowadays, we rarely go to town, and our few remaining friends come out to Stone Hills instead. Of course, they have no interest in spending any time with us. They want to go walking with Badger, though preferably not on the kind of self-inflicted survival course that I just completed.

'So what took you so long?' asks Rich after I've dumped the aerial and the backpack, and cleaned up the scratches on my leg.

'I lost Badger's signal somewhere in the White Hills, so I came back cross-country ...'

'And you got lost!'

I glare at him. 'No, I didn't. I just took a couple of wrong turns, and fell over a grave. Then Badger caught up with me and we came home together.'

I'm certainly not going to tell him how the Southern Cross had miraculously appeared to me in the north.

After dinner, I feed the four bushbuck their dish of leaves through the window of David's old nursery. His collection of model tanks and aeroplanes is gathering dust on the glass shelves; the cupboard is stuffed with games and soft toys, its doors dotted with peeling pictures and blobs of sticky stuff.

It smells different since he moved into the bigger room at the end of the passage. There's a slight whiff in the air, reminiscent of a small badger who resided there for his first six months, and who is also responsible for the large hole in the carpet, and the absence of a skirting board from one wall.

We are locking up the office and preparing for bed when the mobile phone rings.

'Mum?'

'Hello, darling. How are you?'

'Okay.'

'How's school?'

A long silence. 'Fine.'

Well, you know it's not fine when your normally chatty child becomes monosyllabic. And it has been the same ever since he started school in South Africa at the beginning of that year. He isn't alone in his unhappiness: many of the Zimbabwean kids suffer from anxiety and depression in their first year or so away, constantly worrying about what is happening at home, wondering what their parents haven't told them.

'How's Badger?'

'Wonderful and getting very independent. I followed him for miles this evening. We only got back half an hour ago.'

'Did you get lost?'

Father and son – they're always playing the same tune.

'Yes,' I say because Rich can't hear. 'You know me.'

That raises a little laugh, then he's serious again.

'Is everything all right on the farm?'

'Hundred per cent.'

'You promise?'

'I promise – I'll tell you if anything changes.'

Then Rich takes the phone and tells him all about his Badger film, and the leopard that killed the impala by the lodge a couple of nights ago.

Much as we hate David being so far away, we believe we have made the right decision. If he was at school in Bulawayo, he would have to board somewhere in town, and spend his weekends on the farm without his friends. Two hermits are enough in one family; David needs the company of his peers, and some experience of normal life.

It's 10.30pm and Mary starts to bark – a sound that seems far too loud and gruff for a small buck. Standing on the front veranda, I swing the torch beam around the enclosure. Three of them are huddled up near the gate at the far corner, but Mary, always the courageous one, stands out in the milky glow of the half moon, sounding the alarm. The leopard, perhaps, is padding silently around the house, coming back to finish its meal.

The beam picks up two pairs of eyes. Nala and Sarabie, a pair of serval cats, are pacing up and down the fence of their enclosure. They came from Lisa Hywood of the Tikki Hywood Trust in Harare, and they've been with us for four months, becoming familiar with their new environment. We'll release them at the start of the rains, when hunting will be easier for the two novices. Both are radio-collared, so the scouts will be able to keep contact with them, and we hope that they'll come back to us if they are hungry. In the meantime, they can smell, hear and see the wild world outside their enclosure, and they are longing to be free.

Badger had cried for a while after he had finished his supper – he always does – but all is quiet now. He'll be curled up in his tyre inside the little stone house – well, what remains of it after all his chewing.

For tonight, he is safe and we can sleep peacefully. But our cub has a long, hard journey ahead, and his adventures have only just begun.

Chapter Five – Assets In Wonderland

There are all sorts of ways to chat up a girl. A large flashy rock always sends out the right signal, but if that's out of your league, words can be pretty effective. Quoting Shakespeare for example, 'Shall I compare thee to a summer's day? Thou art more lovely and more temperate,' would be a good start. And in America, where God is a greenback, telling a girl she looks like a million dollars is the ultimate compliment. But that's in America. If you had tried the same line on a Zimbabwean chick in 2008, she would have slapped your face. No one likes to be called dirty, infectious and utterly useless – and yet that's exactly what you would have implied. In June of that year, one egg cost 100 million Zimbabwe dollars (Z$), and less than a week later, one US dollar was equivalent to two billion of our worthless currency. Invest in Zimbabwe dollars, said my wit of a husband – it's the viral currency that multiplies exponentially.

Interestingly enough, until their government intervened, the notes were being produced by a German company and flown into Zimbabwe weekly by the ton.

From Independence in 1980 to 1994, Zimbabwe issued only four notes, ranging from Z$20 down to Z$5, and six coins. In August 2008, when the currency was once again revalued, no less than 72 notes were in circulation, one of them being a one cent note, issued at a time when a loaf of bread cost Z$200. As crisp and clean as the day it was printed, it's now a collector's item.

I thought about writing an illustrated book entitled *Assets in Wonderland*. A billion was pure Dallas: a Texas oil man with a red face and a silly hat. A trillion was a toddler on a runaway tricycle. Alice danced the quadrillion with the Mad Hatter, and a sextillion with a long slimy tail smoked Havana cigars and made porno movies.

The very last note to be produced was five octillion dollars, with 27 noughts. I'm still thinking about that one.

Writing a cheque (which most places wouldn't accept anyway) was tantamount to producing a full-length work of fiction: the zeros looped around its back and front like a daisy chain. And to cap it all, the bank added the word 'only' at the end.

In mid-2008, Zimbabwe very nearly made it into the *Guinness World Records* for the highest daily rate of inflation ever – 98 per cent – having only been pipped by 1946 Hungary. And it doubled in just over 24 hours.

We all became obsessed with currency. When David was eight, he discovered that his girlfriend, Millie, had been seeing someone else. 'I'm going to get hold of that boy,' my son threatened. 'And I'll make him tell me his name, his address *and* his exchange rate!'

Doctors' clinics were overflowing with deranged accountants, calculators went up in smoke, and people began hurling buckets of money into the streets. Machines were installed in supermarkets; you handed over your greasy brick of notes and they were fed to the machine, which counted them and spat them out with the staccato rattle of a machine gun.

Most people couldn't keep up. They'd arrive at the supermarket with a handful of notes that would have bought them a few groceries the previous week, only to find that today they couldn't even buy a matchstick.

When Khanye went home to Victoria Falls on leave, he saw a crowd of baboons and people swarming over the municipal rubbish dump, mixing quite companionably as they dug around for scraps from the hotel kitchens. Some hungry people were walking 20 kilometres from home and back every day collecting food for their families.

Even if you had the cash in the bank, it was not freely available. The banks couldn't keep up with the demand, so they limited daily withdrawals, and it took three days of queuing to collect enough to buy that mythical loaf of bread, waiting in lines that stretched up and down and wound around the streets like the daisy chain on the cheque. And when you reached the front of the queue, the value of your money had halved.

Government's response to inflation was simply to chop off

a few noughts. But they introduced the new notes with no warning, giving people just 21 days to trade in their worthless old currency or risk being stuck with it – a fate suffered by many in the rural areas who either hadn't heard about the change or were unable to afford the bus into town. The first of these exercises was dubbed 'Operation Sunshine' by some joker in government, promising that it would 'usher in a new era of ease and greater security', but within weeks the noughts were on the march again, and we were back in the same old spiral of runaway inflation.

One supermarket decided to try a bit of retail therapy. While listless shoppers searched for things they couldn't find, and wouldn't have been able to afford anyway, they were treated to jolly songs from the Chipmunks and even worse, the 'Hokey Cokey' – enjoining them, at deafening volume, to shake it all about – when many hardly had the energy to push their empty trolleys down the aisles.

Survival in the Third World depends largely on the extended family. At 60, Head Scout Mafira takes care of his mother, his wife and three of his adult children, who are either studying or unemployed. He contributes to the living expenses of one nephew and another nephew's son, and two of his grandchildren live with his wife at their home in Masvingo. Johnson, his oldest son, won't be stashing money away for a new car or a trip overseas: as soon as Mafira retires, he will take on the same responsibilities. That is his culture: a tradition of care that unfortunately doesn't apply to many of Zimbabwe's European senior citizens, whose children have had to leave the country to seek work elsewhere.

Of course, many people still support their elderly parents and visit as often as they can, but not all of them. When one old-age home had to increase the rent beyond the means of some of their occupants, they were forced to write to the more reluctant families, asking them to come and collect their parent, who would otherwise face eviction. It was amazing how quickly the money came in after that. Even sadder were those who did receive letters from their families overseas, but never with a return address.

But where some shirked their obligations, others stepped in from the local community: like SOAP, for example – an organisation that raises money both locally and from all over the world to support indigent pensioners; and Maggie Kriel with her *Morning Mirror* – the fortnightly local rag that supports the Edith Duly Nursing Home through its advertising.

When inflation reached 87.7 sextillion per cent, we told ourselves that we must be nearing rock bottom. 'There's no such thing,' said an Argentinian acquaintance of ours who knew all about hyperinflation. 'In my country, we just dug a deeper hole.'

And yet, somehow, Zimbabwe staggered on; you just had to make the proverbial 'plan', some of which were a good deal more ingenious than others.

Rotina Mavhunga, otherwise known as Nomatter Tagira, a self-proclaimed mystic, managed to outsmart some of the craftiest in the land. At a time when fuel was almost totally unobtainable, she claimed that by tapping a certain rock, it would produce refined diesel. A stunned cabinet task force visited the shrine and witnessed the miracle, returning to Harare with the triumphant news that Zimbabwe's fuel shortages were now at an end. The mystic was showered with an embarrassment of money and gifts (embarrassing to the government, that is) to the tune of around a million US dollars, all thanks to an old tank she had found in the bush a couple of years before.

Like most brilliant ideas, hers was exceedingly simple. Rotina attached a pipe to the tank and concealed it behind a rock, then at her pre-arranged signal, a hidden accomplice would open the tap and diesel would come gushing forth. The members of the task force were apparently so awestruck by her spiritual powers that they removed their shoes in her presence.

Unfortunately, Rotina's glory came to an end when some less gullible government officials began to investigate her claims, and she was eventually sprung and convicted of fraud. At the time of sentencing, she was nowhere to be found, and one can only hope that she's had facial reconstruction, bought herself a BMW (much beloved by officialdom) and is now a member of parliament. She deserves it.

For my part, I decided to boost the dwindling family fortunes by writing a block-busting romance set, of course, in Darkest Africa. I suppose the idea had really taken hold with our visit to Hwange Safari Lodge some years before. We'd had a great morning in the National Park, and had come back for lunch and a siesta in our room on the second floor. But soon after we lay down, we became uncomfortably aware of the presence of a third party. A baboon had swung himself onto our veranda, and his nose was pressed up against the glass, his beady eyes following our every move.

'Oh no,' sighed Rich, getting up to close the curtains on our hairy voyeur, 'it's Mills and Baboon.'

But I couldn't write a steamy romance on my own. I knew that, because I had tried it in the early 1980s, when I was unemployed and living in a room over a hamburger joint in Cairns, Australia. Starting it was relatively easy, but when

I got to the bit where Kate and Stephen sat gazing at each other in a river, and I was describing how his dark curly hairs stuck damply and excitingly to the firm muscularity of his broad chest, I found my tongue stuck to my cheek and could go no further.

And then on a trip to Kenya, I met Tash, another bush-based writer fallen on lean times, whom unlike others I had approached, didn't greet my idea with cries of derision. How could we fail? We'd churn out a series of khaki romances and make ourselves a mint. We both collected armfuls of paperbacks, prepared to immerse ourselves in them until we knew exactly what the publishers required. And that was our first surprise – no longer did the door inevitably close on the palpitating hearts and heaving breasts of the hero and heroine as it did when I tried my first romance. No, now the writer has a choice – either to leave the reader outside with her imagination, or to invite her to follow the protagonists into bed for a threesome, and to stay for as long as she likes.

We decided that our reader would be treated to the whole spread, as it were. Tash would write the lead-up, with limited groping and plenty of hyperventilation, and I would be there for the hands-on, grappling, gasping, groaning climaxes that would have our ladies queuing at the shops for the next instalment. Easy.

But first we needed a pseudonym, and that was one of the things that appealed to me most. Why? Because instead of Bookey Peek, a name reminiscent of mutton mislaid, I (or we) could be suddenly be transformed into the mysteriously exotic Gabriella del Monte: brown-skinned, bare-footed, arms jangling with bangles as she gambolled with her pet lion somewhere in East Africa. Tash opted for Gabriella Bruno, but I objected on the basis that it made her sound rather toothsome and hairy.

Our feisty but feminine heroine, Cathy or 'Cat' to her friends, was an environmental journalist, and according to Tash 'dark and diminutive', whereas I pictured her, naturally, as tall and blonde. Small and swarthy won the day, but I made sure I got a look-in with the owner of Thorn Tree Camp in the Serengeti: 'Tall and graceful, Olivia Prescott was obviously the woman in the photograph – a few years older now, but still very attractive.' Such is the stuff of dreams.

Our hero was a challenge. Should he be the ultimate alpha male, an arrogant playboy, 'wearing a discreet TAG Heuer on his wrist' (per Tash)? Or rather a New Man, more human and fallible, but less awe-inspiring?

We settled on Hugo Sommerville: born in the Argentine; 6 feet 2 inches (185 centimetres just doesn't resonate); 33 years old with gentian-blue eyes; 'dark hairs curling on a broad, bronzed chest' (Tash is obsessed with sweat and body hair), and a disarmingly crooked nose.

Cat has won a week at Thorn Tree Camp and Wildlife Sanctuary; Hugo is based there for a few months while he supervises the building of a new lodge on the other side of the river.

The first thing I did was to start a list of appropriately titillating words and phrases culled from the pile of tatty romances strewn around the house. Some I rejected out of hand – 'love's sweet lava flowed', for instance, and nipples described as 'rock-like points' or 'throbbing peaks', which would presumably necessitate some dangerous abseiling by the enraptured hero. On the other hand, I couldn't wait to send Hugo and Cat 'riding wave after wave of ecstasy in perfect rhythm', finally submerging themselves somewhat dangerously in 'a tidal wave of uninhibited passion'.

Slow down, my writing partner admonished me, they haven't even met yet! And so we began – sending our chapters back and forth to each other for approval or demolition, and posting our comments on Skype.

Bookey: 'We'll have to cut down the number of times he laughs "huskily". If we collect any more of them, we'll have enough to pull a sled.'

And: 'She's got to stop pressing her leg up against the solid bulk of his thigh.'

Tash: 'Thigh will be done.'

As a distraction, we couldn't have come up with anything better. Africa, wildlife and the environment – now we had the chance to create our *own* story, set in a place that we could escape to by simply dreaming in front of the computer.

We threw it all in, all the things we worry about the most. We had droughts, wild fires, poachers. And worst of all, developers bent on destroying our pristine patch of wilderness. But this time Tash and I were in charge. We were the rainmakers, the fighters of fires, the saviours of Thorn Tree Camp, its wildlife and the beautiful river that sustained them all.

It was up to us if Hugo kissed Cat in chapter five or six, and whether the final denouement would be up against the wall of the shower or within sight and smell of the moon-washed river. We had the power – something that we tend to lack in real life, especially on a Zimbabwean farm, living under constant threat of dispossession.

Things were very different at Independence in 1980, when government made a point of reassuring commercial farmers that the country needed them and that their tenure was secure.

Then, Zimbabwe was justly proud of its reputation as the breadbasket of Africa – a major exporter of maize to the rest of the continent. But today the basket is empty, and we cannot even feed our own people. Since the farm invasions began in the year 2000, we have had to import hundreds of thousands of tons of maize – some of it grown, rather ironically, in Zambia, by the same people who were chased off their farms in this country and forced to make a living elsewhere.

For a long time, the overseas newspapers kept churning out the same old mantra: the farms were being redistributed to landless blacks to correct a historical injustice – making it all sound quite reasonable and justifiable – when the truth was that in a murderous campaign directed against the legal owners and their staff, viable farms were being distributed to affluent members of the ruling party to keep them sweet; after which the livestock was left to starve, the crops died in the ground and the wildlife was destroyed. And far from being beneficiaries of this grand scheme, the 'landless blacks' were far worse off than they had ever been.

Having lost their homes and livelihood, many dispossessed farmers were forced to leave the country to seek a living elsewhere, though some of the luckier ones managed to start up other businesses or find a job in town, always hoping that some day they could return to their land. There were heart attacks, suicides, broken marriages and drinking problems. Some sank, some swam, and others kept treading water, waiting for a miracle.

And then there were the Kays, who, like many other farmers, ran a clinic and a school on their 5 000 hectare property near Marondera. And that wasn't all they did. With her family's support, Kerry Kay founded an internationally recognised Aids awareness programme; set up a farm orphans scheme for all those children who had lost parents to the disease, and coordinated Eyes for Africa – a project that provides free cataract operations for the needy. The Kays were and still are staunch supporters of the opposition party, the Movement for Democratic Change, which made them a prime target in the run-up to the elections in 2000. In a widely reported incident, Iain was tied up with wire, brutally assaulted by political thugs, and left for dead. There followed months of terror: their staff were beaten, their home ransacked and a landmine laid on the road to their house, until finally the family was forced to flee. And all because they believed in democratic Zimbabwe and had put their lives on the line for it.

The war on farmers never let up, and soon after the invasions began, the Commercial Farmers' Union began to put out a daily report starting with the words:

'Every attempt is made to provide a comprehensive report on the ongoing activities in relation to farm invasions, but many incidents are unreported due to communication restraints, fear of reprisals and a general weariness on the part of farmers. Farmers' names and in some cases, farm names are omitted to omit the risk of reprisal.'

This discretion was essential but it somehow gave the bulletins a touch of unreality. The people were nameless, faceless; it was Zimbabwe, but it could have been the Congo or some other chaotic African country – anywhere but home. Until the focus fell on Komani Farm in Esigodini, south of Bulawayo, home of my old friend Elspeth Goodwin and her family.

Elspeth and I did a secretarial course together at the Cape

Technical College in the late 1960s. We stayed at a hostel for young ladies called Spes Bona – a mouldy old building at the foot of Table Mountain. I don't remember much about it, except the noise of the traffic (I'd never lived in a city before), and the shrivelled black sea slugs the cook matron served up at breakfast in the guise of sausages.

I don't know what I loathed the most – the cheerless red brick of the Technical College and its freezing classrooms with their high, barred windows; the sticky keys of the manual typewriters we battered day after day till we finally cracked 60 words per minute, or the vicious moods of the southeaster that regularly blew our umbrellas inside out and left us drenched.

Elspeth and I both loved the bush and hated town, but there we diverged; for while I was applying false eyelashes and layers of pink Clearasil, desperate for male attention, Elspeth, always the thrifty one, saved her money and sailed happily along, secure in her conviction that one day she would marry a farmer. And by the time I bumped into her again in the Bulawayo Post Office, almost 20 years later, she was indeed married to Paul Goodwin, living on a farm some 25 kilometres outside Bulawayo, and had produced three children (one of whom, Nell, was to join us later in running the dreaded safari lodge on Stone Hills).

The Goodwins were some of the first farmers in their district to be invaded. Paul is a third-generation Zimbabwean: a just, gentle man, who thinks before he speaks. For years, he was one of Matabeleland's premier cattlemen, internationally known for his breeding of Afrikanders and Tulis and his pioneering work with 'Boranders' – Afrikanders cross Kenyan Borans: a breed developed for its ability to cope with drought conditions. Clad in a huge coat and gumboots with a ciggy hanging out of her mouth, Elspeth was at the dairy by 3am every morning. Every inch of the Goodwin's land was utilised.

We paid them a visit soon after the elections in the year 2000. The cattle stud signs on the gateposts had all been taken down. Now only the word 'Komani', painted in black, remained and it was hardly legible. Paul met us at the gate of the security fence surrounded by six large, excited dogs, mostly mongrels, with a touch of Rhodesian ridgeback here and there. We all sat on the lawn in the shade of a Natal mahogany, drinking dreadfully strong tea out of cracked mugs from a kettle covered with a cock-eyed woollen cosy – Elspeth style.

The rhythmic sound of chopping echoed up from a nearby paddock.

'That's all we hear these days,' said Paul, shaking his head. 'If they're not stealing the fencing wire and using it to snare my cattle or my game, they're cutting down the trees.'

He pulled out black and white photographs of the devastation along the river caused by dozens of illegal gold panners. A few months before, the farm was a haven for wildlife, but now almost all had been killed.

At lunchtime, Nell was facing me on the other side of the dining room table. She suddenly stopped in mid-conversation and her eyes widened as she looked over my shoulder. Twelve barefoot men ran across the lawn, accompanied by a uniformed policeman, for what he was worth. The police were merely onlookers, unable to protect the farmers, they claimed, because the invasions, however violent, were 'a political matter'. The dogs were silent.

Paul excused himself from the table, and walked heavily out the door to hear their latest list of demands, while Elspeth got on the radio to rally a few neighbours for support in case there was trouble.

60

'They can do what they like,' she said fiercely. 'I'm not leaving here. Ever.'

Chapter Six – The Land Of Lost Content

Into my heart an air that kills
From yon far country blows:
What are those blue remembered hills,
What spires, what farms are those?

That is the land of lost content,
I see it shining plain,
The happy highways where I went
And cannot come again.

A E Housman

Two months later, over 100 families had moved onto the Goodwin's land. They were breaking pumps, lighting bush fires and killing cattle – around five head a week. 'It started suddenly in my dry dairy cow paddock,' Elspeth told me on the phone. 'Because the cows are so tame, they only need to put a snare around their necks and then kill them with an axe. They're doing it in broad daylight.'

I asked her if they could see the invaders from the homestead.

'No,' she said, 'they're around 90 metres away behind some trees. I can't see them, so as far as I am concerned, they're not there.'

When Paul arrived at a paddock to cut grass for the dairy cows or graze his cattle, the squatters would inevitably be waiting for him, barricading the gate and refusing him entry. One of the staff had been feeding them with information, but despite being constantly threatened and intimidated, the other workers remained loyal to their employers. When foreman John Siwela carted water to the cattle troughs, the war vets demanded that he stop and fill their containers. Heavily outnumbered and at great personal risk, Siwela refused to assist them until the cattle were seen to first.

Komani lies amongst the blue hills and fertile valleys of Esigodini (known as Essexvale prior to Independence). When the Matabele crossed into the country from the south in 1838, they split into two groups – the one led by King Mzilikazi took the route through the Kalahari and into the Zambezi Valley, while the other, including the young Nkulumane, the king's son and heir, travelled directly through the Limpopo Valley and the Matobo Hills, finally settling some 25 kilometres outside the present Bulawayo in the Esigodini area, which was to be their agreed rendezvous. But over a year later, the second group received news that Mzilikazi was dead. The only person able to conduct the annual ceremony of *Ncwala* (first fruits) was the king, so it was decided that 14-year-old Nkulumane should become the new ruler of the Matabele. Unfortunately for them, however, Mzilikazi was very much alive, and not far off. Vengeance was swift. Nkulumane was either murdered or spirited away – no one has ever discovered which – while his supporters were wiped out, and many of them, it is said, are buried in the graves on Crocodile, the farm adjoining Komani.

There are ancient gold workings on the farm, and many years ago, when previous owners were digging a septic tank, they found a grave filled with treasures befitting a member of the royal family. It was thought to have belonged to one of the wives of King Lobengula: another of Mzilikazi's sons and his eventual successor as King of the Matabele.

Nell Goodwin was married on Komani in January 2001, when the family was still living there, giving us a chance to dust off our smart clothes and catch up with a few friends. The turn-off to the farm is at the bottom of a long escarpment where the hills give way to a lush green valley, filled not long ago with maize, flowers, citrus trees and acres of vegetables – the finest in Matabeleland.

Frederick Courteney Selous, famous hunter and explorer, lived there for a while with his wife Gladys in the late 1890s. He describes their 'well-thatched house ... in a very picturesque position on top of a cliff about 80 feet above the Ingnaima River ...' in his book *Sunshine and Storm in Rhodesia*. 'The view from our front door up the river,' he writes, 'with our cattle and horses grazing on the banks, and the ducks and geese swimming in the pools or sunning themselves on the sand, was always singularly homelike.'

As was the Komani homestead – you can see it from the road, set high on a hill, white with a black tin roof. I always loved that house with its sprawling rooms and the large, busy kitchen redolent with the rich smell of Elspeth's marula jelly and the bottles of her special lemon drink that no one can make as well as she can. In the front of the house, her flower beds were shaded with a pair of fine old Natal mahogany trees, wild wisterias and coral trees: a mix of strong African colours – deep green, scarlet and blue – and the gentle fragrances of an English cottage garden. At the back, there was the smell of manure, the gobbling of turkeys, the dairy, the tractors – all the paraphernalia of a working farm.

As we drove through the gateposts on the day of the wedding, a DDF (District Development Fund) truck came hurtling past us, churning up the dust behind it. The last time we had visited, the paddocks along the driveway were neatly fenced. But not now. Thatched squatter huts had sprung up all along the road, and scrawny chickens flew up in front of our vehicle in a flap and flurry of feathers. Women tending their ragged rows of mealies straightened up and stared as we passed – their faces expressionless.

It was a shock, but we left it all behind us when we pulled up amongst the other vehicles parked at the bottom of the hill, craning our necks to see who else had arrived and if we recognised them in their party clothes. Hands were shaken, cheeks were kissed, and rude remarks exchanged between old friends who hadn't seen each other since the last wedding or funeral.

An elegant figure in navy blue chiffon with a pair of very shapely legs stepped out of the white marquee on the lawn to greet us, tottering just a little in her high heels. Only the cigarette and the throaty laugh gave her away as my friend Elspeth, queen of the dairy, and today, the mother of the bride.

Drinks in hand, we all made our way down the steps to the lower lawn, where the service was to be held, taking up our seats on the rows of hay bales considerately covered with stockfeed bags, so we didn't get the prickles in our bottoms.

Snow in the Drakensberg, a rare phenomenon in January, brought fresh, cold mountain air streaming over the blue hills and across the valley. The hymn sheet was framed with a row of silver guinea fowl, and as the priest began the service, we could hear them whistling to their chicks under the feathery green canopy of the thorn trees below us. A small herd of eland wandered by and at that moment, there was no thought of yesterday, nor the dread of tomorrow – only happiness for the young couple standing before us.

Rich took my hand and squeezed it, and I could see other couples smiling at each other, and moving closer, remembering perhaps, like us, their own special day when the future seemed to shine endlessly ahead in an unbroken beam of sunlight.

Nell's dress in crushed raw silk, white with a touch of gold, had something of the Old Testament about it; it was as natural and lovely as the girl herself, walking arm in arm with her father down the aisle between the hay bales with a bunch of roses and flame lilies in her arms. The flowers, the food – everything that day had come from the homes and the farms of the people of the district.

I don't believe anyone wanted to talk about their troubles in the crowded marquee, least of all Paul and Elspeth. Children tumbled barefoot in the grass between the tables, and David dragged me off in my finery through sticky red mud to have a chat with a small pink pig and watch the dairy cows being brought in from pasture.

It was an evening to end all evenings; as the sun set it flooded the distant hills with pure gold, softly backlighting the young couple as they posed for pictures in the garden.

I was facing the entrance to the marquee when one of Paul's workers slipped in during dinner and beckoned to him. They stepped outside, and when Paul came back 10 minutes later, his smile had disappeared along with the magic of the day, and his face was rigid with tension. The squatters had lit yet another fire near the entrance gate, for no other reason but to create a disturbance.

'Oh, for God's sake,' said one of the Goodwin's neighbours. 'Just let it burn!' And with that, the illusion of a perfect day had disappeared as swiftly as a cloud passes over the moon. No matter how much we wanted to believe it, we were not a happy, united little community, making plans for the years to come and playing a part in our children's lives. The children were gone, and we had been left behind, hanging onto our memories.

Nell and Neil were living in Cape Town and would later immigrate to Australia, as would her oldest brother Charles. Younger brother Brian was in Cape Town, studying agricultural management. Nicki and Nigel, Rich's two children, were with us at the wedding, a rare occasion when the family was together. Nicki was married and living in England; Nige was studying chiropractic in Durban, and both of them would end up in New Zealand a few years later. People had started talking about the Zimbabwean diaspora: the wanderers, who belonged nowhere, but always kept Africa locked away in their hearts.

Fourteen months later, we received a phone call from Nell. The war vets had called Paul to a meeting and demanded that they leave Komani immediately. Or else. There was no doubt what that meant – the chief war vet living on the next-door farm had been responsible for the hacking to death of 16 church workers, including a baby, in the late 1980s when dissident activities were at their height. They were members of a Pentecostal group, who were running a cooperative farming venture for the benefit of the local people.

When Nell and her brother Brian heard the news, they jumped into their car in Cape Town and made what was normally a three-day journey home in 24 hours.

The last time we had been at Komani, the path to the house had been lined with milk churns filled with roses. Now, the yard was littered with ironmongery – old beds, cages, engines; everything that could be salvaged was being carried out of the house and packed into trucks. Elspeth's brother, Rob was there with his wife, shifting a cage full of noisy turkeys into their vehicle. We greeted them, but none of us really knew what to say.

Elspeth was sitting smiling in the back of a truck, wearing a pair of long cotton pants decorated with beetles. She looked as though she was presiding over a jumble sale for the Boy Scouts, instead of watching her life being taken to pieces and carried away. In her hand, she held a list of items that the war vets had demanded should be left for them on the farm.

'Thank you for coming!' She gave us both a warm hug.

'Bookey, could you go through my medicine cupboard in the bathroom and sort it out? And Rich, they're dismantling pumps at the swimming pool; maybe you could go and give them a hand?'

I walked into the gutted farmhouse with its bare windows

and walls, followed by one of the hairier old mongrels, his tail between his legs. We negotiated our way to the bathroom between dozens of packing boxes, and I sat down cross-legged in front of the cupboard below the sink. It all looked so familiar: shelves of old bottles; jars and packets never thrown out, whatever their expiry date, just in case – the oldest lost in the back amongst the cobwebs. Tubes of nappy rash ointment last used for Brian, now 19. Nasal drops in the little brown bottle (circa 1896) prescribed for Paul's mother who had died many years before.

I examined each one and then put it in a basket. After all, it was family history, and unless something was obviously useless, I couldn't bring myself to chuck it out.

We stopped for tea at mid-morning, and gathered in the office with other friends who had come to help. I wondered if I was the only one who was aware of the song playing on the radio: 'I'm leaving on a jet plane. Don't know when I'll be back again.'

We hadn't seen Paul. He was lying on his bed, too traumatised to watch the dismantling of his home, his life and 40 years of farming. When he was able to talk about it some years later, he said: 'People ask you how it felt and you can tell them, but you can't actually comprehend until you've experienced it. We'd known for six months or so that we probably wouldn't be able to last, and I thought that I was prepared. But when we actually drove out that night for the last time, I had the feeling that I was totally superfluous, that I'd failed. And when you feel like that, you don't want sunlight, you want darkness in a little cocoon, protected from everything.'

In fact, Paul was heading for a nervous breakdown. 'Why me?' he asked John Siwela.

'Because you are the best, *nkosi*,' his foreman answered.

You may well ask why the Goodwins hadn't left long before, when their lives had first been made intolerable. It wasn't just stubbornness, for the general feeling was that if farmers stood united and refused to break ranks, the law would eventually protect them. After all, the whole exercise had been illegal. When new eviction orders were issued, as legally unenforceable as all the others, their lawyer advised them to sit tight and move nothing from the farm.

'Phone me if you have a problem,' Paul had often been told by one influential politician, the inference being that the invasions had nothing to do with government, but were the work of a bunch of renegade war veterans. But when he made that call as his last resort, the man said that he was unable to help, and asked instead if Paul had any heifers for sale.

When the invasions began, government assured us that only farms fitting certain criteria would be affected. Under-utilised land, for example, or farms adjacent to communal areas. But all the criteria fell away, till it was simply: 'Each farmer will be allowed to keep 1 500 hectares only,' impossible for those with wildlife or large herds of beef cattle, but just manageable for the Goodwins, who reasoned that at least they could keep the dairy going and a small nucleus of Paul's cattle. They could irrigate crops for the cattle and keep going on a small scale. They had no kids to educate. It was possible.

Some were critical of Paul for giving in to the war vets' demands, believing that he should have hung on, regardless of the consequences to his family. But that is not Paul's way, and after two years of a war of attrition, wearing him down, day after day, night after tormented night, he could take it no longer. At the final meeting, the war vets demanded that the Goodwins leave immediately, but Paul bought time by saying that he had to take his cattle to the sale that was due to be held at Esigodini three days later.

I followed Elspeth and Nell into the garden, where they began digging up plants to take to town.

'What about the aloes?' Nell called over to her mother.

'Leave them. They'll survive without water till we come back.'

Elspeth is an old friend and a straight talker. When we were alone for a few moments later in the afternoon I asked her if she honestly believed that they would return to Komani.

'Yes,' she said firmly. 'I do. No one else in the district has been evicted, and our case is coming up soon in the Magistrate's Court. I'm running a very productive dairy, and everyone knows that Paul is a first-class cattleman. We've switched off the machines in the dairy, washed everything down and locked up. The cattle will go to a neighbour till things settle down. We'll be back.'

We stayed at Komani until early evening, when the trucks were packed and everyone was moving off into town. The family was the last to go and we left Elspeth in the yard surrounded by dogs and packing boxes.

'By the way,' I called out of the car window, 'don't forget to leave me those lovely beetle pants in your will. Remember, I'm the entomologist.'

'Good grief,' she said, 'you want them back? You gave them to *me* 10 years ago!'

We left at sunset, when the hills were sunk into deep blue shadow. On our way out we passed a boy of around seven or eight pulling a car made of wire through the dust. I was watching him in the rear-view mirror when he raised a clenched fist and shook it at us.

In a sense, the Goodwins were lucky. They were pushed out before the real madness took over, given a few days to collect their things, and despite the threats, not subjected to violence like so many other farmers and their workers would be in time to come. And they had somewhere to go. Paul's mother had offered to send him and Elspeth to Australia when they were first married to have a look around, but Paul had already been farming for 10 years then, and had no interest in living anywhere else. But his mother was never comfortable with his decision, and she left them her house in her will – because, she told them with a foresight that we have all lacked or refused to accept: 'You won't end your days farming.'

The Goodwins had left Komani, but the nightmare was far from over.

'My darling is suffering from total heartbreak,' Elspeth wrote in an email. 'After 40 years of farming, he had to sell his pedigreed cattle at slaughter prices, and he was there to see it happen. The Boranders we left with Mike Mylne have been stolen, and Paul fears that the farm labour will come and demand the huge severances promised to them by government that we can't possibly afford. He is broken.'

The Boranders were recovered two years later, and brought to Stone Hills for safekeeping. When the court case was heard, the government attorney agreed that the Goodwins should have their land back, but the magistrate then demanded a signed agreement on a government letterhead, something that he well knew would be impossible to obtain. So much for the legal process.

Not long after the Goodwins left Komani, we were having

tea on the veranda when the phone rang. Rich came back to the table, his expression grim.

'The lands officer has begun touring the district. They're going to divide up our farms.' The familiar stone dropped in my stomach, and I could feel my eyes pooling with tears.

'But they can't do that on Stone Hills! It's impossible. Once they're on the land, we'll lose every living thing.'

'Exactly. And we can't afford to fence off our allocation. Anyway, which 1 500 hectares would we choose? If we keep the house and the lodge, we lose the borehole and the compound. Let's face it – there's no way out of this one.'

We sat in silence, looking out at the hills, but seeing nothing. So this was how it was going to end. Not an outright eviction, certainly, but if anything it was worse: a slow process giving us the time to stand witness to the destruction of our land and everything on it.

The phone rang again, and Rich hauled himself to his feet to answer it.

'Oh?' I heard him say, and his voice had suddenly brightened. 'Thanks for letting me know. Maybe they're seeing sense at last.'

He rang off and came back to the table.

'That was Rob Rosenfels with a bit of good news. Apparently, government is removing 12 000 squatters from the wildlife conservancies in the lowveld. They're telling the farmers to return to their land.'

I tried to smile but I couldn't. It was too much to take in. One minute, it was all over; the next we were being offered a crumb of hope that government might end the madness they had started.

Then, suddenly, I started to boil. Of course, they couldn't get rid of 12 000 squatters, nor did they intend to. This was at best a game, at worst a form of torture. The empty words were part of the process of wearing down the farmers – crush them, raise them up, then beat them down again. They did it to the Goodwins, packing up to leave their farm with death threats hanging over their heads. The phone kept ringing: *'Don't go. We'll sort it all out on Monday. Hang on for a few more days.'* The constant see-sawing between despair and hope until they almost wanted it to end, because they couldn't bear to go stumbling on blindly through the darkness never knowing when the guillotine would fall.

We had to go to town the next morning, and I cried all the way there till I was ankle-deep in wet tissues.

Three years after the Goodwins had gone, Charlie Ross visited Komani, having heard that the 'new owner' was selling off some dairy equipment. They stood at what used to be the front door, now torn off its hinges, and Charlie looked over the man's shoulder and into the rubble of glass, wood and plaster that once was the Goodwin's home.

He asked the man if he was legally entitled to sell the equipment.

'Of course! I am a politician, and this has been allocated to me. Everything here is mine.'

'And what about the other people on the farm?' Charlie enquired.

The man laughed. 'I can get rid of them any time I want. As soon as I arrived, I got them all together and took out my pistol. I told them that I'd shoot anyone that gave me trouble.'

The man's wife came out of the house, stepping disdainfully over the debris.

'You can't believe the state this place is in!' she told Charlie indignantly. 'The cupboard doors have been taken; all the windows are smashed; the basins have even been torn out of the walls. *And* they've been keeping their calves in here – the whole place stinks of manure. I can't believe that they would give us a house in this condition – it's disgusting!'

Chapter Seven – The Eleventh Commandment

'It was a sunny day and the birds were twittering happily in the trees when Miss Piggy came and collected us in the car ...'

So began Daisy Moyo's account of a Marula School field trip to Stone Hills.

As a lover of all things porcine, I took it as a compliment.

Sixteen boys and girls from Grade Seven are waiting for us in the school yard, all neatly dressed and carrying pencils and plastic-covered exercise books. Mrs Dube, headmistress, and Mrs Ncube, Grade Four teacher, squeeze into the cab next to me. At a signal from Khanye, the kids scramble into the back of the Toyota, and as we drive down towards the farm ('Fast as a cheetah,' says Daisy) they are shouting, singing and waving to their friends on the side of the road.

But as soon as we reach our gate, the noise subsides into whispers and giggles. The kids know the rules: this is the animals' place and they must not be disturbed. I pull up a couple of kilometres down the track, and everyone jumps out, except little Amanda Prudence Ncube, who waits to be helped. 'Amanda is a lady,' I remark, and she nods. They stand in an excited group in front of Khanye.

'Now,' he says, speaking in a mixture of Sindebele and English, 'everything you see here is important: not only the animals, but the trees, the grass, the stones – they all make up the chain of life. And if you have come here with love in your hearts, they will all welcome you.'

He raises his hand. 'Let's take a moment to listen to them.'

Everyone is quiet, as they become attuned to birdsong and the gentle chirping of crickets: noises that are drowned out by an engine or the sound of human voices. 'Silence' we sometimes call it when we are not really listening. It is anything but.

Khanye leads the way into the trees. 'Use all your five senses,' he says. 'Be alert, and tell me how we know that the animals are here.'

Buhle Dube (Good Zebra), one of the keenest boys, points to a myriad of sharp-tipped tracks – a herd of impala has walked along the path in the morning. And Trymore Ndlovu (Trymore Elephant) finds the midden that belongs to the territorial male.

'What is a territory?' Khanye asks, and almost everyone's hand shoots up. He has taught them well.

The kids don't recognise the porcupine quills they find

on the path, and they can hardly believe that, as the largest rodent in Africa, it's related to the rat. But they all know what's good to eat, and while they help themselves to the sweet black berries of the velvet *Bridelia*, and suck on the tiny sharper tasting fruits of the rock *Rhus* and the donkeyberry, Khanye reminds them of their tradition: always pick fruit with one hand and not two, leaving some for those who follow.

The teachers are lagging. Mrs Dube is always game for an outing, but now her shiny auburn-tipped wig is slightly askew and there are rivulets of sweat running down her face. Mrs Ncube totters unhappily along behind her in a pair of black high heels. I did warn her.

We rest in the shade while the kids go searching for Bushman rock art. Ten minutes later, Walter and Thabo come rushing back to tell us that they have discovered the paintings of the fish – a rare find in the rock art of the Matobo. They've been taught that these were the work of the San people, but they are amazed to learn that they are at least 1 500 to 2000 years old.

Then Dumiso appears with a rusty wire snare, dating back to when we first moved onto the farm, and this gives Khanye an opportunity to explain how cruel this is. And that snaring is illegal, and can lead to imprisonment.

The children have learned that they must extend their appreciation to all living things, and not just to those that are appealing. Khanye stops by the Bushman arrow-poison tree with its leathery foliage and bright crimson berries. The only creatures able to feed on its leaves are the misleadingly named elegant grasshoppers, which in some years breed so well they strip the leaves from acres of trees, leaving the animals hungry. They are so toxic that only a few birds will take them on, like the red-winged starling who whacks them repeatedly on the ground until the poison has dissipated. But, Khanye reminds the children, the tree uses its poison as a defence, and it was invaluable to the Bushmen who would tip their arrows with it for hunting.

I find Daisy Moyo throwing little stones into a hole in an old termite mound, and it reminds me of one of Badger's recent adventures. None of the children have ever met Badger (he's always hiding up in the hills when they visit the farm) but they love to hear about him, so when they gather back at the vehicle at the end of the walk, I tell them the story of how I very nearly lost him forever.

Badge had been full of complaints from the moment I met him for our evening walk: there was nothing to hunt; he was hungry; it was cold and he *still* didn't have a girlfriend. We should have packed up there and then and gone home. And if we had, I told the children, he wouldn't have poked his head into that deep, dark hole in an abandoned termite mound: something I had warned him about time and again. I walked away calling him, but when he hadn't joined me 10 minutes later, I went back to find one paw and a tail sticking up into the air, while the other paw was squeezed between his fat little body and the side of the hole. If Badge had fallen in, rescuing him would have been almost impossible. The mounds are constructed of clay, cemented with the termites' excrement. They are as solid as the foundations of a house.

I took hold of one foot and tried to release the other, but he was trapped. For a moment, I debated whether to leave him to starve for a few days, like Rabbit did to Pooh when he got stuck in his front door, having gorged himself on honey. But there were no leopards in the Hundred Acre Wood, only Tiggers who were not in the habit of eating bears.

A paw twitched. It was dark and I couldn't go and get

help, leaving him totally vulnerable to passing predators. It took ages, but in the end I managed to unscrew him. He popped out like a cork from a bottle.

Of course, the children aren't familiar with Pooh and his friends, but the picture of a small, fat, furry creature stuck bottoms up in a hole makes them scream with laughter. 'More!' they plead. 'Tell us what else he's done!'

This is the final year of junior school for the Grade Sevens, and if they do not make some connection with the natural world now, they may never have the opportunity to experience it again. One day, if stability ever returns to Zimbabwe, we'll build a conservation centre – a place where the kids can come and stay – and we'll develop a comprehensive programme that will extend far beyond Marula to other schools in the country.

At the end of their visit, the children come to the garage to help feed the kudu, gemsbok, eland and warthog who gather on winter afternoons for their ration of game cubes, and then, while they are having their tea, Khanye starts a discussion about what they have seen and learned.

He tries a trick that we have learned from Steve and Anna Tolan, an inspirational English couple who have created a first class educational facility on the boundary of the Luangwa National Park in Zambia. We've never met them, but they contacted us after they had read our first book, *All the Way Home*, with their own stories of the warthogs they had raised and the other animals who have become part of their lives.

A large cardboard box is lying behind the old Land Rover. Khanye lowers his voice dramatically.

'In that box,' he says, 'you will find the most dangerous animal in the world.'

The children eye him to see if he is joking, but his

expression is serious. They shrink back a little.

'Now, I want you to come with me, one by one, to look at it. I'll make sure that it won't hurt you. But you must promise me one thing.'

The children's eyes widen.

'When you have looked inside, you must go and stand over there, under that tree, and don't tell the others what you have seen. Okay?'

They line up, the bolder ones at the front, the others hanging back until they are quite sure that it is safe. Innocent, a day scholar, is first. Khanye opens the box, just a little.

'Now remember,' he raises his finger warningly, '*Bhasopa* – beware! This one can kill you.'

Innocent peers in very cautiously, and then gives a snort of laughter. There's a mirror inside the box, and all he can see is his own reflection.

In the meantime, I go to the house and come back with Max the squirrel, who very obligingly sits on my shoulder and gives me a kiss. The expression of delight on every child's face is worth a thousand frustrations and anxieties. If only you could freeze that moment and fix it forever in their memories.

On the way back to school, they start singing in harmony, their voices carried up and away by the wind: 'Don't kill the world. She's all we have ...' It's Boney M's song and it's become their theme. Amanda is the lead singer; she's tiny but has a strong, husky voice reminiscent of a mini Aretha Franklin.

These kids may forget almost everything else that we have taught them, but maybe they'll remember how they felt when they met little Max, or Mary the bushbuck. Long after the other children had gone back to the vehicle, Amanda was still staring over the fence at Mary, standing quietly below her.

'Mary made me feel like I was with my mother,' Amanda wrote in her composition. 'I was shocked when I saw her; I felt like I was dreaming but I realised that I wasn't. I have never seen a beautiful animal like Mary in my whole life.'

Feelings of empathy, feelings of wonder – these are the emotions that we want to stir in the children. And the knowledge that every creature, no matter how small or seemingly insignificant, has a right to be respected; that they feel pain, sorrow, happiness and contentment just as we do. And even if the only beneficiary of all this is one overworked donkey pulling a scotch cart, receiving a pat rather than a whip around the ears, then we have achieved something.

Nature is not a virtual experience. It is real. It is us. Humans, like every other living being, from scorpions to elephants, are made up of the same elements: water, air, earth – and energy. Although we may often feel like it, we are not merely spectators of the natural world. We are a part of it – but until you stroke the fur of a baby squirrel or smell the fragrance of the earth after rain, how will you ever know that this is true?

'The earth does not belong to man; man belongs to the earth.' The Marula children have memorised Chief Seattle's immortal words – words that their own ancestors might have spoken before the advent of missionaries, roads and Progress. But do they truly understand them?

I've always wondered how different life would be today had there been an 11th commandment: 'Thou shalt protect the earth' – and that message had been thundered out from pulpits all over the world since the dawn of Christianity. For let's be honest, perving over the garden fence at your neighbour's wife in her bikini is a lot less harmful than spraying your roses with insecticide.

But instead the Bible tells us to 'multiply ... and have dominion ... over every living thing that moveth upon the earth' – an instruction that, to the detriment of the rest of the planet, we have obeyed to the letter. And one, sadly, that seems to come very naturally to us.

Back at the school, Mrs Dube pumps my hand: 'You are doing a wonderful job on Stone Hills,' she says.

It's a great compliment, yet she and her fellow teachers are the ones who truly deserve the praise by continuing to dedicate themselves to teaching under the most difficult and financially unrewarding circumstances.

Mrs Ncube also shakes my hand, but less enthusiastically. 'Can't you find me a job in Australia?' she asks. It's the only question she has asked all afternoon.

That's the trouble: it's easy to reach the children – they are receptive and hungry for knowledge – but as adults we tend to be inflexible and closed to new ideas, unless they are of direct advantage to us.

So I am doubtful when Lisa Hywood of the Tikki Hywood Trust calls me to arrange a visit to the school by two girls from the Werribee Open Range Zoo in Melbourne. We have recently been combining our conservation lessons with Lisa's Kusanganisa educational programme, and the visit by Rachel and Katie is the first step in trying to motivate the teachers to include wildlife in their lessons.

On the first day, my fears seem well founded: the teachers have been called to go on a nationwide strike; they are tired, anxious and totally unmotivated. It is almost embarrassing. In contrast, the girls are all fired up: neither of them has been to Africa before; this is their first Zimbabwean school, and they

83

have been preparing for months. They speak to the assembled teachers about their plans for the next few days, but when they ask if they can sit in on their classes, the response is a weary: 'Okay, but for how long?' Even worse, while the girls are talking, the teachers keep on looking at their watches.

I attend their first workshop that afternoon. The children have only just finished cleaning the floor and it smells strongly of Cobra polish. I don't usually notice it, but that day I am only too aware that like all the classrooms, the plaster is falling off the walls, the paint is peeling and most of the windows are broken. Rachel and Katie are anxious, and almost overly polite. They speak to hundreds of people at the zoo every day, so they know what they are doing, but I wonder if they could possibly be prepared for Africa with all its cultural differences and problems so far removed from the comparative ease of life in Australia.

They pin a parable on the board – the one about the seeds falling on rocky ground, and then begin a discussion on how best the teachers can bring wildlife into their everyday lessons, to instill a love of animals in the children, and to make them want to protect and conserve them. For the younger kids, show them pictures, arouse their wonder and make it fun! And for the older ones, make them understand how animals and plants are linked together. What would happen if their habitat disappears? How will they live?

Interest is starting to grow. I can see it. It's not that the message is new. It's the way it's being presented: the girls are passionate; they are reaching out and the teachers are starting to respond. They can't help themselves. Even the reluctant Mrs Ncube has stopped examining her nails and is listening intently. And when Rachel spreads out the laminated photographs of wild animals from all over the world, and shows them the beautifully illustrated children's books, the puzzles and the games, they all leap to their feet and crowd around the table with exclamations of surprise and delight.

The next morning, they are all outside, waiting for the girls and clamouring for their attention.

'Come to my class first, Katie!'

'Come and play games with my kids, Rachel!' Werribee has won them over.

The girls stay for five intensive days. They spend a lot of time tutoring Khanye, and they leave him with suitcases full of ideas and eye-catching educational materials. Now it's up to us to continue the momentum.

On their final morning, Mrs Dube calls a special assembly to thank Rachel and Katie for everything they have done. There are 330 children in the school yard: 80 boarders in full blue and white uniform and black school shoes, and the rest day scholars – a ragged bunch, many barefoot, with hardly a uniform between them. Many are Aids orphans. Learning doesn't come easy on a empty stomach, so for the past few years, through the dedicated fundraising of my oldest friend, Hennie Walton and her generous friends and family in England, we have managed to provide them with a meal a day: just a slab of sadza, cabbage and gravy, but more than most of them will receive at home.

I can see Rachel and Katie dabbing at their eyes as the kids march past them, feet stamping, arms swinging, with the little ones last, in a muddle, completely out of step as they turn to stare at the two girls.

That afternoon, we take the teachers on a game drive around the sanctuary. As if they know what is required, the animals come out in force. The Werribee girls are familiar with many of the animals from the zoo, but this is the first time they have seen them in the wild, as it is for most of the teachers. Afterwards, we bring them back to the lodge for tea and cakes (a rare luxury for all of us) and a final discussion.

Later, we ask them what has been the highlight of their day. Mrs Dube says it was watching a giraffe drinking at the waterhole, head down, and legs splayed out awkwardly. Mrs Lupahla enjoyed watching the pair of Verreaux's eagles at their nest. And for Mrs Ncube, it was simply 'to have been treated like a white person'. It must have been that chocolate cake.

The Marula conservation lessons began simply as an exercise to educate the kids about wildlife, and hopefully, by osmosis, their parents. And, in truth, it was one of the only positive things we could do to try and protect the animals on Stone Hills and the land around us. But over time the weekly exercise has turned into real involvement. Khanye is a natural teacher: he plays the animal games that Rachel and Katie taught him; tells the kids stories and tests them on their knowledge. The children smile and wave as we pass them on the road, and they flock to the Tuesday classes, quite voluntarily. There's the scraping of 60-odd chairs when I arrive at the classroom. 'Goo-ood afternoo-oon, Mrs Pick!' they all shout. I pretend to block my ears, and whisper back, 'Good afternoon, class,' whereupon they all burst into laughter, no matter how often I do it.

It feels good to be a part of the community. And who could be depressed for long with all that laughter and energy around you?

'Please,' Amanda wrote just before she left Marula for good. 'If Mary has a baby, can you name it after me?'

Chapter Eight – Love On The Rocks

I was sorting through a container of mealworms on the kitchen steps one afternoon when I was joined by a pair of Natal francolins and a rock elephant shrew: the same sleek little chap who likes to pick up crumbs under the dinner table every evening. I threw a mealworm onto the lawn and the male francolin picked it up while calling softly to his mate. When she scurried to his side, he dropped the worm, and she ate it. This happened maybe a dozen times before she felt stuffed, as one *might* after a box and a half of Belgian chocolates, and wandered off. And then, but only then, did the male begin to feed himself.

Charm, manners, straight legwork – call it what you like: the fact is that it pays off. Birds do it, boys do it – if they've got any sense – but badgers definitely don't. Like the Aussie male (or so I am told), they haven't got time for all that foreplay nonsense. It's a question of *Brace yourself, Sheila and* (at least in the badger's case) *don't bother calling me when you're up the duff.*

That's not to say that they don't invest time and effort into locating a mate – they do. But once they've found each other, he turns off the music, drags her into the burrow, chucks away the key and gets on with it. In fact, he'll forcibly keep her captive there for around three days, while chasing off any other lecherous males who may be lurking.

It's a shame that it's all over so quickly, when luckier animals like the lions lie about for days in an indolent orgy of sex and sleep, being peered at by shameless people in vehicles who count the minutes between copulations. Fortunately, though, lions appear to be natural exhibitionists – unlike leopards, as Scout Richard Mabhena discovered one fine morning when he saw movement at the top of some rocks. On going to investigate, he caught sight of a female leopard heading off up the hill followed by a male, who stepped out into the open, about 30 metres from Mabhena, snarling and fixing him with a cold yellow-green stare.

'*Hamba Mthakathi!*' he shouted, 'Away with you, sorcerer!' waving his arms, and fully expecting the cat to disappear as they normally do.

Not a bit of it. Still growling, the leopard turned and very slowly started to follow his female, all the while looking over his shoulder at Mabhena as if daring him to follow.

Mabhena was laughing when he told the story. I asked

him if he was frightened and he said of course not; he'd had other experiences with leopards and he was totally confident it wouldn't have attacked him. I wish it had happened to me – I would have extracted every inch of drama from it and filled at least a couple of chapters of my next book.

Anyway, Mabhena hadn't always been so casual. I didn't remind him of his first year on Stone Hills when he walked around a rock, straight into a 'bluddifukkin big cat', feeding on a tsessebe. The predator jumped as high as he did, and gave a roar of fright.

Being essentially solitary animals with very large home ranges, honey badgers can't rely on bumping into each other at opportune moments. It doesn't happen that way. Instead they have a communal noticeboard, which conveys the same sort of messages as the advertisements one sees in the Hitching Post page of the South African *Farmers' Weekly.*

'God-fearing lady badger looking for attractive males with similar interests. Must have hygienic habits. My passions are scorpions, mice and frogs in season.'

Or in Badge's case: 'Small, fun-loving badger with plenty of toys seeking friendship.'

But where we use words, honey badger's use scats and urine deposited at a communal midden, which is regularly checked out by hopeful males. From these scented offerings, he will know who is around and how often, and whether there is any point in pursuing that female who, in the absence of a handkerchief, has left an enticing dab of her perfume on the rock.

Badge found his first midden on a low rock near the Mathole River one afternoon, and he was entranced, intrigued and terrified all at the same time. Big brute badgers leave bold statements right in the middle of the pile: 'I'm boss around here, and don't you forget it!' while little Badgers creep up to the perimeter and deposit a tiny message that can't possibly offend anyone. Which is exactly what Badge did. Then he scuttled off, but a few minutes later, he turned and went cautiously back for another look.

'Perhaps he's checking his spelling,' suggested Khanye.

One of Rich's National Parks mates had similar ideas concerning middens of the human variety.

'If a guy visits you,' he used to say, 'and pees loudly and splashily into the bowl, he's issuing a challenge to the alpha male of the household. But if he's not so sure of himself, he'll trickle it quietly down the side.'

It figures.

Badge's first, tentative foray into romance happened when he was 18 months old. I'd returned from three weeks in Australia visiting my parents just as Rich was about to leave for Durban for his son Nigel's graduation. I arrived at around 7pm with a disgusting head cold, and all I wanted to do was fall into bed, but no sooner had we walked into the house than there was a radio message from Mafira.

'Khanye says that Badger is somewhere in the rocks on Breakfast Koppie and won't come out.' So off I snuffled into the darkness, and luckily, I didn't have far to go. The rest of the story comes from my diary:

I eventually made it to the top of the koppie, guided by Khanye's torch, and found him listening intently to noises directly below us in the rocks. There were two badgers: Khanye saw one diving into the rocks with Badge in pursuit, and glimpsed them both a couple of times by torchlight through a small gap. One, which Khanye was sure must be Badger, was making a soft, purry noise; the other was growling though not angrily – more in a keep-your-distance-we-haven't-been-properly-introduced-yet sort of way. We listened to them for 15 minutes or so, until Badge suddenly realised that Mumsy was around – the Mumsy he hadn't seen for three weeks. He came boiling out of the rocks, leapt onto my lap and then did a bit of Kama Sutra on my arm just to show how much he'd missed me. The girl was forgotten. We tried to lure him back to her but he wasn't budging. So we decided to leave him to it, and when he didn't join us immediately, Khanye thought he must have gone back to her. I knew better. As we reached the path, we heard a rustling in the grass behind us, and there he was at my heels, ready to come home.

The next morning he was off at dawn 'back to the engagement party' as Khanye put it (how does he always come up with these things?). But the girl had gone, and for two very good reasons. Not only is Badger rather portly, to put it politely, but no girl in her right mind would wait for a fellow who would rather go home with Mummy than spend the night with her. Rich gets quite incensed when I suggest that Badge is overweight, but it was my first and lasting impression when I first saw him waddling through the dark towards me. And when I tried to pick him up, I could feel my arms being pulled out of their sockets. Not fat! He shuffles along like a caterpillar. Rich says that he is making Badge grow so that he can deal with the opposition, but this will only work if he sits on their heads and suffocates them. Just before Rich set off for Durban this morning, he accused me of cutting Badge's food too severely, when in fact I haven't touched it. 'Anyway, that's what I should do!' I said, sparking a one-sided row, with Rich yelling and me whispering furiously back with a couple of squeaks thrown in to make my point. That evening, Khanye found a crestfallen Badge back on Breakfast Koppie waiting for 'his madam' to return. He then tracked her all the way to Tshenjela where he made that growly, purry noise again and was set upon by three irate adult badgers. Fortunately, they saw Khanye and ran off, so no injuries ...

Another mystery. Badgers are by nature solitary animals. Or are they? How was it that when our warthog Poombi first went solo at 18 months, having been part of our family since she was a tiny piglet, she was far less emotionally dependent on us than Badger was at the same age? And yet female warthogs are social creatures living in a tightly knit sounder of family members.

Badger's bond with his adopted family never weakened. As mother, I was the prime caregiver, the constant provider of comfort and security. He was more respectful of Rich, but equally as devoted to him, though as adolescent boys will, he would sometimes challenge Rich's authority. With his mates Khanye, David and Nige he was the swaggering leader of the pack, the initiator of rough games and bad behaviour. And poor old Nandi dog? Well, she was his punchbag, on whom he first developed his moves and fighting techniques, all in the spirit of fun, of course, until she could deal with him no longer.

Many a time when we lost each other on a walk, he would eventually catch up with me, having run for miles, and collapse exhausted and crying into my lap. And even when he was spending nights out on his own, often on the next-door property, if I went to find him he would drop everything and follow me back, no matter what the time of the day or how far away we were from home.

Badger made us all a part of his triumphs and his disasters. He was digging into the riverbank late one afternoon when he uncovered a small hole. Rich began filming. There was a slight movement under the soil and Rich mouthed 'mouse', but I saw the tip of a tail sticking out of the hole, and so did Badge. He grabbed it and pulled, and pulled, and out came a long, black, shiny snake.

'Bibron's!' exclaimed the cameraman, whereupon the film crew retreated.

The Bibron's burrowing asp doesn't look very impressive. In fact, it's easy to mistake it for the harmless mole snake, as many an inexperienced snake handler, now short of a digit, has discovered. Its long fangs are horizontal and face towards the back of the upper jaw, so if a Bibron's is held by the neck in the normal way, it's able to twist its head sideways and pierce a finger with one fang. Badge pounced on its tail and began to eat his first poisonous snake without bothering in the least about its head, which was about to come up and strike. Or so we thought.

Having munched his way contentedly through 40 centimetres of writhing snake, Badger arrived at the head, and chewed that up too. It was as if the Bibron's knew that it hadn't a hope against a badger, and had simply lapsed into apathy. A strange reaction from a normally irascible snake.

The Bibron's has a little spine at the end of its tail resembling a fang. This ties in with Rich's observation that when threatened, the snake will hide its head under its coils, cock its tail and curve it over so it resembles its head, then wave this about in order to fool its aggressor into attacking the wrong end. Badger, typically, couldn't have cared less. Heads or tails – it was all dinner to him.

I always feel slightly guilty when I see a Bibron's – but fortunately the feeling soon passes. In our early days on Stone Hills, Rupert, our socially challenged learner guide, and I were in charge of running the lodge alone for a few days. I totally sympathised with his preference for snakes over people, but when he arrived in the office looking rather pale and holding up his finger, having lost an argument with a Bibron's he'd decided to catch, I was furious.

'Here!' I chucked him the vehicle keys. 'I suppose you'd better go into town. But for God's sake, get back later – we've got guests arriving.'

Rupert wobbled off (or so he maintains) and I forgot all about him. I was far too busy to consult a book. He was still on his feet, wasn't he? So it couldn't be that bad.

His mother called me later that afternoon. Our snake handler was in hospital, likely to lose his finger. I checked the book – Bibron's ('Dangerous: an insignificant-looking snake with a potent venom that causes extreme pain') had done it again.

Don't, for heaven's sake, ask Rupert for his version. He'll show you the page in the gate book in which he wrote his spidery, almost illegible name in a shaking hand on his way out. He'll tell you that the burning in his finger continued for two days, and that the pain was worse than the injuries he received from a wounded buffalo a few years later, when it hooked him in the thigh and carried him along on its back for 15 metres. And, with the tiniest bit of encouragement, he'll display the missing patch of skin on his finger (only a patch, mind you, not the whole thing). By all means look sympathetic, but take it all with a pinch of salt. I do.

But back to Badger, and a story that is not for the faint-hearted

– but then again, nor are badgers. It's funny how squeamish we can be when a carnivore is doing what's entirely necessary in order for it to survive, and yet we can quite happily tuck into a roast chicken, for example, that has spent its whole short life crammed with up to eight others into a space smaller than a standard sheet of notebook paper. It's a typically human reaction: if we don't see it, we don't have to think about it.

I spent ages looking for Badge one evening along the Pundamuka River. I could hear the signal from his transmitter very clearly, but he wouldn't come to my call. And then I found him between two small grassy hummocks near the water, grappling with a rock dassie, which was very nearly the same size as himself. It was the sort of situation I dreaded. I could see that the dassie had some severe injuries to its head and its stomach, but it was nowhere near death. This was going to be a marathon struggle.

When Badger looked up at me, the dassie took the opportunity of trying to escape. He didn't get far. Badge pounced and began rolling on him, something he often did to try and subdue larger prey, while the dassie kept biting at him ineffectually.

I watched for as long as I could bear it.

'If only he would let me in there,' I said into my little recorder that, like Rich's cameras, is always with me on my walks. 'I could finish it off. But there's no way he's going to allow that.'

I was wrong. Eventually, I picked up a rock and suggested to Badge that I dispatch the dassie for him. To my surprise, he stepped back and allowed me to do the necessary, after which he dragged the carcass down to the river and began trying to feed. And then something happened that still brings tears to my eyes.

A cat's sharp-edged back molars (the carnassial teeth) work with a scissor action to allow them to cut through meat, but a badger's teeth do this far less effectively – he must tear off chunks in order to feed. It was going to take Badge hours to get through the dassie's skin, and this was a dilemma. Badge was an extremely tolerant animal, except in one respect. No one could touch his food. Even as a tiny cub, he would attack the finger or even the spoon that hovered over his dish of porridge. But I had to try and help, so I produced my Swiss army knife (Be Prepared) and sat down as close as I dared, while he kept twisting and pulling at the skin with absolutely no success.

Very slowly, I put the tip of the knife on the dassie's back quarters. Badge took a little lunge at me, almost playfully, but made no sound, no warning growl. I explained to him that I could help if he would let me, and he kept his eyes on me while I took a couple of gentle stabs at the carcass. Still no reaction, so I pulled out a back leg and made an incision in the inner thigh. Badge moved straight in and once again, tried to rip into it, but with no success. Again, I took hold of the leg and started to cut into it, although this was pretty hard with a small, blunt knife. But Badger knew exactly what to do. He grabbed hold of the opposite side of the leg and tugged it away from me, making the skin taut and easier to cut. Together we had sorted out the problem, and while Badge tucked into his gargantuan meal, I sat back and wept – which, I realise, sounds rather ridiculous. But what a mix of emotions I felt. Never had we dared to go so close to Badge when he was feeding, particularly on something he had killed himself. His most basic instinct was to guard his food from all comers, mothers included, but now I had seen him adapt his behaviour to suit the situation, putting instinct to one side and letting his intelligence take over. Just as Poombi had done when she brought her newly born piglets to me in the bush for an introduction, against all her protective maternal instincts.

It was that display of trust that moved me the most: my acceptance into a place that few people are ever privileged to go. We had absorbed Badger into our world as a cub; now he was making his way back into his and asking us to follow. It was a moment both wonderful and terrifying.

How much more would he show us, how much further could he take us into his head and his heart? What do we really know about *any* animal – and what, God forgive us, have we done to them?

97

Chapter Nine – Stoffel

There are two very interesting things about Godfrey Wells. The first is his enormous red wig, which gives him a rather tropical appearance, as if a baby orangutan has just fallen out of a tree and landed on his head.

The second is his passion for cucumbers. It was thanks to Godfrey that we first learned about the most extraordinary cucumber in the world: *Cucumis humifructus* (the plant that fruits underground).

Now most plants take great pains to advertise their fruit

in order that they have a chance of being dispersed by water, wind or animals. The last thing they should be doing is hiding it away, particularly when that fruit is unable to seed itself as it has a tough outer shell that may remain intact for months, or even years. But that's just what this amazing cucumber does – because it has a secret, which only became known to science in the 1920s, although indigenous people naturally knew about it all along.

The fact is that it's in partnership with, of all creatures, the antbear, whom until this discovery, was believed to live exclusively on a diet of ants and termites.

Something about the fruit is so appealing to him that he digs it up (sometimes from as far as 30 centimetres underground), eats it, and then covers his midden containing the seeds with a thin layer of sand – providing perfect conditions for germination. And after the plant flowers, the shoot drills its way down into the earth where the fruit develops. This is a cunning but also rather a risky ploy. Like all wild animals trying to lead a natural existence, antbears are extremely vulnerable to human activity, being highly prized as gifts for the chief, and killed for their flesh and supposed medicinal properties. So if the cucumber is entirely reliant on the services of the disappearing antbear, it will be in big trouble in time to come.

Khanye didn't know about the cucumber's partnership with the antbear, but he was certainly familiar with the plant. Off we went, accompanied by a delighted Godfrey and his orangutan, straight to a healthy specimen only a couple of hundred yards in front of the lodge. Then we found them everywhere, but always in close proximity to antbear dens or droppings.

Godfrey's devotion to his cucumbers was easily matched by

Badge's fascination with antbears. We'd know if an antbear (or some other incumbent) was at home in his burrow by the cloud of small flies buzzing around the entrance, but Badge only needed his nose to tell him the whole story. And, anyway, apart from hunting, he had a proprietary interest in *all* holes, whomever they belonged to, showing no consideration for the inconvenience caused to the residents. At 6.30am on a frosty winter morning, when they still had at least a couple more hours of blissful shut-eye ahead of them, Badge cruelly evicted five dazed warthogs from a hole in the riverbank. He didn't even bother to chase them, because that wasn't his plan. He just popped straight into the hole, and spent the rest of the day snuggled down into their still-warm bed. If he'd found a bowl of porridge, he would have helped himself to that too.

An antbear doesn't ask much from life. He's a timid fellow, and when he's finished his nocturnal excavations for termites and ants, he goes to bed – having first barricaded the entrance to his burrow with fresh soil, leaving a small air vent at the top. That is normally enough to tell most animals to leave him alone, but not the badger, who regards any rejection as a personal affront.

In a flurry of paws and claws, he tears down the front door until he can see the antbear's thick, powerful tail. And suddenly a great wall of soil hits the badger in the face: antbear is fighting back and he can dig a lot faster than his small pursuer – as a group of men with spades once discovered after they had dug for 32 metres and still were getting no closer to their quarry.

When Rich was in his last year of high school in Harare, the boys woke up nearly every Saturday morning to find an enormous cavern in the middle of their cricket pitch, just in time for the weekly match. Then one night, three of them spotted the antbear, so they took off and threw themselves at it, grabbing whatever part of its body they could. But the antbear didn't appear to notice it had company: it just kept humping along without breaking its pace, till the boys finally gave in, and decided to take up rugby instead.

One evening, Rich arrived back from the walk with his spectacles and beard encrusted with dirt.

'Had a good hunt?' I enquired.

Rich grinned. 'One of the best. Badge found an occupied hole at the Lost Watch Hills and spent about 20 minutes digging. Then he heard the antbear further along the tunnel, so he pinpointed its position from above, and dug there, going back and forth from the entrance to the spot over the tunnel to make sure that it didn't give him the slip.'

Rich took off his glasses and started picking off blobs of red soil.

'And then they were both digging in the same spot – antbear up, Badger down. I had the camera trained on Badge, and suddenly the ground heaved and the antbear erupted out of the earth right under Badger's feet like a bloody great volcano. I got a hell of a fright, but not Badge. The antbear paused just long enough for him to give it a nip on the back leg, and then they were off – antbear shambling along at quite a pace with Badge right behind him.'

Evicting the antbear was never enough: Badge could never resist the final chase. And when the two of them galloped off, weaving their way through the trees, it always reminded me of the frantic tune at the end of the Benny Hill Show, with half-naked women and men in bowler hats, chasing each other around garden hedges at double quick speed.

Of course, Badge was hunting – he would have liked

nothing better than to find a piglet or a young antbear in the hole after he had evicted the parent – but there was a huge element of fun in it too. In the same way that he wanted us to play with him for hours with old shoes, sticks or lumps of grass, the antbears and the warthogs were also part of a game.

Badge was lucky – under our protection, he was experimenting and learning all the time as he prepared himself for life in the wild. But what about badgers in captivity? What quality of life could they possibly have, deprived of natural stimulation?

Much as I hate to see any animal incarcerated, particularly one as intelligent and active as a badger, one has to accept that sometimes this is inevitable, although it should always be a last resort. Rehabilitating and releasing a creature that is dependent on parental protection for around two years, is a major commitment of time and energy. But, given the right environment, it can be done.

For a captive badger, the best one can hope for is that the humans responsible for him will make his life as interesting and varied as possible, which is the philosophy of Moholoholo Wildlife Rehabilitation Centre situated on the border of the Kruger National Park and the adjoining hunting areas. For years, people have been bringing them injured or orphaned badgers. More often than not, hunters are responsible, as they hang their leopard baits in trees and then shoot the badgers that quite understandably come for the meal that's on offer. And it's not uncommon for a client to kill a specimen of the so-called 'meanest animal in the world' in order to display it in his trophy room – the fate of our own cub's mother. Beekeepers are another threat. The Beggs have devised an inexpensive badger-proof stand for hives, but sadly these are not in universal use, and many beekeepers still kill the badgers who find a way to raid them.

Wherever they can, the Moholoholo Centre will treat the badger and release it back into the Kruger area. But this becomes more difficult with those that have been hand-raised because, unless they are far away from humans and totally supervised throughout the long release process, they tend to cause havoc, often with tragic consequences for themselves.

Stoffel is a 13-year-old honey badger who was raised by a farmer in the lowveld and handed over to the centre when he was a cub. Like all badgers, he can't abide boredom for a minute. (Even when they are asleep, badgers are never still: their fingers twitch and they have action-packed dreams that make them roar, rattle and whimper.) So Stoffel keeps himself occupied by hatching plans to escape from his enclosure. At first, he shared accommodation with a female called Cheeky. When Stoffel positioned himself at the gate, she would climb onto his back and then up the struts to slip the bolt, while he pushed it open from below. But this is nothing new: such tricks are hard-wired into the Badger psyche – born of the wisdom of their tribe and perfected through sheer bloody-minded determination.

A hunter of our acquaintance thought that he would outwit potential thieves by hanging leopard bait on a rope from a tree, too high for a badger to reach. No problem. After a few moments' reflection, the first badger to arrive dug a hole near the bait, piling up the earth so it made a handy platform directly below it. Off he went with his prize, very proudly, leaving the hunter astounded – so much so, he tells us, that he has never shot a badger since. And that wasn't his only experience of Badger Brilliance. On another occasion, he saw one standing on the back of the other to reach the bait, exactly as Stoffel and Cheeky had done at the gate of their enclosure.

Most of the time Stoffel and his current companion, Hammy, a five-year-old female, live in a cement-lined pit with smooth walls – but not always. When he feels like a little stimulation, Stoffel pops over the 1.5 metre wall to visit some of the other animals at the centre.

On his first jaunt, he went straight to the lions' enclosure where he gave chase to an adult male. On his second visit, a pair of them ganged up and put him in the centre's hospital for three months.

But how can an animal no more than 30 centimetres high at the shoulder, with very short legs, and minus a trampoline, get over such an obstacle?

Well, he does what you would do – he makes his version of a ladder with whatever materials are available. When there was a rockery in the middle of his enclosure, he rolled the rocks to the wall, piled them on top of each other and climbed out. The rocks were removed, but it didn't take long before little Houdini made another plan. He is always digging, and when the soil was wet from rain or from being hosed down, he began shaping mud balls in his claws. They were not ideal: when he tried to stack them at the wall, he discovered that they broke up far too easily. So Stoffel moved onto Plan B: mixing stones with the mud, in the same way that builders reinforce a cement mix with chips of concrete. This worked very well indeed, until his keepers cottoned on and took them away.

All right – so I'll try something else. Now I am going to put the balls in little piles of two or three all over the enclosure, so that no one will notice them. And then when there are enough and the coast is clear, I'll roll them over to the wall.

Frustrated volunteers resorted to counting the rocks and the mud balls in his house to figure out when he would have enough to escape.

In the absence of that bit of fun, Stoffel spent his time picking away at the concrete walls of his enclosure. When he'd dug out a small notch, big enough for one human finger, he'd haul himself up with those powerful front legs, and over he'd go. The staff bolted the panels onto the walls to cover the holes. Not to be outdone, Stoffel pulled them off, but only partially, simply using them as a lever to lift himself out.

Finally, all Stoffel had left was a stick, which he was given occasionally so that awestruck visitors could see how he carried it to the wall and manoeuvred it into a corner, thick end at the bottom, making quite sure that it was at the right angle to be secure. Then up and over he went – heading for whatever trouble he could find.

Fraser Henderson contacted me after he had read our last book, *Wild Honey*, delighted to have discovered another honey badger devotee. After a career of 14 years as a financial adviser in Scotland, Fraser gave it up to work with wildlife in Africa – something he had always dreamed of. He did three stints as a volunteer at Moholoholo, and was always trying to find ways of keeping the two hyperactive honey badgers entertained. He'd hide meat in rubber balls or in old tortoise shells, paste syrup around interesting holes in the trees, and encourage the badgers to climb onto the stumps and ropes in their enclosure to give them exercise.

'God forbid,' says Fraser, 'that you leave a utensil behind in the enclosure. He loves brooms because they make the best escape tool. Even if just the handle appears within reach from outside, up pops a claw and you can be sure of second place in the ensuing tug of war.'

Once Stoffel has the broom, he simply places it against

the wall and over he goes. Some of the newer students think they can bribe him with food to reclaim it, but Stoffel ignores them. He knows that the broom is far more valuable to him than the food, however much is on offer.

'At this point,' Fraser explains, 'he slides his backside down the broom so his tail merges with the bristles, and even vigorous shaking won't dislodge him. And if you persist, he'll climb up the handle and bite you.'

His favourite story dates back to his first three months at Moholoholo.

Prior to Fraser's arrival, Stoffel had somehow managed to remove and hide the metal gate that separated the two halves of his enclosure. Another gate was fitted, but Fraser knew nothing about the incident. A couple of weeks before his departure, he heard a commotion coming from the badger house and leaned over the wall to see what was going on. A furious Stoffel was beating up Hammy, who had committed the cardinal sin of playing with the stones and mud balls that he'd placed against the wall.

'I knew that I had to destroy the ladder quickly before Stoffel made it out,' says Fraser, 'so I rushed off to get the rake, arriving back just as his claws appeared at the top of the wall. I couldn't believe my eyes. Right on top of the pile was a metal gate! Where the hell had it come from? I looked from him, to the gate on the pile, and then to the gate in his enclosure, which was still where it should have been. Crazy though it sounds, for one second, I even thought that he'd made another one!'

Fraser grabbed the gate away, but as Stoffel was now sitting tight on top of his ladder, he couldn't break it up without whacking the badger on the head.

'As I considered my options (at a much slower rate than

him), he began moving the rocks and balls away with his right paw, one by one, about an inch or two out of reach of the rake. And as he did it,' Fraser laughs, 'I swear he was smirking at me with a look that said: "So whatcha going to do about this, then?" He'd buried the gate and waited for just the right moment to use it.'

Nowadays, Stoffel's adventures outside the enclosure have sadly almost come to an end, as he has become increasingly difficult to handle. Brian Jones, manager of the centre, would like nothing better than to release him, but this is impossible. When they tried it once before, Stoffel kept coming home to inspect visitors' vehicles and to raid the lodge kitchens. It was only a matter of time before he got himself into trouble with neighbouring farms and lodges and so, for Stoffel's own protection, Brian decided to take him back to his enclosure, where the staff try their best to keep him entertained.

Not every member of our staff was as enamoured of the badger as Khanye was: one of our game scouts, Douglas Mkiza, for example, wrote in his daily report: 'Two honey bugger spoors seen today at Pundamuka ...'

People certainly have some strange ideas when it comes to honey badgers. Shortly after our orphaned cub arrived, Rich told a hunter of our acquaintance that I was out walking with him in the bush. 'You must be crazy!' he told Rich. 'You can *never* tame a badger!'

'Foul-tempered things,' wrote Wayne Grant in his book *Into the Thorns*, adding that if a honey badger could be tattooed, his biceps would have MOM and an anchor on them, and his knuckles would read LOVE and HATE.

I wish I'd thought of the tattoos – that's the badger all

right: muscular, tough, determined, swaggering through the bush as if he owns it. And I wouldn't be at all surprised if MOM appeared on his biceps: no animal I have ever met has been so devoted to his family. But the rest is nonsense. The badger is no more bad-tempered than any other mammal: he's a small, short-sighted fellow whose only defence is to react quickly and ferociously against those who threaten him, using voice, claws and teeth. Hate? Only humans waste their energy on such a negative emotion. A badger just wants to be left to himself – and he's prepared to defend his rights with every weapon he has. No questions asked.

Our Badger had a tough time ahead. We had no way of stopping him from visiting hunters' baits on the adjoining property, or indeed the villagers who have taken up residence outside our other three boundaries. They don't kill badgers for fun (in fact, they'd far rather avoid a confrontation with such a belligerent creature) but they do keep chickens, and will readily kill a badger who finds his way into the fowl run. It won't be an easy job – as a child, I remember a local chicken farmer telling my parents that it took 37 shots to kill a marauding badger – but it's possible. And wire snares are another danger, not on Stone Hills, but on all the surrounding farms.

These were not the only threats that concerned us. Badger might be able to avoid humans, but how would he deal with his own kind on their turf, and according to their rules? Without a mother to teach him, he had learned nothing of the code of the badgers. Would he know instinctively how to behave? And how would they tolerate a stranger, particularly a male?

Our vulnerable little cub was going to need an awful lot of luck if he was to survive into adulthood.

Below is an extract from *The Ivory Trail* by T V Bulpin about a pugnacious little badger.

'One morning, after [Bvekenya's] usual walk through the night, the path led him to a small waterhole, half lost in the depths of a mopane forest. This was to be the end of his night's walk, where he would rest until evening came again; and he anticipated sleep and water with a keenness only understandable if your whole body is parched and your feet a hideous ache of cuts and tears from thorns and endless miles of sand.

'As he approached the waterhole, Bvekenya heard a strange commotion. He stood and listened in surprise for some while. It was obviously the shrill noise of an elephant trumpeting against a background of dull thuds: like somebody beating a carpet with vigour, and screaming in the process.

'Bvekenya went on to the waterhole with caution. What he saw bewildered him. There was an enormous elephant, the first he had so far seen, trumpeting and stamping about around the water, for all the world as though it were a woman holding her skirts up and jumping away from a mouse.

'Bvekenya watched the animal in amazement. He carefully worked his way nearer the waterhole, full of curiosity as to the reason for this strange performance. He had half made up his mind that the elephant had gone berserk, when he at last secured a complete view of the proceedings.

'On the ground, offering the elephant battle, was *Shidzidzi*, the tough little honey badger, spluttering and cursing with rage in his harsh, spitting voice. The elephant towered 11 feet above *Shidzidzi*, but he was in a state of complete dismay. The honey badger was nipping the elephant's feet, and then slipping away as expertly as a boxer when the blundering giant tried to trample him down.

'Bvekenya stood watching this strange struggle with fascination. Without thinking, he stepped out of the bush to secure a better view. The elephant saw him immediately. With a dismayed squeal at the appearance of some fresh trouble, the elephant turned tail and fled.

'*Shidzidzi* was completely triumphant. He had not seen Bvekenya. He thought the elephant was running away from him. He practically stood up on his hind legs and shook his fist in defiance. The opportunity was too good for *Shidzidzi* to miss. To have a whole elephant run away from him was a wonderful achievement. With a chortle of glee, he hurtled off through the bush in pursuit of his fleeing enemy.

'Bvekenya walked down to the pool. All around the water the country was trampled as flat as a tennis court. The battle must have been going on for some time. The only explanation he could think of for so unequal a combat was that this was the honey badger's private drinking pool, and he objected to the elephant churning it into a wallow. There was a second pool a few hundred feet away. Bvekenya prudently made his resting place there, in case the pugnacious little animal should return, flushed with victory, and start on him.'

Chapter Ten – A Hoe In The Hand

'Born free, as free as the wind blows …' weren't just the words of a song for many of us brought up in the 60s and 70s. They were the echo of an unforgettable story set in Kenya about a relationship between the Adamsons and their lioness, Elsa, whom they raised and later released back into the wild.

Although the lioness died some months after giving birth to her first litter of cubs, Joy Adamson was convinced that the animal's spirit survived as a guiding presence in her life. And this, as her husband George wrote, 'armed her with a virtually irresistible resolution'. Joy was murdered in 1980, but the conservation work she began continues today through the Elsa Conservation Trust and the international Born Free Foundation.

Joy's own spirit is a powerful presence in her house, Elsamere, tucked into a forest of interlacing fever trees on the banks of Lake Naivasha. With its white walls, green tin roof and vivid bougainvilleas, Elsamere now functions as a conservation centre with comfortable guest cottages set in the gardens around the main house. We stayed there for three days on the first leg of our trip to East Africa, and we felt as though Joy had just stepped out of it. Her furniture is there, as are her photograph albums and her silver. Copies of her tribal paintings commissioned by Jomo Kenyatta and the sketches of her 'gentle lion' hang on the walls. Books on art, Christian Science and the mysteries of animal behaviour line the wooden shelves, as well as the *Writers' and Artists' Yearbook 1958*, which she must have used to find the publishers she hounded with the manuscript of *Born Free* – Elsa's story – a book that, despite numerous rejections, eventually became a publishing phenomenon.

The rooms were refreshingly simple, and the yellow roses on the dressing table were a nice touch. But they struck an uncomfortable note. Picture-perfect and utterly devoid of scent, they were a reminder of the greatest single threat to the delicate ecology of the lake. Naivasha's waters are fresh, in contrast to the salinity of most of the other Rift Valley lakes, and at 6 200 feet it is the highest, and until recent years, the purest lake of all. Hippos graze the lawns of Elsamere at night, and the area is a sanctuary for birds, with over 350 species recorded. But this vast expanse of natural water and the rich volcanic soils that surround it are a major centre for the production of fresh fruit and vegetables, vineyards, and flowers for export.

'The lake is paying the real price,' Margaret Otieno of the Elsamere Conservation Centre told us. 'The water is being poisoned with fertilisers and pesticides, and levels are dropping because of large-scale irrigation.'

Grown under totally artificial conditions, millions of unblemished stems are transported daily to the Nairobi airport, destined for the flower markets of Europe and for a few moments, perhaps, of appreciation by those who have the money to spare on small luxuries. These immaculate blooms are about as natural as if they were made of plastic or silk (and as biologically functional as Pamela Anderson's tits). Raindrops have never splashed onto their petals, and bees have never smelled their perfume – for they don't have any. A few days later, when they begin to wilt, they're tossed into the rubbish bin, of no benefit even to a caterpillar.

And the same goes for our supermarket vegetables: with their bright, appetising colours; total lack of taste; minimal nutritional value and their use-by date (be sure you eat them by the 10th of February or else you or the vegetable will die).

Anyway, this isn't a lecture on organic food. It's a roundabout way of getting to a story about an Afrikaner and his wife from South Africa who left their home near Louis Trichardt (pronounced correctly with a deep rolling 'r' and a 'ch' that gets stuck in your throat) to follow God's call to Zimbabwe – a place they hadn't previously felt any desire to visit.

From Trichardt, where Pierre and Rentia de Jaager lived in a large comfortable farmhouse with their four children, they moved four years ago to a thatched rondavel in the Matobo Hills with no electricity and only an outside kitchen, shower and toilet. And there they began teaching the local peasant farmers a technique that was developed in Zimbabwe a couple of decades ago by a man called Brian Oldreive. They call it 'Farming God's Way' (FGW) and for the ungodly, it works just as well if you substitute the word 'nature' for 'God', for in this case they are exactly the same thing.

Pierre arrived at Marula School one morning in his dark blue Hyundai with a neat little Venter trailer attached to the back – the sort much beloved by many South Africans. He's a big man cast in the Voortrekker mould, with large practical hands and a head of iron-grey hair. He speaks with a heavy Afrikaans accent, which is hardly surprising because as a child, he was forbidden to speak, read or write the language of the detestable *rooinek* (redneck or Englishman for those who, unlike me, are not fluent in the language). In fact, although it's hard to believe now, he only learned English at the age of 30.

The teachers had been called out on strike for the previous few days, but Headmistress Dube had persuaded them to come back to learn about this new method of farming. We all trailed into the dining room – our noses assailed with the sour smell of sadza and boiled cabbage from the adjoining kitchen. These kids were lucky: in Bulawayo, bundles of firewood had taken the place of foodstuffs on the shelves of the supermarkets. One afternoon, I showed the Grade Sixes and Sevens that wonderful movie *The Gods Must be Crazy*. How they laughed, although they did gasp once – when they saw long lines of bread being fed into a high-speed commercial slicer. You could almost hear their stomachs rumbling.

Pierre took his laptop out of its case and opened it up on the table.

'Today,' he said, 'I'm going to show you that a family with a hoe in the hand can be the best farming machine in the world.'

The teachers smiled politely. Then the first picture came

114

up on the screen and we all gathered around it. A woman was leaning on her hoe; behind her was a field of stunted, yellow-leafed mealies produced from our typically arid Matabeleland soils.

'Now look at this. Here is the same woman a year later – in the same field.'

Now it was the teachers' turn to gasp. These plants had shiny, deep green leaves, and they were tall, reaching right over the woman's head.

'See how she smiles!' said Pierre. 'She told me that when the wind blows in her field she hears voices she's never heard before.'

Farming God's Way, it appears, is all about being friends with nature. Forget about the tractor and the ox-drawn plough – those wasted hours spent turning over the soil.

'That's the way you destroy what we call God's blanket,' Pierre explained. 'Those first six inches of topsoil are full of millions of tiny, living organisms and they contain all the riches that plants need to grow.'

Apparently, everything in FGW comes down to the correct timing and preparation, using the most basic of equipment: a hoe, a jam tin, a small baked bean tin and, according to Pierre, the willingness to 'do everything with joy'.

From a field no larger than 10 square metres, made up of a number of holes precisely prepared and measured, a peasant farmer can aim at reaping around seven to eight buckets of maize (around 120 kilograms), provided that he takes care of every individual plant.

'The more you give to the plant, the more it will give to you,' Pierre said, repeating another of FGW's memorable little axioms. 'Now compare this to your typical crop grown on 1.5 hectares of ploughed land, which produces only around two buckets of maize.'

We stopped for tea, and now the teachers were babbling with excitement. Some of them rushed off to use the phone. 'Don't plant till we get home,' they told their families. 'We've got to show you something.' They'd be confronting hundreds of years of tradition with their newfangled ideas, but real inroads had already been made and Pierre's photographs proved it.

He agreed a date that he could come back to the school and plant the first 10-square-metre plot with them and the children.

I'm full of admiration for Christian-inspired teaching that encourages people to work in partnership with nature: one that recognises the land as a living, breathing organism rather than something to be flogged to death and then abandoned like an old donkey, when its heart has finally broken. But it takes a hungry man to listen and, most importantly, to follow such advice. The rest of us hear the words, but still we seem not to understand. If we did, we'd be filling our gardens with indigenous plants, instead of pouring poisons onto our neat green lawns, and spraying our exotic flowers with insecticides, thereby ridding ourselves of 'pests' – the insects and birds that have a far greater right to be there than the flawless blooms of our prize roses.

Without putting a name to it, Rich has been farming nature's way ever since we came to Stone Hills; healing the damaged land has been his first priority. Pierre talked about the importance of mulching: putting a thick layer of cut grass or even dry cattle dung around the plants. It's another of God's blankets, but this one protects the plants, allows the rain to penetrate and then holds the moisture in. And eventually, the grass or manure breaks down into humus and restores the soil.

'Restore or destroy,' Pierre told us. 'It's your choice.'

Rich mulches by leaving mown grass where it falls, which not only protects the ground from drying out but also provides perfect conditions for germination of the seeds.

In FGW, fallen leaves and other natural detritus are part of nature's bounty and should not be swept away, but left to protect and enrich the earth. On Stone Hills, we use only a minimum of dead wood for fires and boilers; the rest is left for fungus to work on and eventually convert into topsoil, while providing shelter for numerous little animals and plants.

'Conservation is harmony between man and nature,' said Aldo Leopold in his *A Sand County Almanac*. He was an extraordinarily far-sighted American naturalist whose prophetic writings are even more relevant today as when he penned them in the 1940s.

The crop at Marula didn't do well. The ground was poor and needed far more enrichment than we had provided in that first year. And the school had closed a couple of weeks after the maize had been planted, so it didn't receive the attention it needed. But the children, the teachers and some of the local people had dug the holes, brought in the topsoil and manure, and planted the seeds under Pierre's good-natured instruction, and they had learned something. When they looked at Grade Three teacher Lydia's bumper harvest in her 10 by 10 on the other side of the railway line, they could see that FGW really worked.

Pierre and Rentia came back to see us early the next year, at the time when Hennie and her partner Pete, a 100 per cent pedigreed Pom, were visiting from England – bringing with them, as always, donations and boxes full of equipment for the school. I was worried. Not on account of Pete, but in case someone let on that I was born in Norwich, England and christened Elizabeth Anne – a name chosen by my fiercely royalist father, then a career soldier in the British Army.

The best tactic was to distance myself from Pete as quickly as possible. When I was 17, I'd read Wilbur Smith's *Where the Lion Feeds* (about 20 times) and decided that if was ever to be a true child of Africa, an ability to read a menu in French wasn't going to qualify me. No question about it, I would have to learn to *praat* the *taal*.

I was due to leave school in less than a year, but somehow I managed to scrape through my O Level Afrikaans with the assistance of the domestic science teacher, Mrs de Villiers, who knew all about the value of an encouraging word.

'*Ag*, my dear, your accent is so good,' she told me. 'You must have an Afrikaans *ouma*.'

I laid it on thick for Pierre and Rentia, dropping *Ja's* and *Nee's* all over the place to prove my credentials, and smiling or nodding whenever they spoke in Afrikaans, even if I didn't understand what they were saying (which was most of the time).

In retrospect, I may have been trying too hard when I told Pete what a *soutpiel* was – but once I had started, it was too late.

'You see, Pete, that's what they call a Pommy who lives in Africa – a salty dick – because he's got one foot in each continent, so his penis hangs in the ocean.'

Fortunately, I was laughing so hard that I didn't see how Pierre and Rentia reacted to this bit of totally inappropriate humour.

After lunch, we went up to our vegetable garden where Mafira and gardener Ronald were waiting. Rich's mother,

Pat, a great believer in the benefits of earthworms, started the garden on organic principles in the early 1990s, and so it has continued ever since. Pierre was impressed, but especially when he saw Mafira's mealies planted after he had attended the FGW course at the school. They were magnificent: so tall and densely leafed that we could crawl into the shady tunnel between the plants to turn over the dark, fragrant earth with our hands and see it writhing with life.

Not long ago, Zimbabwe could not only meet its own needs, but was also a major exporter of maize to its neighbours. But now we are out with the begging bowl, because like the rest of Africa, much of our country has been broken up into small plots worked by subsistence farmers, struggling against poverty, drought and lack of education in basic farming skills.

FGW works on two levels: first, because it is a simple natural method, using basic equipment specially designed for subsistence farmers; and second, it's taught as God's way – an avenue that appeals to a people who are naturally worshipful, in one form or another.

Unlike me, Pete was perfectly relaxed at lunch, being blissfully unaware of his dodgy status. It paid off. When the De Jaagers were leaving later that afternoon, Pierre gave Pete's hand a powerful squeeze.

'You know,' he said, 'you're the first *Engelsman* I've ever liked!'

Pierre was called to Zimbabwe by his God, but unlike so many of the earlier missionaries, frustrated by their lack of real progress, he preaches from the fields instead of the pulpit, giving practical and lasting help to the local people.

Although Christianity has a huge following in Africa,

more often than not it is closely interwoven with traditional beliefs, despite the disapproval of the church.

Unlike the Christian God, *uNkulunkulu* (the one who dwells in the clouds) is a remote being who cannot be contacted directly by the living. He can be reached only by way of a kind of spiritual ladder, the first rung of which is occupied by the spirits of the most recently dead.

If the head of the household dies, for example, his spirit takes up residence with the family, and he will become their adviser and guardian. He will attend to most of their problems, but if he can't, he will seek the assistance of the ancestors who died immediately before him, and so on, until, if needs be, the original ancestor refers to *uNkulunkulu* himself.

The spirits communicate with the living through dreams and omens – both of which are vastly influential in a person's everyday life. If Johnson Sibanda accidentally drops food off his plate while he is eating, it's a sign that his ancestors or his children are hungry. So he leaves it where it falls, so they may eat too.

Traditionally, any bad or strange occurrence inevitably happens for a reason, more often than not because of the influence of bad spirits.

Scout Mabhena is particularly aware of omens:

While I was on patrol today, I nearly stepped on a 3-metre-long black mamba, he wrote in his report. *The snake rose to almost level in height with me. When I tried to strike, using my axe, it swiftly rushed to the other side of the fence and disappeared. Just some 200 metres away from the first one was an Egyptian cobra. It was struggling to swallow another dead rotting snake that I could not identify. I armed myself with a long stick, intending to kill it. Still shaking from seeing*

120

the black mamba, I missed the cobra, striking close to its head.
It crawled 2 metres away and started vomiting the dead snake.
Then it rose up to charge. I stepped backwards, running around
trying to get a chance to strike. But then the snake disappeared
into the long grass.

Frightened, shaken and thinking what this could mean, I
carried on with my patrol.

Khanye is a practising Christian, who also has a healthy
respect for omens. On his way to the laundry, he noticed a very
thin female baboon eating the remains of a honeycomb. Three
times he saw her in the same place, and then she disappeared.

'She could be an *indangula*,' he told me. 'That's a baboon
who is used by witches to thieve and to send out spells.'

One of our streams on Stone Hills is called *Swelikhuba*
(the one without a hoe) – after a witch who used to farm there.
By tradition, it's very unlucky to loan out your possessions, as
your power will then pass to the borrower, but because they
were frightened of her, the local people lent her their hoes.

'Then,' said Khanye, 'she took the power from their hoes
for herself. Her crops were always successful, while theirs
were poor.'

Khanye and I were discussing honey badgers in traditional
medicine and witchcraft on one evening walk with Badger.
Unfortunately for honey badgers, they are considered to be
good *muti* (medicine). In a sort of backhanded compliment,
a strip of badger skin may be tied around a baby's waist so
he will grow up to be strong and courageous. And, Khanye
told me, witches use nocturnal animals like badgers to run
their evil errands.

'Oh, by the way,' he said, 'there's been a lot of trouble next
door on Syringa Vale, and witchcraft is suspected. Remember

when Induna the thatcher died? Well, MaNdebele saw him alive amongst the mourners on the scotch cart coming back from his own funeral. They've called in some prophets to smell out the witches, and they start tomorrow.'

In Africa, life is a constant conflict between good, represented by the spirits of the ancestors, and evil in the shape of witches and wizards, who unfortunately often turn out to be a close relative. Witchcraft is fascinating enough, but smelling them out sounded positively sinister. According to legend, if a witch was caught, long wooden pegs were driven into her anus, which remained there until she died.

'Strange things have been happening,' Khanye told me. 'Antbears have been digging up graves, and owls calling. And there's been one ghostly incident when a bowl of fire came out of the earth and exploded in the air.'

I had to find out more, but I certainly wouldn't be welcomed at the proceedings. So Khanye went, very willingly, to observe, and he reported back the following evening. He caught up with us on the Mathole River, where Badger was hunting for frogs.

There were two male witch hunters, or 'prophets' – one Shona and one Ndebele – Khanye told me, along with four local assistants. They had taken up temporary residence in the house on Syringa Vale – a farm that had been taken over by government some years previously for a 'village scheme'. Now around 50 families lived there, each on a small plot of unproductive land.

The two prophets, Khanye reported, were attired in red robes with a white cross on the back. They carried cow tail switches and wore a cloth in leopard print wrapped around their heads. Thirty-six families had been called to the proceedings, and each had to pay Z$10 000. I asked Khanye what would happen if they chose not to attend.

'They would be suspected of being evil spirits,' he said. 'No one would dare to refuse.'

A crowd gathered to watch as the prophets danced, their red robes swirling about them, their eyes rolling. When he was in what seemed to be a trance-like state, the senior one disappeared inside the house, while the other called each family member in turn over the age of 14 to stand in a box full of soil with their hands raised above their heads. Then, when instructed, they stepped onto a piece of wood, holding onto the two poles placed on either side.

'We could hear the prophet inside talking in a trance,' said Khanye. 'When someone had finished the procedure, he'd call them in and announce if any of them were witches or wizards.'

'And did they name anyone?'

'Oh yes, a number of people. But unfortunately, he discovered that one of our workmates is also a wizard.'

Black magic on Stone Hills? It didn't seem possible.

'Who, for heaven's sake, Khanye?'

'Kephas Dube.'

Chapter Eleven – Witches, Wizards
And Friendly Ghosts

Kephas, the alleged wizard, is in his 80s; a little bent leprechaun of a man, with a radiant smile that creases up his whole face. He's a traditional herbalist, and his work mates believe that he is related to the *amasili* – the Bushmen of long ago, who roamed these hills and left their stories painted on the rocks.

I'd seen him on my walk the previous evening, herding the Goodwin's cattle back into the kraal.

'*Yebo*, Kephas,' I called out to the red woollen beanie bobbing up and down in the long grass. '*Kunjani?*'

'*Ngiyapila!*' he had called back, raising a hand. 'I'm well!'

He never replies any other way. He doesn't walk – he trots everywhere, and he's hardly changed in all the years we have known him.

Khanye was standing amongst the expectant crowd when Kephas was taken inside the house on the following day, having gone through the procedure between the sticks. A few minutes later, the prophet led him out.

'Triple X, zero one one!' he shouted. 'This man is a wizard!'

He instructed Kephas to go and wash, then he cut three Xs into his forehead with a razor, and rubbed some special *muti* into them.

'If you try any more witchcraft,' he warned the old man, 'you will die.'

'But why Kephas, Khanye?' I protested. 'I've never heard a bad word about him, and he's nearly blind. He'd have a head-on collision with a tree if he rode his broomstick around at night.'

Khanye gave me a stern look. 'Our witches and wizards don't ride broomsticks. They use antbears or hyaenas.'

He picked up a frog that had come flying out of the hole Badger was digging, and we watched as it frantically burrowed back into the sand.

The problem, he told me, stemmed from Kephas's relationship with Emily Sibanda: one tough lady and the self-appointed keeper of the rain rock on Stone Hills, where dances are held annually to honour the ancestors and to pray for rain. For some reason, Emily had become very unpopular with the other residents of Syringa Vale who had long been convinced that she was a witch.

According to the prophet, Kephas had taken 'bad *muti*'

from her, and together they were responsible for Kephas's wife's death, his one son's imprisonment, his other son's madness, and even his daughter's marital problems.

'But that's rubbish!' I said. 'Why would he do that to his own family?'

'He admitted it in front of everyone. He doesn't remember doing any of it, but he says that he must have been asleep when he was bewitched.'

'And now what happens?'

'He'll be shunned by everyone, including his family, because he might want to use the blood of a relative to give him power – maybe even one of his grandchildren.'

So, henceforth, old Kephas Dube would be a marked man.

The prophets announced to the crowd that they had discovered a syndicate: two males (one of them Emily's brother, nicknamed Madliwayidonki – the one who was bitten by a donkey) and five females, including Emily and four of the other women who danced at the annual rain rock ceremony.

Now the real witch-hunt began. With a steadily swelling crowd at his heels, the senior prophet led the way to the hut of MaNdebele the sister of Kephas's dead wife. He ducked in through the door and after poking about for a few minutes, emerged holding something over his head.

'It was a child's leg bone,' said Khanye, 'with two horns attached. The witches can open doors with it. I knew the little girl, Talent. She was MaNdebele's grandchild, and she died mysteriously. They say that six women went to the grave to dig up the bone and they've been using it to get into people's huts. And that's not all.'

He gave his foot a shake and managed to dislodge Badger, who'd become bored with frogging and decided to bother us instead. The cub dived at the other leg and clung on. Khanye continued as if having a ball and chain attached to your left leg was perfectly normal as, of course, it was. We began to walk slowly down the riverbed.

'They also found a hyaena tail used to make people fall asleep so they don't hear the witches come in. And there were two razors at the end of the bone, facing out, that they used for cutting people. Everything was wrapped in a pair of underpants belonging to MaNdebele's oldest son. He says he lost them long ago, and since then he hasn't been able to have sexual relations with his wife.'

From there the procession went to Emily's brother's hut, and this time the prophet appeared with a pillow. He cut it open, and, presto, there was a second hyaena tail wrapped in black cloth. It was being used in the bed of a sick person who, very mysteriously, wasn't recovering. Madliwayidonki immediately admitted his guilt.

The prophets moved to Gogo Manleya's home, where they found a horn full of sinister powders and potions, some of which could conjure up the hyaena that the witches would ride at night, and others that would make them invisible as they went about their evil deeds.

'There was one more very strange incident,' said Khanye. 'Gogo Manleya had a black chicken that she turned into an owl at night, so she could send it out with her spells. The prophet went and collected the chicken and told Gogo to put it on her head. If it died, then she was using it as an owl, but if not, she was innocent.'

'It died, didn't it?'

'Yes, while we were all watching. And I'm sure the prophet didn't do anything to it.'

Emily had the worst of it. She was accused of killing some of her children. The prophets raided her hut and then burned

127

all her precious drums, switches and the *muti* that she used for the rain dance. Despite this, there was a dance later that year, but it was marred by suspicion and violent disagreements amongst the participants.

Call it witchcraft or call it the devil, bad things happen, and people need a scapegoat.

I confronted Mafira the next morning when he came down to the house for his daily powwow with Rich.

'So what do you think about all this smelling out of witches?' I asked him.

Typically, his answer was crisp and straight to the point.

'It's bullshit.'

But I wasn't going to let him off so easily.

'What do you mean? They found all sorts of strange things in people's huts. There has to be something in it. Come on, Mafira, you're the one who told me that when a person dies, his shadow does too. And that if he has a problem with his family at the time of his death, his shadow will appear on the walls of the hut. I thought you *believed* in the spirits.'

'I do, Mrs Peek, but I don't believe in witchcraft, and specially this smelling out rubbish. And I know about it, because I have a bad cousin who also used to call himself a prophet and do the same thing. He's now in jail. These guys spend time with the young men in the community to find out what their problems are, and then they know exactly who to target. They plant things like those hyaena tails in people's homes. You wait, now there will be even more trouble on Syringa Vale. The "prophets" make a fortune out of people, and they destroy their families. And when they leave the place, they often take the young girls of the village with them.'

It made sense. People would be looking for someone to blame for the miserable state of their lives, particularly at that time, when *Operation Murambatsvina* (Clean up the Filth) was in full swing. We had watched some of the footage on South African TV. Bulldozers came rumbling into the high-density suburbs, ostensibly targeting houses or extensions erected without municipal authority. Shacks, some of which would have belonged to the farm workers and their families evicted in their thousands during the land invasions, were razed to the ground. But so were solid brick buildings, smashed in minutes into a pile of rubble. Sick people were thrown out onto the street, sitting there dazed, their belongings strewn around them. And others camped for days outside the wreckage of their houses, scared to go to work in case someone stole the few possessions they had managed to salvage.

'Informal' vendors were the next to be cleaned up. Streets of stalls, which had been operating in the same place for years without hindrance, were destroyed, along with their owners' only means of livelihood.

It was mid-winter. More than 300 000 of the homeless sought refuge from bitterly cold nights in churches and temporary camps, but they weren't allowed to stay there for long. Officials went around checking identification documents: people were to be returned to their district of origin, no matter how remote their connection with it. Each person was allowed to take one suitcase and a bucket of maize, and then they were herded into army trucks and dumped, maybe hundreds of kilometres away from home, in a place where they had no job, no shelter, and very likely, not a soul who knew or cared about them.

Some died of cold, others of hunger. And Khanye told me that the older people wandering around looking for help would have been shunned as witches or wizards.

The intimidation went much further. Buses were stopped

and searched at police roadblocks. Those who were carrying more than Z$2 million (a paltry sum at the time) were relieved of it as 'it should have been in the bank'. And anything over 1 kilogram of sugar was also taken – simply because the owners were in no position to protest.

In house-to-house searches, TVs and other electrical equipment for which receipts could not be produced were confiscated, and videos were simply taken away, with or without the paperwork.

Marula was not the only place under the influence of spirits in those harrowing days. Strange things, too, were happening in my friend Maureen's house in Bulawayo. At night, her children would see lights flashing on and off, and hear footsteps and the whirring of electric toothbrushes, switched on by unseen hands. They called in a psychic who identified the visitors as Christine, a 43-year-old woman who had apparently been strangled (but not in Maureen's house); two children, one of whom was a 12-year-old called Ryan, and Ben, an Indian spirit guide. The psychic could sense where they were. Guiding Maureen's hand in her own, she directed her to a place in the dining room that felt cold – far colder than the surrounding air.

'They mean you no harm,' she assured the family. 'They just like living in this house.'

But Maureen and her sleep-deprived family decided that the ghosts had stayed long enough. She called in a group of Christian exorcists who persuaded them to leave, having learned, we trust, never again to borrow anyone's toothbrush without asking.

All his life, Kephas's 18-year-old son had suffered from epilepsy and mental illness. He had tried suicide a couple of times: once by cutting himself with glass and another by trying to hang himself with wire. I knew nothing about it, so when Mafira told me that Kephas had asked that we get some pills from town, I told him that we would do so on our next trip the following Friday. By then, it was too late. Kephas didn't come to work one day, and his son died very early the following morning. And the unfortunate old man had to deal with the tragedy all alone.

'The boy hadn't been eating,' Mafira told me, 'but none of the family would come to help because they believe their father is a wizard.'

I felt a terrible sense of guilt. Could he have been saved if we had brought the pills earlier? Why hadn't I listened more carefully, and sent him off to Plumtree to get the medication instead of putting it off till Friday? If only Kephas had told us how serious the situation was and demanded help – but that was something he would never have done.

I heard hammering from the garage and went out to see Big Fight, who was making the boy's coffin. None of the family would attend the funeral. I asked him what he had thought of the prophets on Syringa Vale.

He straightened up and wiped his hands on his overalls.

'I don't believe all of it. They told me my family was clean, but that someone was trying to bewitch me. And if I wanted to find out more, I'd have to give them a cow. I wasn't going to do that. But that old woman with the black chicken that died on her head? That was true; we've all known for a long time that she is a witch.'

Things didn't settle down on Syringa Vale. A few months later, we heard reports that a man was found dead there, and that one of his legs was missing.

Kephas's other son, Tommy, died in jail a couple of

years later, probably of starvation like many other prisoners. According to everyone around here, he was falsely accused of rape by someone with a score to settle. This time, though, his family was on hand to help the old man. I gave him and a few relatives a lift to town so that they could go to the jail, make a coffin on site, and bury him.

I turned to Kephas as he climbed into the back of the car: 'I'm so sorry.'

He leaned forward shaking his head, his old eyes hurt and bewildered, and I wondered whether he had made peace with the spirits, or if he still blamed himself for all the misfortunes of his family.

The Goodwin's cattle have long gone, and nowadays Kephas spends most of his time manning the main gate and making very sure that every visitor signs the book, even if he can't read what they have written.

He still has the red beanie, but now he wears a dark blue pullover that Hennie brought for him a couple of years ago. On the front, it has a picture of a horse and the words: 'British Horse Society, Cambridgeshire Pony Club'. It makes us smile and he smiles back, just like old times.

I often wonder how the headman's wife on Syringa Vale fared after the prophets had declared her to be not a witch, but a bad spirit on account of her moodiness and antisocial behaviour. She certainly wouldn't have been able to get Prozac or pills for her PMT at the local clinic.

'African women can be very dangerous,' Khanye remarked after he had imparted this bit of information.

'Believe you me,' I answered. 'We're all the same.'

Chapter Twelve – Old Hat And Other Adventures

It was all very well for Badger to read other people's messages, and to leave his own pee mails at the midden, but he still wasn't getting any experience with other badgers and we had no way of providing this. The three infuriated adults who rumbled him as he was serenading his girlfriend might well have done him some serious damage, had Khanye not stepped in and frightened them away. Three more incidents with lone badgers followed and each time they were aggressive. Badger, however, was not deterred. On the day after the incident at the koppie that became Three Badger Hill, he was back sniffing around and looking for trouble. And often, he'd insist on spending the day there.

Although it looks quite innocuous from the outside, the rocks of the koppie conceal a low-roofed, rather sinister warren of caves. Years ago, when we were searching for Bushman paintings, we crawled in through a narrow entrance, and then climbed down into it over piles of loose rocks. It was damp and dark, and filled with the sickening stench of ammonia.

'Bats!' said Rich, and with that, the air was alive with hundreds of them, gusting around our heads like a whirlwind, stirring up the air and making the smell even worse. Then we noticed something up against the far wall. Rich pushed at it with his foot: some rags and a couple of tins – most likely belonging to a dissident hiding himself and his weapons in the early 1980s.

After 14 years of the Bush War, Independence was declared in 1980, but that was not the end of the violence. The Mashona ZANU (PF) had taken total control of the country, leaving the Matabele faction of the liberation army, ZIPRA, out in the cold; a situation that their leader, Joshua Nkomo vowed to change. So began the era of the dissidents, which led the people of Matabeleland to far greater suffering than they had ever experienced during the Bush War.

The dissidents were very active in the Marula area: they hid in the koppies, just as the Matabele had done during the Rebellion in 1896, and they stashed their weapons amongst the rocks at the end of the conflict. Many are probably still there, buried under mounds of dassie dung.

We didn't want to spend long in that cave, and we've never been back, but Badger, despite his highly sensitive nose, was a regular visitor. For the fact is that all animals, including ourselves, are compulsively drawn to their own kind, whatever the consequences. Nature's aim is to ensure the continuation of the species, so she can't allow us to wander off aimlessly instead of focusing on the serious task of procreation. After all that's the only reason we're here.

I've always felt desperately sorry for Mowgli. There he is in the jungle leading an idyllic life with his friends Bagheera and Baloo, until one day he catches sight of some little tart at the river. And at that moment, his hormones (which up till then he wasn't even aware of) leap into life. Besotted, poor fool, he follows her back to the village, where he ends up with a mother-in-law, three little brown babies and a steady job picking coconuts nine-to-five. What a rotten trick.

Anyway, back to the social life of badgers. Males sometimes gang up when they are out in search of good-time girls, and Mabhena once saw three of them on Stone Hills trotting along a dry riverbed quite companionably. We also know that when the alpha male drags her off into seclusion for his version of a romantic weekend, he is often disturbed by the other males hanging hopefully around the burrow. This irritates him no end, but when he rushes out to chase them away, one of the intruders may take the opportunity of ducking in and stealing a bit of the action for himself.

Badge was much more at ease with people than other honey badgers. Once he had been properly introduced, he adored company, particularly children. But it was best if they came on the morning walks, or in the early part of the evening, because as the sun began to set, the transformation would begin from a relatively biddable Badger to a bouncing, badly behaved ball of fire.

Limbering up usually commenced with wrapping all 10

kilograms of himself around the nearest foot and attaching his mouth to one's Achilles tendon, only in play of course, as we assured his victims who suddenly found the walk becoming a bit of a drag.

'If you can't hop along on one leg,' we advised them, 'then just pull him along behind you.'

Sometimes, when he became completely out of hand, Rich would swat him on the bum. If he did it too softly, Badge would ignore it, but if it stung, he would roll onto his back and vigorously rub his bottom with both paws, glaring at Rich defiantly with those little black eyes. You can't hurt me! And then he would rush off and demolish a grass plant (he really had it in for them), or dig up the large, onion-shaped bulb of a *Boophane* for a hectic game of football. Or, as happened on one memorable evening, he would take his revenge.

The walk had started badly. We'd left him at the Grain Bin cave in the morning, but he wasn't there at 4.30pm, and he only caught up with us half an hour later, tired and irritable. Instead of his usual welcome, he began a very rough game with Rich, who eventually found a long stick and poked him in the bottom, normally an effective deterrent to mischief. Unusually, Badge responded by biting him hard in the heel, whereupon Rich hauled him up by the scruff of the neck and carried him along – something that would have subdued most animals. But not the flexible Badger, who immediately put his two front legs over his head and tried to dislodge Rich's grip. After 10 minutes or so, Rich dumped him back on the ground, and at that moment, the wind came up and blew off his hat, providing a God-given opportunity for one with a score to settle.

Badger roared after it with Rich in pursuit, then once

he had the hat between his teeth, he lay down holding it firmly with his claws and began tearing at it. Rich stood over him cursing, which was exactly what Badger wanted, so we decided that the best tactic was to ignore him. 'Hat? Oh, that old thing? Have it, Badger, I didn't like it anyway.' As if he'd believe *that*. We wandered off chatting and within minutes, the thief was trotting along in front of us, but rather haphazardly, with the brim tilted over his eyes.

He stopped for a moment, adjusted his grip, and then continued bouncing along, tail up, every inch of him daring us to challenge him. But when we refused to respond, he started to become annoyed. While Rich was filming, he began rolling around at our feet and inviting us to play, those strong white teeth still firmly clamped over his prize. At first, I wasn't game to put my hands anywhere near him, so I shuffled my foot around a bit and then, when he looked more relaxed, I began to tickle his bottom, hoping he might lose concentration.

What happened next was completely unexpected. One minute Khanye was standing next to Badge, the next he had leaned down and snatched the hat away. Well, Badger sailed right into his reputation. In he went for the attack: roaring at Khanye who bounded away like a springhare, waving the hat over his head. Badger went after him, ready to kill.

They didn't go far before Khanye's sense of self-preservation prevailed. He flung the hat back at Badge, who grabbed it, and immediately the excitement was over. Everyone was rattled, even Badge, who crawled into my lap, hat forgotten, for a bit of comfort and reassurance. And after a few minutes, Khanye came over to make his peace. All was forgiven – but not forgotten. We were all slightly awed by this reminder of what a badger could be, and how important it is that one should always respect the instincts of a wild animal, no matter how well you believe you know him.

Ever since we moved onto Stone Hills, I'd always longed to explore it at night, but somehow, once the generator wakes with a roar at 7pm, and the lights come on and the fridges start to hum, life seems to concentrate itself in the house to the exclusion of the world outside that is just starting to wake up.

Badger, bless him, changed all that. We'd take off at around 4.30pm, hopefully locating him quite quickly, if he was still where we had left him in the morning, and then walk with him until around 8pm, when I would insist on heading back for my supper. So much happens at night: leopards hunt, badgers bother, brown hyaenas shamble out of their dens. And there's that magic hush at dusk, before the darkness comes flowing in to fill the empty spaces of the land; a time when, strangely, the animals seem to lose their fear and are at their most approachable.

The river is the most enticing place of all, especially on nights when the full moon drifts up behind the trees like a balloon released from its string, silvering the water, and throwing out long shadows in front of the trees that line the riverbank, all the while growing brighter till you no longer need the light of your torch.

Well, that's what you think until you step on a puff adder – a snake most active after dark, and notorious for its quick temper, long fangs and lightning strike. Unlike other dangerous snakes, it's sluggish and likes to lie in wait for its prey. This one was curled up on the path I was taking, at speed, in order to catch up with Badge and Khanye. I registered it in mid-stride – lying in a fat coil exactly where my foot was about to land, and its body yielded like soft rubber under my weight. But fortunately, the snake was as shocked as I was and anyway, at the speed I catapulted off him, he didn't have a chance to retaliate.

Walking with Badge at night gave us the gift of hours: it stretched out the days into the darkness, especially in winter when we would otherwise have pulled the curtains and lit the fire when the sun went down. The night was truly his place, his time, and to be alone with him, encapsulated in our own little intimate world, was an indescribable privilege.

Mornings were mostly for bothering – warthogs, antbears, mongooses – Badger's way of leaving his personal signature on the day before he retired to bed. Hunting began in earnest in the evenings, and in summertime, it was pretty uncomplicated, even for a small badger of little experience (I always wanted to write a poem beginning: 'Have you seen a badger, small and fat?' but I could never come up with a really good second line).

Once he got the hang of immobilising their powerful jaws before they bit him, sand crickets were easy prey, and winged termites were there for the picking, either as they emerged from the nest, or as they fluttered clumsily about on their maiden flight trying to get airborne.

Lizards hiding under rocks are tricky critters to shift, but Badger had a plan for them too. When we first saw him chase a skink under a rock, then stand on it with his back feet, putting his head on the ground while trying to lift the front edge with his claws, we thought he was being an idiot. Of course he couldn't get under it that way: he could only lever up the rock an inch or so, before it dropped back onto the ground.

But that's exactly what Badge intended, and we should have been clever enough to see it immediately. When the edge of the rock came up, the skink moved forward to make its escape. It didn't get far. With Badge's weight behind it, the rock snapped down like a rat trap, stunning the skink and making it much easier to catch.

Tool-using? You could certainly see it that way: Badger was using rocks as weapons, in the same way that Stoffel used sticks, rocks and mud balls to make his ladders.

As time went on, he graduated to other prey that taxed his ingenuity even further, like mice, tortoises and snakes, all of which required different hunting and dispatching techniques and not a little acrobatic skill.

Badgers are perfectly equipped for digging: their claws are powerful yet sensitive, and they grow up to 4 centimetres long. Those same claws can support their entire weight, enabling a badger to pull himself up almost sheer rock surfaces. But you would never think, looking at his short legs and solid body, that he would be a natural tree climber. And you'd be right – he isn't. It takes him months of falling, often on his head, before he gets the hang of it, but with typical bloody-mindedness, he masters it in the end – and then nothing is safe.

After a boisterous welcome when we met up one evening, Badger trotted off along the river, having already decided on his first port of call. Five minutes later, he was halfway into an antbear's hole, bum up and digging furiously – the same hole from which he had evicted the poor creature on the previous evening. But this time, it wouldn't be shifted. As fast as Badger dug, so did the antbear, showering him with red soil till his eyes, ears and coat were caked with it. This was fun, but when it was clear that it wasn't going to play ball, Badge decided to move on to something more challenging. Giving himself a little shake, he trotted off, tail aloft, with Mother as always right behind him.

A kilometre or so further on, another hole, stuffed with dry grass, beckoned. This time Badger approached with a little more caution. Working quietly but intently, he began pulling the grass away, till an infuriated rumble from within made him jump backwards. Ah-hah, this was more like it! When the entrance was clear, he pushed his nose inside, whereupon, with a roar, an enormous warthog burst out of the hole, knocking our cub clean off his feet. Then he tore off into the darkness with a dusty but delighted Badger on his tail.

For Badge, this was turning into the perfect action-packed end to his day. It was by then 7pm, and I'd begun thinking longingly about dinner – a special one that night: roast beef and Yorkshire pudding, which Ruthie, former head chef at our safari lodge, has mastered to perfection. And Badge was also in for a treat. If he came home with me, which he normally did, he would find half a spitting cobra waiting for him inside his enclosure – an unwelcome guest we'd recently found lurking in our dining room. I called him, and headed for a path that wound homeward through the hills. If Badge didn't find anything too distracting in the meantime, I'd be there in an hour. But he didn't join me, and after 10 minutes, I followed the tick-tick-ticking of the receiver to the foot of a tall duiker berry tree. There he was, wedged in a fork about 3 metres up, pleading for help.

I walked around the tree a couple of times, looking for an easy way up, but there were no low branches within my reach. The whining became louder, but now the sound seemed to come from a slightly different direction. I shone my torch upwards to find that he had moved to another fork a little higher than the last.

'Badger!' This was ridiculous. 'That's it,' I threatened. 'I'm going home without you.'

I strode off purposefully for a few yards, then sat down

under a tree to wait, trying to banish the unpleasant mental image of Rich pouring the last of the gravy onto his roast potatoes.

There seemed to be some vehicle activity from the Mangwe Road – at this point, only a couple of kilometres away from us. And that was unusual, as it's a quiet dirt track that is generally used only by other farmers in the district. Then it stopped, and all I could hear was Badger. I couldn't possibly leave him there, as well he knew, so I'd have one last try at climbing up to him, and then I was definitely going to radio Rich and ask him to bring a ladder. So we'd both have a cold dinner.

My only option was a slender mobola plum growing very close to the duiker berry, with branches so thin that I didn't think they could take my weight. They did, just, and by stepping up and off them as quickly as I could, I managed to reach one of the lower branches of the duiker berry. With much grunting and muttered threats, I swung myself onto it, just a few metres below The Most Fearless Animal in the World, who sat there holding out one limp-wristed paw and moaning. Using a branch as a backrest, I reached up and put my hands under his armpits. He responded by pressing himself tightly into the fork and becoming a dead weight.

I heard a soft chirping, and my torch lit up the enormous yellow eyes of a night ape, bobbing up and down behind the leaves. Whenever something entertaining happened on our nightly walks, one was sure to be watching, like some disapproving old lady peering through her curtains at the neighbours from hell.

By this time, Badger was howling, and it struck me that if there had been an axe handy I would have been very tempted to chop the tree down, with or without him. But there was no point in losing my temper: the boy sounded genuinely distressed and from hard-won experience, I knew that gentle persuasion worked better than four-letter words. Eventually, I managed to manoeuvre him around so that his backside was facing me. Then I winkled out both back legs and put them on my lap, while Badger hugged the tree with his front legs like some frantic Greenpeace volunteer defying the bulldozers.

'Come on, darling,' I said encouragingly, talking him through it as one would to a frightened child. 'Just relax and do what I say. Now, down we come.'

But having managed to prise one leg free, and then the other, I found that the first one was back gripping the branch as tightly as the tentacles of a hairy octopus. This went on for another five minutes, till I finally had him in my arms, and just as I was figuring out how best to guide him down to the ground, he slid off my lap and made a leisurely but effortless descent all on his own.

'Good boy!' I called after him. And I reckoned I also deserved a pat on the back for my rescue efforts. We were quite a team.

Then in the distance the traffic noise began again, but this time it was louder and there seemed to be more of it. I'd better get back quickly in case there was a drama on a neighbouring farm. It was 8.15pm; if I walked fast enough, I might even arrive back in time for that hot dinner.

But first I had to get myself down, and I could see that Badger had found it a lot easier than I would. I caught hold of the branch above me, and from that moment, things began to happen very quickly. In an instant, what I had mistaken as the hum of traffic became a roar, and then I felt a needle-sharp sting on the back of my hand. Sometimes, I can put two and two together with impressive speed. Badger had discovered a beehive deep inside the tree and he'd lured me up there under false pretences, hoping that I could help him get to it. And the bees were sick and tired of being bothered. Another sting in the hand had me swinging from branch to branch at a rate that would have stunned the most agile orangutan, and then I was off at a run, flailing my arms, with a buzzing line of angry bees in hot pursuit. And there was Badger, loyal as always, lolloping happily along beside me.

'Good on yer, Mum,' he was saying. 'I knew you'd get them out in the end!'

Chapter Thirteen – The Mellow Months

Even in Africa, autumn has its own melancholy beauty. The velvet *Commiphora* is always the first to lose heart, its dull golden leaves fluttering like banners amongst the green koppies, heralding the end of summer.

On a morning in mid-March, I see what I think are three Wahlberg's eagles gliding high over the house. Then suddenly there are more of them, flying through stormy clouds and coming from the south-east. Rich arrives on the lawn with his binoculars.

'No, not Wahlberg's,' he says, 'look at the red tinge to

their tails with the light behind them.'

They're Steppe buzzards. Hundreds of them – maybe more. After a summer in southern Africa, they are once again gathering in great flocks for the journey back to their breeding grounds in Russia and Finland. As we squint up into the sky, the birds sweep out from one huge grey cloud into another, wings folded back like dark arrows, high in that silent, airy world above us. Sometimes we can hear their faint calls as the message goes out: join us, we are on our way. It's time to go home. And while we fight and jostle and worry ourselves to death, believing that the world revolves around us, these birds are doing what they have done for millions of years, as unconcerned with our existence as we are, sadly, with theirs.

Are they renewing old acquaintances up there in the blue beyond? Do they look out for each other at the full moon, knowing that it's time to leave?

'Look!' we call to each other, 'more, coming this way!'

They are circling over Dibe, catching the restless winds that will lift and carry them northwards across the continents.

Their glorious freedom stirs us beyond words, but as the last birds drift away out of sight, our hearts are as empty as the sky. Some will travel up to an incredible 13 000 kilometres between their two homes. Will they survive their marathon journey to be back here in September? And if they do, will we be here to welcome them home?

March is the month of marulas, and when the fat yellow fruits hit the ground with a loud thud, Johnson Sibanda is always ready. I was chatting to Badger on a walk one evening, miles away from anyone, or so I thought, when a voice came from the top of a tree, making me jump.

'*Litshonile, Gogo!*'

'*Yebo*, Johnson, *wenzani?*'

I didn't have to see him to know what he was doing – only Johnson makes a serious hobby of collecting wild fruits in season, and there he was, perched in the middle of an *Umbumbulu* tree, picking the golden, bullet-shaped fruits for his special 'bread', that lasts for six months or more.

And only Johnson calls me *gogo* – granny. Oh yes, I know it's a mark of respect, blah blah blah, but I don't like it and I'm sure he only does it to annoy me. I advised him long ago that I am *not old*, but now he makes it a habit, and it's all the more irritating because he is the same age as I am.

He's lean and tough as a length of chorded black rope. The other workers complain that he is 'full of I know', because no one can ever contradict or correct him. But the fact is that as an old poacher, he knows the secrets of these hills better than anyone.

He called me from the house one morning to show me the nest of a Jameson's red rock rabbit in a shallow hole with two babies tucked into a bed of silky down. And it was Johnson, on his way to crank up the borehole engine every day, who always managed to spot the bushbuck ewe, hiding in the woodland shadows, when we believed they had all been taken by leopard long before.

There's a nonchalance about the man, a careless confidence, that the animals pick up on immediately. Bushbuck rams are notorious for their aggression, but where other people are understandably wary, Johnson strolls into the bucks' enclosure with a dish of leaves, inches from Willy's magnificent horns, whistling as if he wasn't there.

When a swarm of agitated bees took up residence in an empty hive at the garage, we decided to move it to the top of the old generator house after dark, well away from the house.

Rich asked Johnson to fetch a ladder, and he went out later that evening to decide on the best course of action. No need – before he had knocked off at 4.30pm, and without being asked, Johnson had plugged up the hole, carried the box down the drive and put in on the top of the genny house.

The marulas provide a bonanza for everyone: the larger antelope like eland and kudu chew on the fruit and then swallow them whole; while the warthogs, with their gin trap jaws, crunch up the scoured nuts that come out of the other end for the taste of the tiny but delicious seeds inside. Squirrels hoard them for winter and Kephas, little Bushman that he is, piles them up in the corner of his hut.

Johnson hefts sackfuls of the ripe fruit back to the compound, and after soaking them in a little water for a couple of days to help separate the hard skin from the nut, he pounds the pulp into a viciously alcoholic juice, from which he appears to suffer no ill effects.

March is the time when good housewives, like Elspeth, my friend from Komani Farm, make marula jelly. Rich is addicted to it, and one year he decided that he would make his own. I objected on the grounds that it would be a waste of sugar, and that we would be depriving the animals of their food (not a very convincing argument as the road was thick with fallen marulas that burst open under the tyres of the vehicle). But it was no good: soon the kitchen was reeking with sacks full of fermenting fruit, and black pots were bubbling away on the solar cooker in the garden – a glittering silver disc reminiscent of a Star Wars spacecraft.

The making of marula jelly is more of a science than an art, and its consumption requires the close proximity of a dentist. First, the fruits have to be picked at exactly the right time;

then the liquid must drip slowly from inside a pillow case or a piece of muslin into a container. That's the easy part. It's in the boiling and re-boiling that things go wrong, for if the consistency is not exactly right, you're likely to lose your teeth in the glutinous toffee that results.

Rich could chat away for hours about it to my girlfriends, comparing notes on successes and failures, boiling times and the exact amount of sugar to be used. And he would glow with pride at breakfast as he produced his jars of shining amber jelly, to be spread lavishly and deliciously on toast. Secretly, I felt as though I had failed as a woman, but when he had to chip away at his last efforts with a hammer, he gave it up, much to my relief. Now we're back to begging for a couple of jars from Elspeth every season.

I wish the birds that have been a part of our lives since the start of summer would at least say goodbye, or give us some hint that they are on their way. Instead, you're suddenly aware of a certain quietness. You can't put your finger on it, but the hills seem to have retreated a little, and you feel as though you are standing in an empty playground after the children have gone.

The gentle summer wind is changing her tune: still playful, but more assertive now with an edge of moodiness. By the time April comes, the great towers of shifting cumulus sending shifting shadows across the hills have disappeared, and the skies are clear. It's as if the vivid tapestry that has lain so softly on the land since the first November rains has been whipped away, taking the smells, the sounds and the colours with it.

You start listening out for the soft melodious trills of the European bee-eaters, hawking for insects, and you can't quite remember when you last heard them. And what about that spotted flycatcher, who faithfully returns to her favourite spot on the fence in the front garden every summer? She wasn't there yesterday and she isn't there today – so she too must have woken up one morning, preened her feathers and hitched a ride with the wind, all 20 grams of her, to the same English garden in which she raised her chicks last year. Or so I like to think.

She comes to us as a welcome visitor from overseas, whereas the paradise flycatcher, our most exotic bird, belongs only in Africa, even though it somewhat disloyally heads towards the equator in our winter months. As the leaves begin to fall, their neat little nests decorated with bits of lichen garnered from the rocks sit exposed in the forks of the trees around the house. Their tastes in nesting material are certainly eclectic, as Rich discovered when one innovative little male hovered in front of him one day, fluttering his long russet tail feathers, as he tried to pluck hairs out of his beard.

The end of summer means the disappearance of crickets, toads and termites – all those tasty tidbits that make a well-fed Badger's life just that little bit more enjoyable. But the cooler weather suited him well, and with more energy and less to distract him, his thoughts invariably turned to mischief.

So when, one April morning, Badge discovered a bush pig sow asleep under a rocky overhang, it was just the sort of diversion he was looking for. She was so still that at first Khanye thought she might be dead. Badger knew better. Giving Khanye his 'watch this!' look out the corner of his eye, he tiptoed up and sniffed her. With a resounding snort, the pig leapt to her feet and whirled around ready to attack. But when she saw that it was only a small badger, she flopped down again and went back to sleep.

Badge stretched out behind her, and all was peaceful for a few minutes, which is about as long as it takes for a honey badger to get bored. He rolled around a bit, looking for something to play with, and then stretching out his head, he lifted the pig's tail with his nose and sniffed her bottom – a liberty that she greeted with justifiable outrage.

This time, she jumped up and gave Badge a good shove with her head, but instead of running away, he began dancing around and presenting her with his neck.

'They went on like that for five minutes,' Khanye told us when he came back to the house. 'Then the bush pig lost her temper. She pinned Badger against a tree and hit him hard with her tusk. It would have been very painful for any other animal, but he didn't seem to care. I didn't want her to do it again, so I chased her away.'

'Do you think she hurt him?' I asked.

'Of course not! As soon as she had gone, he went down an antbear hole and he's been there for the last hour trying to dig it out.'

As darkness falls, a Labrador's thoughts turn to food (even more than usual), and the hungrier he gets, the less he is able to concentrate on anything else. Badge, on the other hand, was just winding up, and if he was focused on hunting or bothering, it was very hard to persuade him to come home.

When he was older, and more able to take care of himself, we would just leave him to it, knowing that he'd be panting at our heels 10 or 15 minutes later. But as a totally inexperienced youngster, he needed our protection, which sometimes meant hours of twiddling our thumbs outside a cave, or watching clods of earth fly out an antbear hole.

Nandi could sit around for so long before something snapped. When Badge emerged for a breather, she'd take a run at him, whereupon he'd retaliate by snapping at her feet. Then, she'd begin circling him, still on the run, ears back and pink tongue flapping, herding him towards home – and supper. It worked, but it wasn't long before Badge had the upper hand, and Nandi settled for the comfort of her bed and regular mealtimes.

In fact, Badge was beginning to demonstrate that he had the upper hand in most situations.

Every single day of his life was a page in history, reported Khanye in his little story entitled 'Badger's Plan', *and I was fortunate enough to appear in some of those pages. On one of the evening walks, we found an unfortunate juvenile tortoise who happened to have grazed past his time of going to bed. Badger picked him up as if playing, and started pulling one front leg. I felt sorry for the tortoise, and tried to spare its life by hiding it in a little forked tree. Blessed with a special nose, Badge easily found it, dropped it down and started his torture routine.*

I hid the tortoise again and again but he kept doing the same thing. For the fourth time, Badge had his other plan. He climbed the small tree where the tortoise was, dropped it down by pushing with his head, then began breaking the two small branches that had securely held the tortoise up, so I could not hide it there again.

Determination is Badger's motto.

The upper hand also extended to games, which more and more, were played subject to Badger rules only. Where once I could escape from his grip around my ankle by shaking my leg or throwing it forward so he flew off as if fired from a cannon, he was now so bulky that if I tried any of those old tricks, I'd lose my balance and fall over – which was exactly what he wanted. We got tired of waiting for him one evening when he was frogging in the river, but as soon as I started walking away, he rushed over and grabbed me by the leg.

'I'm stuck,' I called out to Khanye, 'Could you give him a swat for me?'

Khanye got hold of a leafy stick and shook it at Badge, who immediately let go of my leg and lunged at it, turning the whole thing into a wild game, with Khanye baiting him with the stick and then whipping it away from those snapping teeth just in time.

Naturally, Badger won in the end, and we expected him to parade around with his prize in his usual fashion. But not this time. He took it straight to the river and held it under the water. And as far as we were concerned, there was only one explanation.

'He's trying to drown it!' laughed Khanye. 'Making sure that I can't use it again, just like he broke the branches that held the tortoise.'

Badger had foiled one plan, but he was going to use every trick he knew to try and induce us to stay. Next, he whacked me across the legs with a stick, inviting a game according to another set of Badger rules. He would lie on his back, twiddling the stick between his feet, or do the shuffle-bum routine, dragging it underneath his belly and chewing on it – daring us to snatch it away. I managed to grab hold of it a couple of times, but it was so knobbly and bent that I couldn't wrest it out of his mouth.

It was 9pm – way past suppertime. 'This is it, Badger! We're going home!'

Ten minutes later, he'd caught up with us. It looked as though we had finally won – until Khanye dropped his glove, and Badger pounced on it. Ignoring him wasn't an option, as he kept weaving between our feet and tripping us up. And when the glove was reduced to two fingers and a ball of dirty wet wool, he picked up a stone, then another stick – and after every little game, he galloped off and I could see his eyes shining in the torchlight, waiting along the track with another toy.

Getting Badger home at night was as much in our interests as his. Only then could we sleep peacefully, knowing that his belly was full and that he was safely asleep in his Houdini-proof enclosure outside our bedroom window; rather than ripping out the pot plants on the veranda (no loss, I might add), upending the box of rubbish in the garage, or stealing the tools from the workbench.

I saw a light out in the garage one evening and on going to investigate, I found Rich smiling indulgently, as he filmed our wayward cub shredding the tractor seat with his claws. Anyone else guilty of such a crime would have been pursued with roars of rage and retribution, but not Badge. He was immune from prosecution, even when he tore into the seats of one of the safari vehicles. Rich never had them mended, and today when people climb aboard, he points to the holes in the tattered canvas, and says, proudly:

'Badger did that!'

Chapter Fourteen – Jailbirds

There's a curious affinity between small boys and rats that is generally not appreciated by their parents, so when David's friend Kevin Marillier begged his mother to let him have a couple of pups from the Peek's owl-feeding programme, I was certain she wouldn't agree. But to her great credit, she did, and the family became so enamoured that the rats were allowed to join them every evening after supper to watch TV. Rats are, of course, amongst the cleverest of rodents, and are just as endearing as any other animal once you get to know them (which is why ours were delivered from the chop and put into early retirement).

Kevin's Dad, Ron, was particularly fond of Lucky and Snowy. This stood him in good stead when he made the unexpected acquaintance of the gigantic rodents in the prison block of Bulawayo Central Police Station in February 2002.

For some months, Father Noel Scott of the Anglican Church had been arranging regular interdenominational rallies, always with police approval, to pray for the suffering people of Zimbabwe. Churchgoers, including the Marillier family and John and Joan Stakesby-Lewis, would walk from one church to the next, hearing a short service in each. This was quite legal until government passed the Public Order and Security Act (POSA) making it an offence to hold a public gathering without police permission.

A 'Walk and Pray' had been organised for Saturday the 16th of February, and Father Scott went, as usual, to the Hillside Police Station to get their approval. This was granted. Then late on the Friday afternoon, he received a letter from the local commander telling him that permission had been withdrawn as there was concern that the rally 'would cause unrest'.

Father Scott wasn't going to let such a minor hiccup disrupt his plans. He told the commander that instead of walking, the congregation would go by vehicle from church to church. Bingo.

The rally began at the Catholic Church, where the congregation of around 200 was advised of the change of plan. Led by Father Scott, they drove slowly onto the road, their hazard lights flashing, only to be stopped by the waiting squad of policeman.

An officer put his head through Father Scott's window.

'This procession is banned,' he said.

Once again, the priest explained that only the walk had

been banned, and that there could be nothing wrong with the congregation driving from church to church in order to attend services.

'You have been warned,' replied the officer, but he let the vehicles continue nonetheless.

'People along the road raised their hats thinking that it was a funeral,' recalls Father Scott. 'And they weren't far wrong. Only we were mourning the death of democracy in Zimbabwe.'

The police vehicles continued to follow them and Ron noticed that they were in frequent radio contact with headquarters. Then, during the final service at the Anglican church, the police officer strode down the aisle and told Father Scott that he was under arrest. The priest replied that he certainly wasn't going to leave the pulpit until the service was over. And if the policeman would kindly back off, he would see him outside the church in due course.

There was a fair amount of tension amongst the congregation as Father Noel Scott marched outside surrounded by church elders. Discussion with the police turned into an argument, and eventually they all walked to the nearby Hillside Police Station, where on the orders of the commander, Father Scott was handcuffed, bundled into a police car and driven away. If convicted, he would very likely face a spell in jail. That was bad enough. But what really worried the others was the very real possibility that he might have been taken to one of the many township or rural police stations, where he could be bullied or even tortured – with no recourse to a lawyer, nor contact with his friends. At the very worst, he could disappear altogether: the fate of many other unfortunate Zimbabweans.

In fact, Father Scott was taken to the Bulawayo Central Police Station, where he was first interrogated before being led barefoot into an office where three of the 'top brass' were sitting behind a desk with a rickety chair in front of it.

'Being mindful of African culture, I sat down on it,' says Father Scott, 'but this was greeted by a roar from the officers. "Who do you think you are?!" they shouted. "Get off that chair and sit on the ground!"'

'I complied, and for the next hour they harangued me, before sending me off to have fingerprints taken. Then I knew I was going to be locked up. I was driven to Nkulumane Police Station, stripped of my possessions and pushed into a cell with 15 young Zimbabwe lads, a mixture of rapists, cattle rustlers and shoplifters.'

Father Scott's support group, including four church ministers, drove to the Bulawayo Central Police Station. They were told at the charge office that Father Scott wasn't there, so they decided to wait outside in case he arrived. In what seemed to be a good idea at the time, they linked hands to pray, but considerately, so as not to block the pavement. A few minutes later, Joan Stakesby-Lewis arrived and joined them.

They were halfway through the Lord's Prayer, when a policeman appeared and hustled them inside. For the whole of that afternoon, they sat in the criminal investigation department office, until 6pm when they were informed that they were being placed under arrest 'for causing a disturbance liable to cause a breach of the peace'.

The CID office was upstairs, and when the 'Hillside Eleven' (as they came to be called) looked out of the window, they could see a wire cage in the yard below filled with prisoners.

'We were appalled,' says Joan. 'We were eventually led downstairs where watches, glasses, rings, shoes, and even my bra, were taken from us. Then we were ushered barefoot into the cage, and from there into the cells.'

It was a day of stifling heat. The bare cells reeked of urine, and were filthy: their blackened floors and walls were thick with grease from decades of human sweat. A broken toilet sat in one corner, in full view of the adjacent occupants. Toilet paper was not provided. The cells had been designed for a maximum of 10 people, but by evening, there were 19 in the men's cell, including a youngster of 14 who had been picked up without identification papers.

From time to time, one of the inmates was allowed to fetch water from the yard in order to try and clear the toilet. And that's where Ron made the acquaintance of the biggest rats he had ever seen, running up and down the drainpipes.

'I'm rather fond of rats, so they didn't bother me at all,' he says, 'They were so bold that I could have reached out and touched them. But what a dangerous source of disease in such a foul place.'

Joan was separated from her husband and the rest of the men.

'When the cell door opened for me to go in, my stomach lurched. I was going from the light into the dark, and couldn't see very well,' she recalls. 'The smell from the toilet was overpowering. There were bodies lying all over the floor, and I kept stumbling over them, as I couldn't see where I was putting my feet. There were 13 of us, myself and 12 ladies of the night. They were very kind to me, and at their request, I prayed with them.

'Eventually we settled down to "sleep" on the concrete floor. We had four very dirty blankets that stank of urine and heaven knows what else. The cell was about 2.5 by 4.5 metres, and a least a square metre was taken up by the toilet area. The floor was very hard. I started the night by lying on my side with my nose, elbows and knees touching the wall.

Being on the edge, I ended up with less and less space, so eventually I turned around and used someone's legs as a pillow, draped my legs over someone's bottom, and squeezed mine in a small space between.'

The Hillside Eleven looked upon their unexpected incarceration as an opportunity. Since there was only standing room in the men's cell, they spent the night singing hymns and praying with the other inmates. In fact, they probably scored more converts to Christianity in two days than the old missionaries had in 20 frustrating years. Their singing annoyed one of the guards so much that he threatened to turn the water hoses on them. They ignored him.

'We were let out into the "cage" early on Sunday morning,' Joan recalls. 'Having been in the cells all night, we were thrilled to be there – it was bliss! The ladies from the churches brought us wonderful food, which was a great morale booster, and there was enough to share with the other prisoners too.'

As his wife Liz was leaving, Ron lifted his hand in farewell.

'Don't wave!' the guard snarled at him. 'You had an open *pum*!'

This mystified the fledgling convicts, until one of the other inmates reminded them that the open palm signified the opposition's version of a salute.

The Hillside Eleven spent the weekend in jail before being moved to the crowded basement cells in the Magistrate's Court early on Monday morning. There they waited for hours, sitting with hundreds of other people awaiting trial, some of them young boys of no more than 11 or 12.

They were led into court late that afternoon and, to their

intense relief, they were released on bail, on condition that they report once a week to the Hillside Police Station. After three more court appearances, they were taken off remand – although the charges against them were never dropped. In November 2005, three and a half years after the rally, a determined effort was made to convict Father Noel Scott (who was clearly a dangerous man). His lawyer had no trouble in showing that the case was flawed, but the magistrate refused to drop the charges, and the case was postponed, just as it had been for the Hillside Eleven. A lesser man would have left the country, and Father Scott certainly had the opportunity to do so. But only six years later did he take final retirement in Ireland.

'On reflection,' Ron wrote to me recently, 'what impressed me the most was the love that came about amongst all of us who were incarcerated that weekend. Zimbabweans are a warm and caring community – across the races. Our suffering was very small compared to what others have been through. Many have lost everything – even their lives.'

Having completed primary school together, David and Kevin, Ron's son, moved onto the same high school where girls replaced white rats as the companions of choice. Through the years, the Marillier family were regular visitors to Stone Hills. But by 2006, with Kevin and Lara to put through university on salaries that were barely enough to feed the four of them, they realised that they would have to move.

After a long paperchase, they were finally accepted as migrants into the UK, a place they had visited once on a brief holiday. They found homes for their dogs and tenants for the house, and on a chilly winter's morning, five weeks before they were due to fly, they came out for their last visit to Stone Hills. Badger made sure they would never forget it.

All four of them accompanied us on the morning walk; the grass was heavy with dew, so Badge led us along the centre road, tail up, and swaggering. Once he was sure that all eyes and cameras were focused on him, he picked up a piece of wood and dropped it at Kev's feet, and they played a hectic game of shuffle-bum and grab – with Badge as always on the winning side.

Only Ron and Lara accompanied us on the evening walk, by which time Badge had moved down to the banks of the Pundamuka River. He came straight to my call, but instead of greeting me first as I would have expected, he headed straight for Ron and the squeaky new, highly polished (and as we discovered later, rather smelly) buffalo-hide boots that had been presented to him as a leaving present from the school where he had worked. Ron was very proud of them and as this was their maiden voyage, he was understandably distressed when Badge wrapped himself tightly around one ankle.

'Badge!' I picked up a stick and swatted his bottom. He grabbed on tighter. Then, I tickled him and for one moment, he relaxed his grip.

'Run, Ron! Get a head start!'

With Badge struggling in my arms, Ron sprang out of his embrace and took off through the long grass, with Lara pounding along beside him.

I held onto the twisting and wriggling Badger for as long as I could, and then he was away, surging out of the starting gates with all the explosive energy (if not quite the shape) of a greyhound after a hare.

A honey badger's usual relaxed gait is a bouncy, rollicking trot – at times so springy that he appears to be floating along. But they can also run like the devil, and it took Badge just

162

a few minutes to catch up with Ron's boots, despite the fact that their owner regularly jogged 10 kilometres a day and was as fit as anyone we knew.

By the time I reached them, Ron was sitting on the ground with one leg in the air, desperately trying to retie his shoelaces, a complicated business involving hooks rather than holes, with Badger wrapped around his arm. When I arrived, he gave me his beadiest look and clutched on even harder.

'Playful little chap!' gasped Ron. 'He tripped me up and then somehow got my laces undone. I wonder if you could ...'

Somehow, I managed to wrestle Badger away, and then off we all went again, in a fashion.

'Try high-stepping. That might work.'

Ron pranced through the grass like a participant in the Sydney Mardi Gras, with Badge bouncing up and down after him until once again he captured a boot.

'What about goose-stepping?'

Now, Ron threw his legs forward till he was in danger of dislocating his pelvis, and to his great delight, Badge suddenly found himself airborne.

I tried hanging back in the faint hope that Badge would return to Mother, but of course he didn't; in fact he was glad to be rid of me. Catching up with the little circus was no problem, even in the dark. I just followed the cries of 'Badger, no! Get the little sod off me!' until finally when we reached the road, I radioed Rich and asked him to come to our rescue with the vehicle.

Ron's and Lara's smiles of relief from the back of the Toyota were premature. Badge scrambled up onto the bonnet via a front wheel, hauled himself onto the roof using the windscreen wipers as a ladder, and landed between them. Somehow I managed to manhandle him to the ground, then

Rich did a quick turn and took off. Seconds later, Badge slipped out of my grasp and went haring through the dust, chasing those boots all the way home.

The Marilliers left for England on the 9th of July. I can't imagine how they were feeling, but for us it was emptiness: the bleak sensation of being alone on our island, while our friends swam away to face a different set of sharks.

We were sitting on the veranda of the lodge on their last afternoon on Stone Hills, when Lara made a comment that I try to remember when I'm feeling down.

'Five years ago,' she reminded me, 'we were all sitting here, in exactly the same place, looking at the trees around the lodge, which were hiding the view of the hills. You said that in five years' time, they would have grown so much we'd be able to see through them – *if* you were still on the farm.' She smiled. 'And look, there are the hills!'

Mother-in-law's breath – that's what our neighbour Julius calls the bitter-sharp winds that drive the winter in, making the grass sparkle with ice from the first frosts, and sending white ribbons of early morning mist drifting over the dam and along the riverbeds.

It's a time of dripping noses and frozen feet, especially for those on after-hours perambulations with a badger. But while the day is full of human distractions, the night, at last, belongs to the animals. And as darkness falls, they slip out of their caves or holes, or down from the trees, and go quietly about their business. It was then, when the world had narrowed down to just the two of us, that I felt as though we were floating in our own little bubble, Badger and I, somewhere in the vast blackness of the universe. And as long as I knew he was around, I felt safe amongst the sudden squeaks or grunts, and the rustle of unseen feet amongst the dry leaves.

Often I could feel that he was close, even though I couldn't hear or see him, but there were occasions when I was sure he'd gone, and just as I was wondering how on earth I'd get home without him, I'd suddenly hear a reassuring little prrt! – or he would appear out of the darkness like a phantom, as if he had been there all the time.

I'd like to think we suffered more than Badge did at bedtime, after his supper, when he disappeared into the bunker in his enclosure. I'd done my best to make it comfortable: first with a blanket, which he tore to pieces, and then a pile of dry grass, which he immediately kicked into a pile and flung outside. In the end our little Spartan settled for a tyre, giving him both something to chew on and a place in which to curl up. And when the wind was shrieking around the house and trying to squeeze itself through the gaps in the windows and doors, I'd pull up the blankets around my ears and try not to think about him, only 10 metres away in his mean little house.

A lot of sensible creatures, particularly the amphibians, dig in for the dry season. Wrapped in a waterproof cocoon with only his nostrils showing, the bullfrog can remain underground for years – until conditions are just right for a re-emergence. Pre-Badge, I'd only ever met a *Tomopterna* – a sand frog – once, when David was playing in the builders' sandpit close to the house. We dug out a fat mottled ball with bulbous eyes, identified him and then watched as he frantically shuffled back into the sand for the rest of the winter. And we'll never forget his name: he's the little man, twirling a mop attached to his big toe.

Badger sniffed out his first sand frog in the Mathole riverbed, 20 centimetres underground, and he liked the taste of it so much that he was there the following evening, all evening, until he had at least 12 under his belt and a bad dose of hiccups.

Mining, Khanye called it, and it became an addiction. Badge would feel around for frogs with his claws, and then dig huge holes in the riverbed with a funny humping movement, his hind legs bouncing backwards while his front ones flung out the sand, together with a few unexpectedly airborne frogs. The only drawback to his meal was the wet sand that stuck to their bodies, but Badger simply lay on his back and raked them across his belly till they were clean before dropping them into his mouth.

There is nowhere chillier than a riverbed in mid-winter. I can vouch for it. When I got fed up with marching up and down and stamping my feet, I thought I'd try a bit of yoga on the bank about 20 metres away from the current excavations. My first few stretches were fine, but when I stood on one leg with my hands in the prayer position on top of my head, oozing peace and tranquillity, Badge came roaring out of the darkness and nipped me on the foot. Next, I tried listening to my iPod, but the minute I started moving in time to the music, he'd was there, clutching onto my ankle. I think I must have embarrassed him.

We'd keep score by listening out for each satisfied smack of his lips, and he was up to 35 frogs and counting one night when I decided that I was going home for supper, with or without him.

Moments later, he was lying in front of me demanding to be picked up. And as I staggered on with 10 kilograms of wet cold Badger bunched up in my arms, his paw resting in my hand, he puckered up his nose and gave heartrending little cries – which he kept up for five minutes until he was absolutely sure that I had been moved to tears. Then off he trotted back to the river, tail up, knowing full well that he had won and that I'd be close behind. After all, how can you compare the pleasures of a hot dinner with the honour of being considered indispensable to the meanest animal in the world?

We were on our way home after one of Badge's frog-fests when we heard the hoarse deep-chested barks of a kudu, and almost immediately Badger found cheetah spoor, sharp and fresh in the sand. He stopped and sniffed at it for a few moments with total concentration – then followed the tracks until they veered off into the long grass.

My heart sank. Only a few hours before we'd been giving the kudu, eland, giraffe, warthog and gemsbok their cubes. Betty, the oldest kudu cow, had brought us her new calf for the first time, licked clean and fresh as a newly opened flower, and we'd laughed at her antics as she charged around, discovering just what she could do with those long, uncoordinated legs. I worried about Betty though; she was bony, ragged and tired. A calf would be a real drain on her, particularly in winter. But there's no blessed menopause for the ungulates, as there is for us lucky primates: they are programmed to breed every year until they drop.

Betty was the first of her little group to give us her trust, she led the others to the house each June, looking for the game cubes we had stored to help some of the needier animals through the lean months. One Friday afternoon, we'd arrived late back from town and everyone had already scattered, tired of waiting for their food. But at 6.30pm when I went to draw the curtains of the lounge, there was Betty, at the top of the stairs, staring at me reproachfully through the glass door, while the rest of her little group stood in a patient line on the other side of the fence.

Kudu gaze out at the world with soft, trusting eyes. Stately, serene and yet so vulnerable, there's something ephemeral about the way they dissolve into the dusk like puffs of grey smoke. The cows give birth throughout the year, and the mother hides her calf amongst the koppies, which is exactly where leopards are likely to be. And if it escapes that threat and emerges safely into the open, a cheetah may well be waiting for it in the long grass.

The eland are far more canny: they all give birth at around the same time, and almost immediately put their calves into day care under the supervision of an adult female, where they stay together in a tight bunch, making it very difficult for a predator to take them by surprise.

Kudu barking and fresh cheetah spoor – it was unlikely to be a coincidence. The scouts climbed the cheetah's favourite lookout rock the following morning, and found fresh dung filled with matted kudu hair. At feeding time at 4pm, the adults were waiting, but the calf was missing. Betty looked as though she had suffered a stroke: her ears were drooping, her back legs were knock-kneed and she could barely stand. When I walked up close with her bowl, I could see that the life had already gone from her tired old eyes. She wandered off alone, very slowly, and I knew that I wouldn't see her alive again.

Badger disappeared at the end of his walk that night – but with the help of the receiver, we soon picked up the sweet cloying smell of fresh meat, and the reflection of the calf's eyes and her enormous ears in the torchlight. There were no signs of a struggle. But it was another reminder of our cub's misplaced confidence in his own invincibility. This was the first carcass he had found on his own at night, and he was tucking into it without paying the slightest bit of attention to what was around him. As we arrived, something heavy crashed away into the long grass. It could have been a brown hyaena, but

Badge didn't even look up.

A week later, when I was doing the 4pm feed, I saw vultures circling along the Habhe River. It was Betty, and she'd died, as they so often do, close to water. Her neck was twisted awkwardly under her and her lips were pulled back over the worn yellow teeth.

By feeding her in winter, we'd kept her alive for perhaps four or five years longer than her natural span. But she had been steadily losing the battle, too weak to defend herself when the other, younger females chased her away from her food. She knew when her time had come, and she left us quietly to die alone. The circle was complete.

The rest of her little herd continued jostling over their food every evening, and then drifting off back into the bush as they had always done. They couldn't weep or dress in black, or play with her bones like the elephants do, and we'll never know if they missed her or what thoughts lay behind those unfathomable brown eyes. We don't know, and we should never assume that we do.

Khanye and I were walking with Badge, who was around nine months old, on the other side of the wall of a small weir on the Mathole River. We heard a noise and went around to the other side to investigate. A waterbuck bull was standing on the bank and below him, stretched out in the mud, was a waterbuck cow. If her ears hadn't twitched slightly, we would have thought she was dead. I stepped back, horrified, but as I was pulling the radio out of my rucksack to call Rich, I realised that Badge was also deeply distressed. Crying continuously, he lay down on the grass and refused to move. I knelt in front of him and he crawled into my lap, his head between my knees, quite inconsolable. Khanye waited with the cow until Rich came; he tried to pull her head out of the mud, but she was old and weak, and it was too late. He said that he felt she knew he was trying to help her.

I took Badge off to Grain Bin Koppie, one of his favourite spots, hoping to distract him. He wouldn't leave my side, and even refused to eat his apple: his usual treat at the end of the morning walk. Instead, he followed me back to the house, tail down and belly to the ground, and I had to leave him in his enclosure till Khanye arrived home and carried him back to the rocks at Grain Bin Koppie, where he stayed for the rest of the day.

It was an unnerving experience. Was he just responding to my distress (which was minor compared to his), or did he somehow recognise the imminence of death, or even the concept of mortality? And why would this affect a carnivore, who kills for a living?

Whatever the explanation, his sensitivity and the depth of his feelings were terrifying, I wrote in my diary that evening. *One little animal – if he began talking to us, I wouldn't be surprised.*

Chapter Fifteen – Victims And Cannibals

One of Badger's favourite hors d'oeuvres was fresh mouse lightly rolled in grit and served warm and squeaking, direct from the hole. But the mouse is nobody's instant takeaway. It has a warren of subterranean tunnels with a number of handy exits, giving it a sporting chance of escaping predation – until the honey badger comes along.

At first, when the delectable smell of rodent wafted into the nostrils of our young Badge, he would begin frantically digging down one hole, as the wily rodent shot to safety out of the back door (with much silent cheering on my part).

But it wasn't long till he figured out a couple of elaborate and highly successful techniques, both of which appear to be part of the standard honey badger *Mousetrap Manual* (12th edition), as follows:

First: locate main mouse exit, or where the smell is strongest.

Collapse all other holes and proceed to stuff them with soil or leaves, carefully tamping them down with your paws.

Commence digging at full speed into main exit to retrieve trapped mouse.

Or: The Two Hole Tango: Lie flat on your tummy with back legs dangling into one hole and your nose at the lip of the other, but not visible from inside.

Commence brisk tail wagging and foot wiggling. If done correctly, panic-stricken prey will rush out, straight into your mouth.

Bon appetit!

Badger would usually deliver the coup de grâce with one snap of those iron jaws, but sometimes, when his tummy was already full, he would first (despite my strict instructions to the contrary) have a little game with his victim. As the mouse was on the whole an unwilling participant, Badge would trap it between his interlocking claws, making a convenient little cage from which there was no escape. And once, having caught a very small pouched mouse, he rolled onto his back, and dangled it over his mouth like a bunch of grapes.

'I'm going to play with you,' he announced, whereupon the mouse responded: 'Like hell you are!' as it slipped out of his grasp and scurried away.

He failed far more often than he succeeded – as in the time he was lying in ambush at one exit, while two little climbing mice crawled out of another looking rather dazed, like a couple of survivors emerging from a bomb shelter. And while Badge lay drooling at the hole, they scampered up to the top of the nearest bush and sat watching him and washing their faces.

Environmentally incorrect as this might be, I have to admit that it was much easier witnessing the last moments of a scorpion rather than a Tom Thumb or a Mrs Tittlemouse. I always felt that I owed the doomed mice an apology, which (combined with the fact that they have the most delightful names) led me to write something in their honour.

ODE TO A SINGLE-STRIPED MOUSE
(*Lemniscomys rosalia* – pronounced 'Lemniscomiss')

If a rodent called *Lemniscomys*
Is occasionally promiscuous,
It's not her fault:
It's how a mouse is meant to be.
For it hardly can be heaven
Giving birth to up to seven
And to care for that enormous family.

And then:
ODE TO A TINY FAT MOUSE
(yes, that's really what it's called – *Steatomys parvus*)

The legitimate grouse
Of this little fat mouse
Is that people make fun of her name.
For they keep pointing out
That she's overly stout
As if somehow the mouse is to blame.

From a properly scientific viewpoint (inescapable with a husband like mine), Badger's rapid mastery of honey badger mouse-trapping techniques in the absence of any maternal tuition, showed us that once again, he was capable of drawing on a combination of instinct, experience and straight ingenuity.

Even those who view all furry rodents as common or garden rats are likely to have a soft spot for the dormouse. The name alone, conjuring up something small and fluffy, peeping blearily out of its warm nest, is enough to elicit Oohs and Aahs from the hardest heart. I admit I am no exception. Yes, they have destroyed the frill around our bed (what good is it anyway?), and shredded a few clothes for nesting material, but when I heard a noise from the top of the corner cupboard in our office and saw a mother dormouse teetering on the bar of an aluminium frame with a baby stuffed into her mouth, those minor misdemeanours were forgotten. After rocking indecisively back and forth for a while, she took a sudden leap from the top of the frame to the ledge under the thatch, a foot or so above her. But the baby was too heavy, and after five aborted attempts, she gave up.

A couple of days later, I discovered one of the babies fast asleep on top of a concertina file on my desk, abandoned and clearly needing my help. I leapt into action, with more success than I had had a couple of weeks before, when I had wandered around the house for most of the day trying to pinpoint the source of a pathetic but insistent squeaking, only to find that it was the sound of the water trapped in the sole of one of my sandals.

The dormouse submits to being picked up, I wrote in my diary, *and even takes a few drops of ProNutro mixed with milk from a syringe. I make up a nice little bed in a shoebox and close the lid. A few minutes later, I hear the sound of debris falling from the thatch onto the top of the corner cupboard and there amongst a thick layer of poo sits Dormouse Number Two, a bit livelier than the first. Nothing could be quite as adorable. The thick, soft grey fur, slightly snub nose, delicately pricked ears, wide black eyes, round tummy – and fluffy tail, just to finish it off. And now I have two! We can bring them up together and release them as a pair. Later, one takes a little milk, but when I pull back the towel to find the second, it springs out of the box, onto the floor and away, not to be found again. Now I'm in a quandary – can such a tiny creature cope on its own? Should I release the other one to keep it company? I decide to keep it for a few days and feed it up, hoping we can relocate its sibling. So very lovingly I carry it to the kitchen, and make up its bed in one of the bird cages. But as I am putting it ever so gently inside, it bites my finger, which is surprisingly painful. But surely I am imagining this from something so small? The dormouse casts a contemptuous look around its new quarters, and walks straight out through the bars towards my outstretched hand. It cocks its head, steps daintily onto my fingers, and sinks its teeth into my thumb. And before I can stuff it back into the cage, it really latches on with what feels like a mouthful of red-hot needles.*

How shallow we humans are, so totally duped by appearances. If it's cute and kissable, we reason, then surely it has a personality to match. We're just as silly when it comes to our uncritical adoration of movie stars, those masters of deception, who simply glow with health and happiness and never get wrinkles, piles or halitosis. It's not possible. And it's the same with the darling little dormouse, until that shocking moment when your severed finger drops to the floor, and the creature's inner monster is revealed.

I am not exaggerating. Dormice pull the heads off baby birds and eat their brains. And they dine on their enemies. If a dormouse family happens to covet their neighbour's nest, they won't do the reasonable thing by negotiating a rental or even simply evicting the rightful residents. Oh no, they march in, attack and then *eat* the lot of them, kids and all.

So, the terrible truth is that a dormouse is a cannibal, far better suited to horror movies than to bedtime stories. And think of the unfairness of it: the honey badger, tough, aggressive but with a heart of gold, is the one who has the terrifying reputation.

Not all rodents are similarly ill-disposed. The largest in Africa is the porcupine and although it's reputed, quite erroneously, to have poison-tipped quills that it shoots like arrows, it is actually quite a peaceful creature. In truth, the male, at least in the opinion of the dormouse, is a bit of a pansy. To start with he is 100 per cent faithful to his partner. Even worse – he's far too polite to initiate sex, leaving it to his prickly boss lady to make the first move in their somewhat hazardous lovemaking. And he's a devoted family man, always ready to accompany his offspring on foraging expeditions, and protect them against predators – like the honey badger.

At 16 months old, Badge had collected his fair share of quills as a consequence of tangling with irritated porcupines, but up till then, there had been no serious encounters between them. So, when Khanye came rushing down to the house one early morning to report that Badge was 'fighting with *inungu*' in a cave behind the lodge, Rich grabbed his video camera and ran.

He couldn't see a thing under the low, dark overhang, so he lay down, holding his camera out in front of him. Now he could make out the shapes of two bristling adult porcupines in full display: growling, roaring, foot stamping and rattling their quills like a pair of frenzied flamenco dancers. And weaving around them amid billowing clouds of dust was Badger, wearing five quills, Mohican-style, stuck in the top of his head and his neck. As always when he was in hunting mode, he was absolutely silent.

For a moment, the dust cleared, and then Rich saw the cause of all the fuss: a youngster, maybe a month old, hiding behind his parents who were trying to shield him with their bodies. The quills didn't bother Badge until they began catching on the roof of the overhang – then he emerged and began pulling them out.

Now if the leopard or the lion are stuck with quills, they have only one recourse – their teeth. And if the quills break off and the remnants are left in the skin, the wounds fester and can very often be fatal. You won't be surprised to hear that the honey badger has no such problem. His natural defensive attitude is to present the top of his head, his neck or his bottom to his adversary, where the skin is rubbery and thick, making penetration difficult. But when the quills do lodge themselves in the top of his head or the back of his neck, in places inaccessible to most other animals, he merely reaches up with his two flexible front legs, and either grasps them between his paws, or locks them between the alternate digits of one paw, effectively clamping them tight before pulling them out.

There was only one quill in his neck that Badge couldn't reach, so Rich pulled it out for him. For a change the porcupine had stuck him a good one: around 4 centimetres into the skin. But when Rich checked the spot half an hour later, he could find neither a hole nor any bleeding, probably thanks to the lack of large blood vessels in that area (a feature that was very useful when he was raiding beehives).

Badge gave up after a couple of hours, but the incident proved to us that there was a very serious side to his relentless bothering of porcupines, warthogs and anyone else in occupation of a hole or burrow.

I could write an entire book about Badge's adventures with warthogs – like the time an enraged female lifted him up on her tusks and somersaulted him out of her den. Or when he suddenly vanished on a walk, and then reappeared on the other side of the Pundamuka River heading for an antbear hole. He crept around the back, pushed a bit of soil in from the top, then dug a little around the entrance, before venturing briefly inside and rapidly out again. He was being so cautious, I thought there might be a snake inside. Nothing happened for five minutes or so, until a low subterranean rumbling announced the arrival of something resembling a supersonic bulldozer, which exploded out of the hole and began mashing him into the ground. I'd already decided where to bury him, when the warthog suddenly stopped. Up jumped Badge to face her, challenging her to another bout. But unexpectedly she backed down the hole again, and only with much clapping and yelling did I finally get him to leave her in peace.

He's in-de-bloody-structible, I wrote in my diary. *How is it that he can get into these life-threatening situations and trot away without a scratch? Perhaps he is made of Indian rubber, or maybe he relaxes completely when he's having fun. Piggy showed great restraint by not coming after him sooner, but she was probably torn between wanting to crush the life out of him and protecting the piglets that were no doubt in the hole. Lucky I wasn't any closer. I'll be on crutches soon, while Badge trots off into the sunset.*

Months later, Khanye and I were watching him do his treacly tiptoeing routine around another group of holes, criss-crossed with tree roots. He'd managed to open up a small entrance, no bigger than two fists, at the base of a tree, when there was a growl, and a warthog's head emerged almost directly underneath him, sending Badge into rapid reverse. But instead of rushing out, she lay there quietly, with only her head visible, while her tormentor kept digging furiously until the side of the hole collapsed on top of her.

She had to be sick or dying, or perhaps trapped by the root across the hole, so we tried to call him away. It was hopeless, as we knew it would be – he was on a mission and nothing would deter him from it.

Now he whipped around and began digging backwards, piling more and more soil on top of the poor hog's head. Sometimes she groaned, and bubbles of mucous came up through the sand, followed by long, ragged breaths as if she was breathing through her mouth. And then silence. Badge kept throwing sand onto her, but each time her head was completely submerged, he'd step back for a few moments, and then start digging her up again, presumably to check if she had suffocated.

'No patience,' said Khanye.

Just when we thought it was all over, a pair of tusks and two sand-encrusted eyes appeared, and the warthog took a lunge at him, while Badge ducked back behind the root. This went on for two long hours, like some ghoulish, never-ending funeral. Most of the time, the warthog lay completely still, and we were quite sure that she was near to death. Then she'd summon the last of her strength to have another go at Badge, and he'd present her with his neck; steadily getting bolder, till he was climbing over the root and pressing his whole body against her head – before entombing her again.

Then, at last, he went too far. When he began nibbling at the sand around her eyes, she threw her head sideways and nicked him with a tusk. And big, bad Badge came rushing back to Mother and threw himself into my lap, complaining about the unfairness of it all. I shone my torch onto the warthog – she was shivering, but still alive.

All the while, I had kept calling Rich on the radio but there was no reply. Only when the whole performance was nearly over did I realise that it was on the wrong channel. As we followed Badge down to the river, the lights of the vehicle swept through the trees and illuminated a family of warthogs: mother and two babies, charging away and into the darkness.

Our resurrected pig had won. Now the hole was empty, we could see that she had wedged herself into the entrance to protect the youngsters in the chamber behind her. Such is the strength of maternal love, and such also is the tenaciousness of the badger.

In fact, Badge wouldn't have been successful, even if he had managed to get past the formidable mother hog. It was July and her piglets were already around seven months old, too large a meal for a small carnivore. But Badge wasn't to know that, and he was only now beginning to learn that there comes a point when it is better to save your energy for something achievable rather than to expend any more of it on a venture that is likely to end in failure.

Chapter Sixteen – A Taste Of Honey

Ever since we first saw photographs of the Ngorongoro Crater and the Serengeti as teenagers, paging endlessly through Bernhard Grzimek's book *Rhinos Belong to Everybody*, both Rich and I had longed to visit East Africa. And in January 2005, we finally made it.

Dreams have a habit of disappointing, but not this one. We saw the Ngorongoro Crater in shadow, storms and mist, but nothing will ever compare to that first clear day, when we drove through the ancient trees that line the rim and stood looking hundreds of feet down onto the vastness of the crater floor, its soda lake shimmering pink with flamingoes, its forests and swamps, and the tiny figure of a single elephant bull pacing slowly along, thinking his elephant thoughts – on his way, as Karen Blixen put it, 'to keep an appointment at the end of the world'.

It was the first time we had both left Badge for any length of time, and although we were sure that he would be well taken care of by Khanye, we also knew his propensity for trouble. We arrived home three weeks later when they were already out on their evening walk, and waited impatiently for a call. Finally at dusk, Khanye radioed in to say that Badge was busy with a beehive and wouldn't come home. So we went to fetch him.

There is no room in a badger's life for muted shades or delicate nuance. He is black and white inside and out. And our cub was always a man of strong emotions. When he heard our voices, he came running out of the bush and threw himself into my arms, making little cries of welcome, and hugging me tightly with his sticky paws. In fact, he wouldn't let go, and I had to haul him up and carry him, still hanging off my arm like an outsize furry fashion accessory.

The hive was under a rock, and Badge had been there for two days, digging his way into it, and receiving plenty of abuse from the bees in return. But no amount of buzzing and stinging could deter him; like any addict, he'd have his fix no matter how much it hurt. This was the first opportunity for Rich to get some footage of Badge seriously tackling a hive, so very early the next morning when we thought the bees would be less active, we all set off – Badge in the lead as usual, Rich and Khanye clonking along behind, festooned with camera equipment, and me, trailing behind.

Fortunately, writing is a lightweight pursuit – a small recorder in my pocket, a pair of binoculars, and that's it. In any case, as I always tell Rich when he tries to get me to take photographs, there are times when you can no longer distance yourself by staring at something through a lens – you simply have to let those sensations wash over you, merely allowing the magical moment to happen, unimpeded.

That's where a recorder is so handy, although I often cringe when I get home to hear the heavy breathing, the excited whisper, like the soundtrack of some awful film.

We were around half a kilometre from the hive when Badge began running back and forth in front of us, panting with what seemed to be extreme excitement. At first, we thought he wanted us to hurry, but the closer we got to the hive, the more worked up he became. Then he lay down in front of me and refused to move.

'Try going on ahead,' Rich suggested.

That worked for a few minutes, until Badge grabbed hold of my foot and wouldn't let go. We were in the middle of a stand of *Ililangwe*, and the combined effort of trying to drag Badge behind me while climbing rocks, and coughing and sneezing from the millions of tiny hairs flying up my nose, was just too much. He'd made his position quite clear: he didn't want me to go any further. Rich and Khanye managed to get a quick look at the hive, but I wasn't allowed to go anywhere near it.

As soon as we started walking in the opposite direction, Badge released his grip. We sat quietly on a rock for a while at the top of a rise over a green valley ringed with hills – 'our crater', Rich called it – and Badge curled up in my lap for a few minutes, as he used to do as a small, insecure cub. Then he went in search of a stick, and invited me to play, but not too boisterously. *No hard feelings?* he seemed to be asking. The message couldn't have been clearer if he'd brought me a box or chocolates or a bunch of flowers. Badger was apologising.

But what had it all been about? It would have been quite understandable if he'd felt the need to protect his food, but he'd led Khanye to the hive where he had fed quite happily for the two previous days, so that wasn't it.

Something had been different about our visit. Could he sense that the bees were particularly active on that day and therefore dangerous? If that was the case, he was not only protecting us but also himself, as he didn't show any inclination later to re-visit the hive. We'll never know what Badger's real intentions were that day, but we still believe that it was simply another expression of his devotion – keeping me away from clear and present danger.

A honey badger does have some defence against stings. His external ears are tiny, reduced to a hard ridge of cartilage, and his eyes are small. His back and neck are covered with a fairly dense mantle of white fur, plus the skin is thicker there and lacks large blood vessels, thus slowing down the dispersal of toxins.

The white of his back may also give him some protection. It's generally thought that the contrasting black and white fur simply acts as a warning to a badger's enemies. But Badge preferred to raid hives at night, when bees are almost blind, and Rich has observed that when they swarm out, they are immediately drawn to the white fur rather than to the rest of the badger's body, which is covered with sparse black fur, and thinner, more sensitive skin.

How doth the little busy bee
Improve each shining hour
And gather honey all the day
From every opening flower?

So wrote Isaac Watts in the 17th century in his *Divine Songs for Children*. Bees fascinate us – from the complexity of their social organisation, to the dance the scouts perform when they return to the hive to give detailed information to other workers about the amount and quality of the food they have found, and its direction and distance away.

They are, of course, the major pollinators of flowers, but this is a two-way transaction. The flower benefits and so does the bee, who collects the pollen stuck between the hairs on its body to feed its young.

Some of the social bees have a truly beautiful method of carrying their precious cargo home. Using special brushes and combs on their legs, they fill up two tiny pollen baskets attached to each of their third legs, pinning them securely with a special bristle – like two tiny saddle bags filled with gold.

Flowers that rely on insects (*entomophily* – insect love, in bio-speak) put a huge amount of effort and not a little cunning into making themselves attractive. Petal shape is important; alluring colours are essential, and perfume, well, if you really want to score, darling, it's a must.

Interestingly enough, in some instances, bees, and humans have quite different perceptions of colour. Yellow petals are a favourite, but red is spurned because to a bee, this shows up as black.

The male, in some species of non-social bees, is a romantic fool who is attracted to a flower's perfume solely for its effect on the ladies. He collects it in drops of fragrant oil, but instead of patting it onto his face or spraying it under his arms, he transfers it into special containers on his hind legs filled with absorbent hairs. Then, drenched in perfume and thoroughly intoxicated, he flies unsteadily onto a suitable perch, and sits flexing his abdomen, waiting to be mobbed by a swarm of nubile females.

On the other hand, the flowers that are wind-pollinated (*anemopily* – wind love) don't need to bother much with their personality or looks: the wind will do the job however shy and unobtrusive they are. All the female flowers have to do is to hang there, waiting to be knocked up by any old passing breeze.

So doth the little busy bee go about his business, filled with appreciation for the finer things of life – which is more than one can say for Action Badge (The Terminator), whose attitude was always: if you can't eat it, shag it or at least chase it up a tree, then it's a waste of time.

Badge, too, had a particular smell of his own. But it was stored in his anal glands, and hardly likely to be a chick magnet. He did, however, exert a real attraction for another kind of bird – the greater honeyguide.

Honeyguides eat bee larvae and wax, but they can't break into a hive on their own, so they must solicit the help of a third party, most often a human – as far as we know. We've all experienced it on Stone Hills: first you hear a frenzied non-stop chittering, and then the bird is flying from tree to tree ahead of you, flashing its white tail feathers and making sure you can't misread its invitation to follow.

Often it behaves so erratically that you can't find the hive, but sometimes it will lead you to it, and having fulfilled its part of the bargain, it will sit by quietly and wait for its reward. In

African folklore, you'd better not forget to repay the favour, or next time, the bird will surely lead you to a black mamba or into the jaws of a lion.

It's also widely believed that honeyguides will invite badgers to follow them to hives. Johnson Sibanda told me that he once heard a badger making a peculiar hissing noise while it followed the bird, and I saw this story repeated in a couple of the reference books. This makes perfect sense, but the trouble is that the badger/bird connection is supported only by numerous anecdotes, and has therefore not been given the nod by the scientific fraternity.

Badge provided us with two very interesting experiences. We were walking around 50 metres behind him, when a juvenile honeyguide landed on a tree next to him. The bird was silent, but it followed him for 15 minutes while he fossicked about. Not surprisingly, Badge ignored it.

On the second occasion, when we were also a good distance away, an adult honeyguide arrived, and spent the next frustrating half hour chattering dementedly, and circling around a totally unresponsive Badger. This time, Khanye managed to find the hive in the hollow of a nearby tree, about a metre off the ground. With the bird in attendance, we led Badger to it, but it was inaccessible.

Both times, Badge ignored the bird but, remember, he hadn't had the benefit of a natural upbringing when, as a cub, he may well have learned from his mother to take note of the bird's behaviour.

In fact, it's quite easy to see how a partnership might have evolved between bird and badger. In both instances, the honeyguide was soliciting Badger rather than us, and although he didn't actually follow it, he may, through experience, have learned to do so over time.

Spotted hyaenas can locate carcasses by watching vultures circling over it. As another highly intelligent animal, why shouldn't the honey badger learn to make the connection between honeyguides and food?

And what about vice versa? Do badgers really need honeyguides, or is it the other way around? The birds are certainly impelled to solicit help in breaking open hives, as we saw from the instinctive behaviour of the juvenile bird, which Badge ignored. So aren't they equally as likely to follow a badger in the hopes that he would lead them to a hive?

If only we had had more time with our Badge to find out.

Chapter Seventeen – Kimba's Story

I feel a prickle of fear. The sun has suddenly disappeared and I'm trapped in the shadow of two enormous elephants, one on either side of me – close enough to touch. The larger of the two turns and takes a step towards me, and I stand absolutely still, feeling tiny, and totally intimidated. She begins to explore my face with the tip of her trunk, very gently, and then she smells me all over.

'Don't worry,' I hear Theresa's voice from somewhere behind me. 'Chitora's just getting to know you.'

A fire was burning in the grate on the morning we arrived at Wasara, Gary and Theresa Warth's ranch in Zimbabwe's south-east lowveld. And warming themselves in front of it were an African grey parrot, a tabby cat and a fox terrier-cross, all sunk into a gigantic beanbag. The reason for its size became apparent when we looked at a picture on the mantelpiece: there was Theresa, tickling the chin of a hippo, who was wearing a smile that split her face in two.

'We had the beanbag made specially for Hippy,' Theresa explains. 'She used to share it with the warthog, and they were always vying for the best place. Before that, she spent a lot of her time on the couch or our bed, all 1 400 kilograms of her. She'd always slide off when I arrived, but then she'd go waddling down the passage and spend the rest of the day sulking.'

Hippy's mother was shot by a hunter when she was just a few hours old, and she became totally devoted to Theresa.

'I couldn't do anything without her. Hippos love contact and she always liked to be touching me – her head on my foot, or on my lap. If I was down with the elephants, she was there; if I was cooking, she was in the kitchen. She used to lie under the dining room table with the dogs, and she was quite content for our black Labrador to clean her mouth out after she'd finished her meal.'

Hippy was just one of the numerous wild orphans that Theresa has cared for over the years. While we were there, two young eland bulls wandered around the garden, pushing their heads through the stable door of our rondavel and looking for snacks. A newly released coucal called from the garden, then flew through the door for his daily ration of frozen termites and mealworms. And a few days after we left, a blind buffalo calf came in from the surrounding conservancy, presenting

Theresa with yet another challenge.

Most of the orphans come and go – but others, like the three elephants, Chitora, Mungwezi and little Kimba, represent a lifetime commitment for the Warths.

In the disastrous drought of 1991/2, Clem Coetzee (pioneer in the translocation of elephant family groups) and Gary started capturing starving animals in the Gonarezhou National Park, including sub-adult and young elephants, in order to try and take the pressure off the remaining cows. It was an exercise that lasted for around six months.

At the same time, the Warths were raising money to provide food for around 50 hippos living in the Esquilingwe Dam.

'Luckily, not many people in the town knew that this was the sole source of their water during the drought,' laughs Theresa. 'It was pretty revolting!'

Then the first load of 12 young elephants, most of them around two years old, arrived from the capture. Some were so weak that they didn't survive one day. Theresa describes them as: 'skin and bones, too weak to get up once they were down. It was heartbreaking. But the survivors thrived on a good diet, and they settled down very quickly. It finally rained in December 1992, and it was wonderful taking all the baby ellies for walks and watching them play in the puddles and find the new green shoots.'

But after about a year, when the little elephants were strong again, they were all sent away to various parts of the country, most of them destined for elephant-back safaris. Theresa knew that this would happen, but it was a terrible wrench. She'd formed a particularly strong bond with a little female who was so weak that she had to be helped to her feet every morning in order to feed. She christened her Miss Elly, and when she and a young male were taken away, they were sent to another conservancy where they successfully joined a wild herd. Tragically, their freedom was short-lived. Three years later, they were recaptured and transported to the Midlands, where they are presently also being used for elephant-back rides. Theresa hasn't seen Miss Elly since 1993, but she's determined to check up on her soon.

Will Miss Elly recognise her after all this time?

'Of course she will!' Theresa laughs at the question. 'Elephants don't forget! In fact, the more I learn about these animals, the more they amaze me.'

And Theresa has learned a great deal. After the 12 orphans, came Marula and Lewa, two females around two and half years old, rescued from the Gonarezhou National Park during another drought.

Training and discipline are essential. 'You have to be strong,' asserts Theresa. 'Elephants are like children: they need constant contact and the security of knowing that you are in charge. But you have to lead – not subjugate.'

Training is different for every animal according to its temperament. Marula was the clown, who liked nothing better than making people laugh, whereas Lewa was constantly up to mischief. Her greatest delight was trying to unseat Theresa by rubbing up against trees or scraping her off her back under a low branch of wait-a-bit thorn bush. But although Theresa was learning all the time, she constantly questioned her homegrown training methods.

So, in 1999, she attended an intensive two-week-long elephant training course at an animal sanctuary in Little Rock, Arkansas, where she worked with four Asian and six African elephants, most of whom had come from Zimbabwe. The course was attended by people from all over the world, and it gave her some invaluable experience. For instance, she was taught a set of commands – like relax, quit, trunk down – that are now in use universally – in English – for elephant trainers.

Marula and Lewa lived with the Warths for seven years, and they were devastated when, once again, the elephants were moved away to be used for elephant safaris. And then, at the end of 1999, two three-year-old females arrived. The Warths named them Chitora and Mungwezi after two of the rivers on the ranch, and Theresa swore that this time, they would never be taken from her.

The two are very different in character. Chitora is more docile, and has an air of serenity about her, while Mungwezi is a comedian, constantly scheming and testing her boundaries. Both cows are very maternal, and Theresa often used to find them with the dairy herd, mothering the calves. That is, until Kimba arrived, when at last they had a real baby of their own.

Kimba and a young male calf, were captured in the Bumi area, on the shores of Lake Kariba, victims of the drought of 2005. They were the only remaining calves in a herd when Paul and Kerry Berry, who ran a kapenta fishing outfit, took them in. Thirty years ago, calves under six months didn't have a hope of surviving. Cow's milk kills them, and no one was able to come up with the right formula. Then, after years of trial and error with orphaned elephants in Kenya, Daphne Sheldrick discovered the secret: a mixture of coconut oil added to a fat-free milk base.

The calves were making good progress when on Christmas Eve, without any warning, they were borne away by the authorities, destined for China where they were to be exchanged for two tigers. Luckily for Kimba, that didn't happen; instead they were sent to a small national park in the Umvurwe area in the north of Zimbabwe, where they immediately escaped. Within a couple of days, the little male had been killed by dogs, watched by Kimba who had escaped the same fate by standing in the middle of a dam. She was recaptured 10 days later, in horrific condition. Lisa Hywood from the Tikki Hywood Trust was called in by National Parks to assist.

'When I saw her, my heart broke in two,' she recalls. 'There was this tiny baby, pacing up and down the line of the fence. Her physical condition was horrendous; her spine was protruding at least four inches from her back. And the look in her eyes was one of fear and pleading not to be left on her own again.'

At the time, Geoff Hoddy from SAVE Australia was in Zimbabwe, and when he heard about the calf, he offered to assist. A price war was already in progress between some of the elephant-back safari outfitters, but after days of negotiation, culminating in a very generous donation by Geoff and his wife Kim, Kimba (her namesake) was moved to the Mavuradonha Wilderness area under the care of James and Janine Varden. She couldn't have gone to a better place. James has run Natureways Safaris for the past 23 years, and is one of the best-known safari guides in the country. And Janine used to be an animal keeper and educator at the Werribee Zoo in Melbourne, Australia, where Rachel and Katie were working when they visited Marula School.

Together, James and Janine run riding safaris in both Mavuradonha and Hwange National Park, using horses that in many cases have been rescued from farm invasions.

Kimba was now so weak that the Vardens doubted very much that she would live. For weeks, Janine didn't leave her side. She slept with her at night, later alternating with two of their staff members, so the little elephant was never alone. But although her physical condition improved, Kimba was terribly depressed and showed little will to live. On walks, they would try to encourage her to play in the mud, and do the things that usually come naturally to baby elephants. She wasn't interested. They introduced her to a calf, then a goat, and in desperation, a chicken – hoping that one of them would cheer Kimba up. She ignored them all, and then Whiskey arrived – a small pink piglet who, as James puts it, 'finally cracked the code'. They adored each other. Whether they were wallowing in the mud or walking in the veld, they were never apart. At night, they lay stretched out back-to-back in Kimba's stable.

'Whiskey became very protective,' says Janine with a smile. 'If she felt that Kimba was being threatened, she would try to bite you and chase you away.'

At first, Whiskey accompanied Kimba on her daily walks, and when the piglet got tired, Kimba would lie down with her to rest. But inevitably, piglet became porkly, and although their friendship continued, Whiskey could no longer keep up. Then Kimba found another friend in Mahobohobo – a dun gelding who had been rescued from a farm. And the little elephant loved the visits of the children from the local school.

The Varden's intention was to rehabilitate Kimba and release her into Mavuradonha to join a wild elephant herd. But politics intervened.

'During the elections, we were forced out of the area at short notice, and had to leave our animals behind,' James recalls. 'It took months to get them all out, during which time, our staff were beaten up by the invaders and forced to go hunting for them. We then received a message that if we didn't move Kimba quickly, they would kill her as bushmeat.'

Finally, with the help of the SPCA, permits were obtained, and Kimba was moved to the Warth's ranch, where she has been for the past two years.

On the morning we arrived, we met up with James and Janine, and together with Theresa, we went out to meet the three elephants, who were already feeding in the bush with a keeper. Under normal circumstances, the first thing you'd notice about Theresa Warth is her startling blue eyes. But when she is with her elephants, all you can think about is her size. She is diminutive, barely reaching the top of Chitora's leg. One swipe with the elephant's tail, one kick, push or stomp, even in play, could injure or maim her – and yet Theresa is totally at ease. In fact, she's never happier than when she's with her elephants.

I asked her if she had ever experienced any moments of real fear.

'No,' she replied. 'But on the odd occasions when they challenge my authority, I do wonder if I am doing the right thing. You have to find a way to handle it so that they don't feel they've won; somehow you have to change the subject or distract them.'

Even before we saw them, we could hear branches breaking and the contented sighs of the elephants. They sounded like steam engines. Then suddenly there they were, a couple of metres away. They came straight towards me, and when Chitora stretched out her trunk and gave me the once-over, I almost expected her to wrap it around me and pick me up.

Obviously, the best thing to do was to act unconcerned. Which isn't too hard when you are eye-to-eye, but a pretty tall order when it's peering down at you from a great height. But this was a kind eye framed with long luxuriant lashes, the sort of eye you felt you could trust. Especially with Theresa behind you. Once the two adult females had met us, they lost interest and carried on feeding – unconcerned with yet another crowd of star-struck humans.

But Kimba – now five years old – had a completely different agenda. She loves company, and is always looking for a game. Rich homed in on her, all a-dangled with cameras, and Kimba was intrigued. When Theresa ordered her to stop following him around, she would ambush him from behind a tree, determined to get hold of one of those things around his neck.

Then Rich discovered that he'd left the video at the house, and when he thought Kimba was busy elsewhere, he sneaked off to fetch it. The little elephant let him go 50 metres, and then she was off, thundering after him, with Theresa in hot pursuit. To Rich's credit, he didn't run. He put both hands on Kimba's head and pushed, just managing to keep her at bay till Theresa arrived and turned her back. And that's when she had a mini-tantrum. Ears flapping, she tore back to the others – stopping en route to lay into a couple of bushes, and squealing with rage. I can't speak for Rich, but the rest of us were helpless with laughter.

It was a momentous day for Wasara when Kimba arrived. For her own safety, in case she might be overwhelmed by the welcome, she was put into a separate boma where Chitora and Mungwezi, hesitant at first, but rumbling with excitement, could push their trunks through the wooden poles to touch and smell this miraculous new arrival – their own baby! But far from being pleased, Kimba was cocky and almost aggressive to her new family – until a few days later, when all three were released together. As her adoring foster mothers rushed towards her, trunks outstretched and longing to make contact, Kimba turned and charged off into the bush screaming in terror, her tail stuck straight up in the air. And the other two thundered off after her with Theresa behind, adding her yells to the general pandemonium.

They didn't take long to catch up with her and then, after much rumbling, milling about and careful inspections, all three elephants suddenly calmed down and started browsing, as if they had known each other all their lives.

Chitora and Mungwezi took their maternal responsibilities very seriously.

'If Kimba lay down in play, they'd try and pick her up,' says Theresa. 'She only had to give a little squeal, and they'd rush to her assistance. Kimba, of course, caught onto that very quickly. She'd often squeal on purpose, when nothing was wrong, just for the fun of working them up.'

A herd of around 40 wild elephants often visits Wasara. They originate from 12 captured animals who became unmanageable and were released into the conservancy some years ago. Chitora and Mungwezi often play with them when they come to drink at the dam, separated by the fence that runs through the middle of it. And sometimes the herd will follow them home in the evening.

Then, one day, Mungwezi decided to take the relationship a step further.

'Both females were in season,' recalls Theresa. 'We could hear the wild herd, and suddenly they were with us, and Mungwezi, followed by Chitora, pushed down the fence and ran off to join them. I didn't try to stop them. I don't believe they were running away: they were just caught up with all the excitement.'

Under different circumstances, the Warths would have liked nothing better than for their elephants to go free. But this was in 2005, when land invasions were at their height, and all wildlife was under threat. (In 2009, the wild herd numbered 60, but a year later only 40 of them were left.)

For five weeks they searched. Often, the elephants came home during the night, only to disappear again before morning; and then there were reports that they had approached villages and people had chased them away. But not once were they ever seen with the wild herd.

'We eventually caught up with them,' says Theresa. 'And that was one of the happiest moments of my life. They were overjoyed to see me, and when we were walking back, it was as if we were one big family again, heading home.'

They still meet up regularly with the wild herd, but have never again tried to join them.

Having visited the Warths, I have to say that ambling with elephants, as opposed to riding them, is now top of my list of favourite occupations. To walk with these amazing animals, watching their feeding, interacting, and behaving quite naturally is an incomparable privilege. It's their enormous size and power combined with such gentleness that is so overwhelming.

We were watching Theresa feeding the elephants in the evening, when Mungwezi picked up a tiny twig and offered it to her in exchange for her dish of cubes. It's something she does, unbidden, every day.

'They are such thoughtful animals,' says Theresa. 'They have every reason to hate and fear humans for the unspeakable things we do to them, but still they accept us.'

We walked back to the house at sunset, leaving the elephants contentedly munching their game cubes, sweet potato leaves, maize stalks and sugarcane.

A herd of cattle trudged passed us, sending up a cloud of dust. Theresa pointed to their deeply eroded tracks in the bare ground.

'It shouldn't be like this,' she says. 'But we've got so little land left, there isn't an option.'

I ask her what her greatest hope was for the elephants.

'If they could go back to the wild,' she replies without hesitation, 'but still keep contact with us. That would be wonderful. And education – that's an area where they've already contributed so much. I want local people to understand that they aren't just a lump of meat and ivory – they have feelings, just like us, and they are highly intelligent.'

And her greatest fear?

'What will happen to them, to us? If we have to leave, where will they go, and will we be able to keep them? These are the questions that haunt me. But the ellies are the reason that I go on. I wake up every morning, longing to see them, and I ask myself: who in the world can actually do what I am doing? It is such an amazing privilege.'

We left the Warths the next morning and we travelled home in silence, mulling over all the impressions of the past two days. I had expected that the elephants would affect me most, but it was in fact the Warths themselves, hanging on, battling for survival against seemingly insurmountable odds.

One of Theresa's stories keeps coming back to me, and it has happened more than once. She was with the wild elephant herd at the dam when something frightened them. As they turned to run, Theresa called after them: 'Relax!' And at the sound of her voice, they stopped, listened, and came back to drink – reassured that all was well.

Wasara is part of the Chiredzi River Wildlife Conservancy, but now the elephants, rhinos and other animals that are left are no more than refugees in their own home. The wild elephants know Theresa and have learned to trust her over the years. Who will protect them if she is no longer there?

Chapter Eighteen – A Walk
In The Wilderness

In May 1966, a young man aged 25, carrying a rucksack, his camera and a rifle on his shoulder, set out from the Angwa River in the north-west of Rhodesia, intending to walk 150 miles to Kanyemba: a small tented police outpost, miles from anywhere, on the banks of the Zambezi River bordering Mozambique.

Much of his journey would take him through the Chewore Game Reserve, at that time an uncharted wilderness inhabited only by the fabled Vadoma: the nomadic 'two-toed tribe', of whom very little was known.

He had no radio or other means of communication. With the help of a 1:250 000 map and a prismatic compass, he reckoned that he and his one-eyed Malawian companion would reach Kanyemba in around two weeks.

Between them, they carried two water bottles, a fishing line with some hooks, a few tins, some packets of rice, dried meat, soup powder, sugar, powdered milk, tea and mealiemeal. Medical supplies, such as they were, consisted of a few bits of sticking plaster and a snakebite outfit, which they might as well have left behind. The anti-venom would have been ineffective against mamba and cobra bites and very quickly destroyed through exposure to heat.

That young man was my brother David, who was born in Denmark and, for the most part, educated in England. He was 15 when we moved to Rhodesia, completing his education at Peterhouse School in Marondera.

He'd always been a pest. At 12, when we were living in Buckinghamshire, he used to blast away at the rabbits in the woods opposite the house with a 12-bore shotgun. At 15, he arrived by plane at Salisbury (now Harare) airport with a loaded .25 semi-automatic pistol in his pocket, given to him by the South African couple who had bought our house. At 16, he was hiding Dad's folding butt single shot .22 rifle under his mattress at school, and sneaking out at weekends to cause alarm and despondency amongst the local guinea fowl.

And at 18, he shot himself in the hand while cleaning his pistol, which slowed him down a bit, but not for long.

At the time of his walk, David was managing a tobacco farm for Pip and Sue Rogers in the Doma area, and although he had done a bit of hunting, he had no experience with big game. He enjoyed farming, but his dream had always been to take off alone into the bush – 'just to keep on walking to see what was over the next hill'.

Barrie Ball, the local National Parks Warden gave his consent to the trip, on the strict understanding that David would not use his .375 rifle except in an emergency, and that he would take a companion. None of the workers wanted to go with him except Boniface, who agreed only after David offered him a hefty bribe.

Of course it was crazy. My brother had no back-up, no contact with the outside world, few supplies and not even a bandage or an aspirin in his rucksack. If he had been injured or fallen sick, there was no way that Boniface, unarmed and in totally unfamiliar country, could have found his way to help. And if the situation were reversed, David would have had to leave Boniface alone in the bush perhaps for days in an area teeming with big game.

Today, 44 years later, he would have been equipped with the latest GPS, a satellite phone, a cellular blanket, hi-tech hiking boots and a full medical kit. All very safe and sensible, but hardly the adventure that David had intended: the sort of adventure to which a certain F C Selous, the great African hunter, explorer and naturalist, whose books David had devoured as a boy, would surely have given his blessing.

What makes a young man leave a comfortable life in England to journey to the 'Far Interior' of Africa, hundreds of miles inland, with only the vaguest idea of how he will get there and the dangers he will face? Inspired by the writings of Gordon Cumming and Baldwin, Selous left home in 1871 at the age of 19 and did just that, disappearing for three years into the wilderness without a word to his family, who eventually gave him up for dead. Certainly, ivory and their love of hunting were the lure for many of those early travellers, but more than that, it was the sheer challenge of confronting hardships and danger alone, and the thrill of exploring wild places 'never before paced by civilized foot', as William Cornwallis Harris put it.

In all the 13 days of David's journey to the Zambezi, they never saw a track or a sign of another human being. They had no communication, no fixed route and no firm timetable.

Once they had crossed the Angwa River, only the wilderness lay ahead.

'Then I suddenly realised that we were completely on our own; the walk had started and there was no turning back,' my brother recalls. 'And I have to admit that at that stage I did feel a bit apprehensive. It wasn't long before we came across elephant spoor, and we had our first taste of tsetse fly – or at least, they had a taste of us.

'It was magnificent, unspoiled country, but pretty rough going. If I'd had access to more detailed maps, I might even have had second thoughts about the trip. Most of the time we were traversing the mountain ranges running parallel with the Zambezi. To plot my position, I'd climb a high feature and take back bearings on known hills. One time, it took me about an hour to climb a very steep hill, and only when I came down did I realise that I'd left my compass behind. Up I went again and luckily managed to find it. But even if I had lost the compass and the map, it wouldn't have made much difference. I knew all I had to do was to carry on north till I hit the Zambezi River.

'I'll never forget our first night out. There was a full moon and everything was wonderfully calm. We made a small camp, built a log fire and cooked our supper – a good meal of sadza and tinned meat and vegetables. I wanted to use up the tins quickly to lighten my pack, which was already becoming very uncomfortable.

'In the mid-afternoon of the next day, we met a large herd of buffalo: the only ones I had seen outside of a National Park and definitely the first that Boniface had ever encountered. Even though the wind was blowing our scent directly to them, they were not in the least bit afraid. Apart from the elephants in the area, it's most likely that none of the other animals we saw had ever been hunted or even come across another human being. The buffalo started trotting towards us, which was rather unnerving. I didn't know what to do, so I shouted and waved my hands about, which stopped them for a few minutes. Then they began coming again. I'm sure they were just curious and wouldn't have harmed us, but to be on the safe side, we climbed a hill to get out of their way. Halfway up, we stopped to look back, and there they were, grazing peacefully. They had already forgotten about us.

'It's hard to believe it now, but there were black rhino all over the place and, like the buffalo, they were also totally unafraid of us. On our sixth night out, we were very rudely awakened by a loud snorting and puffing. A rhino charged through the camp, very close to where we were sleeping, giving us both a hell of a fright.'

David was exhilarated by every experience: after all, this is what he had yearned for since childhood. But Boniface, who had never before seen any big game, and wouldn't have had much faith in the ability of this inexperienced young lad to protect him, was petrified, particularly when they disturbed a leopard, which fortunately took fright and ran off.

'Thank goodness he never panicked, screamed or ran away from the animals,' says David. He just froze and stared at them.'

They heard lions almost every night, and once terrifyingly close.

'We were settling down to sleep when we heard them roaring in the distance, and the sound kept coming nearer. With nowhere to hide, we built up the fire and got as close to it as we could. The noise became deafening, till I was sure that the lions were only a few yards away from us. I clutched my rifle and cocked it with the safety catch off. Then there was a sudden silence, which was almost worse, and about 10 minutes later, the roaring began again, but this time on the other side of the camp, slowly fading into the distance. What a relief! When I checked the spoor the next day, I saw that they had passed by about 20 yards away from the camp.

'That morning, I could see that Boniface was nervous and unhappy. I was worried that he might be sick, perhaps even coming down with malaria, so I asked him if he was okay. He looked at me very sadly through his one eye, and said he was not at all okay, and that wanted to turn back and go home. I felt terrible. He was a simple farm labourer from Malawi, and he was completely out of his element. I knew I'd have to handle the situation very carefully so as not to upset him further. We'd already come halfway, and there was no way in the world that I was going to turn around. So I told him that if he really wanted to leave, he'd have to go alone. I showed him the map and tried to explain where we were and where we were headed, but naturally this meant nothing to him. So I tried to persuade him to trust me and promised that I would get him home safely soon. I'm not sure whether he believed me or not, but eventually he agreed to continue.'

An unrelieved diet of sadza and vegetables does get a bit tedious, even for the hardiest explorer. Sometimes they would stop at a pool and catch barbel using grasshoppers as bait. Then they'd gut the fish, push a stick through it, and suspend it over the fire. And twice, they followed a honeyguide to a beehive and managed to collect some honey and a number of stings. I just hope they left some for the bird.

Mid-morning on the twelfth day, David picked up a whiff of sulphur and realised that they must be nearing the Tunsa Hot Springs. Not long after, they rounded a bend and in front of them were a series of clear, deep blue pools. The water in the first was almost too hot to touch, but around 25 yards further on, it was comfortably warm and inviting.

'Boniface was very suspicious until I told him that the water was good *muti*. We didn't bother to take off our clothes – they were just a filthy as we were – we just pulled off our boots and jumped in. We must have stayed in the pools for around three hours: it was heavenly, and we didn't want to leave. While we were playing around in the water, two black rhino came down to drink about 100 yards below us.

'That night we slept on a sandy spit on the Zambezi, just below Mapata Gorge. But at about midnight, we had to beat a hasty retreat as we were sleeping on a hippo path and one ran right through our camp scattering the remains of our fire.'

Two days later, they reached Kanyemba, to an enthusiastic welcome. The police had been notified of their journey but had been expecting them some days earlier. They radioed Pip Rogers, who flew in to collect them the next day.

'For dear old Boniface, this was his final adventure – he'd never been in an aeroplane before. But he went home well rewarded, and I like to think that he felt like a bit of a hero when he told the story to his workmates back on the farm. I wonder if they even believed him. For me, the greatest pleasure was to sleep in a decent bed again, with a belly full of good food and a couple of stiff whiskies.'

Like his hero Selous and the old timers before him, Africa was David's testing ground, for it drew on all the resourcefulness, courage and self-reliance that he could muster.

'I joined the Department of National Parks and Wildlife shortly afterwards,' he says, 'but even today, over 40 years later, I still think of that walk as the most thrilling adventure of my life.'

So little is left of the true wilderness: we have run it through with roads and railways, slaughtered its wildlife, dug out its heart for gold and diamonds and made it bleed. And yet still we hanker after the fragments that remain: the smell of the veld after the first rains, the warmth of companionship around the camp fire, and the sheer majesty and mystery of Africa all stir in us some primeval sense both of longing and of loss.

A couple of years ago, Johnson ran back to the house from his morning patrol in an uncharacteristic fluster to report that the game fence had been flattened in two places. We could hardly believe it: occasionally strands are broken or supports bent, but it would have taken something like a tank to crush seven feet of steel fence strung with 20 strands of high-tensile wire.

Mafira was already there when we arrived at the scene, and from the look on his face, you would have thought he'd just tripped over a lump of gold. He bent down and scooped something up into his hands.

'Elephants!' he breathed ecstatically, holding a pile of warm dung up to his nose. 'Oh, that *smell*, takes me back to the old days – it makes ...' he paused, searching for the right words, 'it makes my body feel free!'

Until he was booted out of National Parks to make way for an inexperienced war veteran, Mafira spent most of his 24 years as a game ranger stationed at Gonarezhou (the place of the elephants), and in Hwange, 14 500 square kilometres of wilderness on the edge of the Kalahari – where close encounters with lions, buffaloes and elephants were almost a daily event.

Two bulls, one large and one slightly smaller, had broken in through our game fence, fed briefly on some marula trees, then crashed out again, clearly in a panic. We don't know where they had come from, but we could be sure that they were refugees, displaced from their normal home range by the activities of the hordes of new settlers taking up land right through the country.

It wasn't the first time elephants had been in the area: in a good season, they come in search of marulas and the pumpkins people store by their huts, but they are in constant danger and are soon driven away.

Mafira took a packet of dung back to the compound, just to remind him, and Mabhena boiled some up with cooking oil, and drank it to relieve his cough.

I planted marula nuts in the fresh dung and put them on our veranda. They didn't germinate, but for days afterwards that musky evocative aroma of the lowveld came floating in through the house.

'There are some who can live without wild places,' wrote Aldo Leopold, 'and some who cannot.'

Perhaps it's as simple as that.

Chapter Nineteen – Africa Fever

One of the first Englishmen to hitch up a wagon and head north was 'little Mr Burchell' whom, until he set off from the Cape in June 1811, couldn't read a map and had never spent a night in the open air. He was frail and small (5 feet 4 inches in his stocking feet), and if ever there was an unlikely adventurer, William Burchell was it. Passionate about botany, painting, and playing the flute and harpsichord, he was anything but the picture of a rugged outdoorsman, which made his achievements during his time in the wilds of Africa all the more extraordinary.

In 1805, he left England for the island of St Helena to take up a post of schoolmaster and acting botanist, there to await the arrival by ship of his fiancée, Lucia Green. Two long years later, she arrived, only to tell the heartbroken Mr Burchell that she could not marry him as she had fallen in love with the ship's captain.

We can't be sure if his disappointment contributed to his decision but in any event, he left for South Africa in 1810, totally unsuited, or so it seemed, for the journey that he was to make: up to the Orange River and then north to the interior through parts never before visited by a European. Two other explorers, a Lieutenant Cowan and a Captain Donovan had set out on the same route a couple of years earlier and disappeared without a trace. It was thought that they must have been murdered by hostile tribesmen or Bushmen, but that didn't deter little Mr Burchell one bit.

From the beginning, he was entranced, later writing in his book: *Travels in the Interior of Southern Africa* that the 'perfection of nature in the wilds of Africa was the irresistible motive that led me on'.

During his four years of wandering, he collected around 63 000 specimens of plants, birds, and animal skins, making detailed maps and studying, sketching and recording everything from wildlife to the native people he encountered – their music and their ceremonies. He loved his 'unshackled existence' on the move in the wagon with his faithful dog Wantrouw, and was captivated by the 'spirit of enthusiasm which seemed like some fascinating power emanating from the strange objects which everywhere surrounded me'.

He was the first person to record for science the white rhino and the blue wildebeest. And it was Burchell who described the differences between the quagga and the zebra that now, like a number of other species, bears his name: *Equus burchelli*.

He was a collector, not a hunter – and what's more, he was an enlightened ecologist, although that name and the principles it embodies, only reached the public consciousness around 150 years after his time.

'Nothing is wanting, nothing is superfluous,' he observed, 'The smallest weed or insect is indispensably necessary to the general good. Nothing more bespeaks a littleness of mind, than to regard as useless all that does not visibly benefit man.'

Even today, we still fail to recognise and act upon this basic truth.

After leaving Africa, Burchell spent five years collecting and exploring in Brazil, another prodigious feat of resourcefulness and endurance. Then for the rest of his life, he filled his time working on his collection until his death at the age of 81, by his own hand.

It was a tragic end for a brilliant and heroic man. He had never married, and perhaps loneliness played a part in his decision, but I wonder if he had ever really settled down back home in England. Did he dream of Africa? Did he miss the smell of the oxen's sweat, the rumble and creak of the wagons and the life of a wanderer for whom each day brought fresh discoveries and adventures?

I'm quite sure he did, and his words confirm it:

'To me every spot on which my wagon stood was home; there was my resting place; there was my abode ... Few as were the comforts of such a dwelling, and though they might be such as the luxurious would think very little deserving of that name, they were accompanied by health and contentment, and have often afforded greater enjoyment than more splendid accommodations.'

Burchell paved the way for the next English adventurer, who bore the same Christian name as himself, but had a very different agenda. Tall, elegant and well educated, Captain William Cornwallis Harris, ex-Indian Army, came to Africa quite simply to shoot. And at that time, the game must have seemed limitless. '... Here a grand and magnificent panorama was before us, which beggars all description,' he wrote, about an area near present-day Rustenberg. 'The whole face of the landscape was actually covered with wild elephant. There could not have been fewer than 300 within the scope of our vision ... their colossal forms being at one moment partially concealed by the trees which they were disfiguring with their giant strength, and at others seen majestically emerging into the open glade ... a picture at once soul-stirring and sublime.'

Cornwallis Harris had the eye and the appreciation of a gifted artist, and his detailed watercolours are a fascinating record of his experiences, but, unlike Burchell, the preservation of the animals he painted was the last thing on his mind.

In his first year in Africa, he shot 400 animals. He witnessed the migrations of millions of springbok (the 'trekbokke') and joined the Boer hunters in riding amongst them, shooting wildly and randomly into their midst.

Ivory was the first prize – although it seems that many of the early British adventurers were more interested in covering their expenses than making a fortune. It's been estimated that the latter part of the 19th century saw the annual export from Africa of around 45 000 tons of ivory – and the Arabs, the tribal chiefs and the Boers had been hard at it long before the likes of Cornwallis Harris arrived on the scene. It was in demand all over the world for trinkets, knife handles, piano keys, billiard balls, jewellery and even for false teeth, before it was replaced by porcelain.

Cornwallis Harris recorded his experiences in both his paintings and his books, as did the unspeakably murderous Roualeyn Gordon Cumming who hunted in a kilt and deerstalker, and toasted new acquaintances with a full glass of gin. Then there are the stories of the pint-sized William Charles Baldwin, who at only 5 feet 2 inches hunted elephants for six years before he finally brought one down.

'Poor Baldwin,' his friends used to say, 'his trouble is that he cannot see over the long grass.'

And there was Henry Hartley, born with two club feet, who hunted with the best (or worst) of them and gave no hint of his deformity.

Unfortunately, we have no such records from the tough and taciturn Boer hunters, who unlike the *rooinek* Englishmen, didn't have an adoring public hanging on their every word back home, and probably didn't see what all the fuss was about anyway.

Petrus Jacobs shot 110 lions and 750 elephants in his lifetime, and collected more than 36 000 kilograms of ivory. Selous met him shortly after he had been attacked by a lion (who had every justification) at the age of 68. He sustained horrible injuries to his arms and thighs, which his wife treated with milk and castor oil, and within a couple of months he was back on his horse and off hunting again.

Selous is often called the greatest hunter of them all or the 'Mighty Nimrod', a title that he found both embarrassing and inaccurate, referring to himself as 'a moderate shot'. What he did have in full measure were guts, endurance and a great personal magnetism, which enabled him to mesmerise an audience with his stories. By the time he arrived in Africa in 1871, the great herds had already been wiped out, and the best hunting was to be found north of the Limpopo, in the area ruled by Lobengula, king of the Matabele.

Even as a boy at Rugby, one of Britain's oldest public schools, Selous had always known what he wanted to do. When he was found by a master sleeping on the floor by the side of his bed wearing only his nightshirt, the boy told him that he was merely hardening himself for his future career as a hunter in Africa.

In April 1872, he set off on the 700-mile journey to GuBulawayo, Lobengula's headquarters, with two companions, Dorehill and Sadlier. Thrilled to see his first giraffe, he galloped after the herd for miles, eventually being thrown from his horse and colliding with a tree. And then he realised that he was lost. For five days and four nights, he was alone without food, water, blanket, or even his horse, which had wandered off. The nights, he said, were 'piercingly cold'. He couldn't feed himself as he had used the last of his gunpowder in an abortive attempt to make a fire. It would have been a terrifying ordeal for an old hand, let alone a raw young Englishman with no experience in the bush. But with characteristic optimism, Selous forced himself to carry on, until on the fourth afternoon, when he was 'devoured by a burning thirst' and very close to expiring, he came across two Bushmen hunters who fed him and helped him to find his companions. Later, he was to write: 'I was never a bit the worse for my sufferings.'

Lobengula laughed dismissively when Selous told him that he had come to hunt elephants.

'Was it not steinbuck you came to hunt?' he asked. 'You are only a boy!'

But Selous persisted, and eventually Lobengula gave him permission not only to hunt elephant but also to go where he pleased, a privilege he had not granted to any of the other, more experienced hunters. But if the king believed that the lad would soon give up his grandiose ideas when faced with the dangerous reality of hunting big game, he was mistaken. When Selous came back to GuBulawayo at the end of the season, he had the satisfaction of informing Lobengula that he had shot 12 elephants.

'Why,' exclaimed the king, 'you are a man. You must take a wife.'

Selous had always been a keen naturalist – even as a boy he was collecting butterflies – and yet he killed a total of 31 lions and 106 elephants, with many others wounded. This was a paltry number compared to Petrus Jacobs' 750, but it was probably more attributable to the relative paucity of the animals than to any restraint on the part of Selous.

I readily accept that hunting is an ancient and unquenchable instinct in mankind. But what happened in Africa in the last part of the 19th century was simply slaughter: a crazed lusting for blood in the name of sport, deplored by missionary/explorer David Livingstone as 'the hunting form of insanity'. Despite this, and perhaps because of it, Selous became an ardent conservationist in later years, but the deed was done, and the wild animals left on the continent today have never stopped running from the gun.

Others have written about the psyche and the motives of the old hunters. What fascinates me is the old Africa, as they saw it, and the often eccentric characters, many of them 'gentlemen by birth and education but Bohemians by nature', who made the wagon their home.

Those early adventurers didn't come to Africa to build brick houses set about with neat hedges. They didn't import the house sparrows or plant oak trees and English flowers to assuage their longing for home, as the settlers did in years to come. It was the essence of wild Africa that stirred their souls, in spite of all its dangers and discomforts – most of all the ever-present threat of malaria, with its devastating fevers, chills and hallucinations, which so often proved to be fatal.

Selous suffered from it numerous times, and a serious bout could put him out of action for months. When George Wood, his sometime hunting companion, led a party of 18 up to Mashonaland in 1870, all of them contracted malaria, and seven people died, including his wife and child.

Not until the turn of the 19th century was the connection made between 'Africa fever' and the mosquito. There were plenty of theories and quack remedies to be had: some believed that the disease was caused by sleeping out in the moonlight or in one's wet clothes. Others associated it with drinking stagnant water or inhaling noxious fumes from marshy ground, which at least did something to keep them away from the mosquitoes' breeding grounds. Africa truly was the 'White Man's Grave' until the introduction of quinine, and even then it was not always available.

But still the young men came, and stayed, drawn irresistibly to the 'roving, careless, wandering life' as Baldwin put it, that kept them captive to the continent, in spite of the terrible hardships they faced.

I think of those times as living history. My grandfather could well have attended Selous's lectures in London and shaken his hand, as thrilled by his tales as we are today.

In May 1916, 50 years before my brother's epic walk, Selous had been in East Africa for a year as a captain in the 25th Battalion of the Royal Fusiliers. Despite his 63 years, he was still fit and in remarkably good health.

'I think that I am the only one of our officers who has not suffered from either bad diarrhoea, dysentery or fever,' he wrote to a friend. 'The long marches do not tire me at all, and the men now say that when I fall out no one else will be left standing in the battalion.'

He was killed the following year by a sniper's bullet, and is buried in what is now the Selous Game Reserve in Tanzania. It is said that he was mourned by the British and the Germans alike.

Selous collected numerous mammal specimens for the Museum of Natural History in London. His bronze bust stands at the top of a flight of steps in the main hall, and I got to know him well on my regular weekend visits to the museum during my three, miserable years as a trainee lawyer. Little did I guess that 10 years later I would be living amongst the same hills that he described so vividly in *A Hunter's Wanderings in Africa*:

'... the scenery ... is very remarkable and exceedingly picturesque. In many parts the country is covered with small hills composed entirely of huge stones, piled one upon another in the most fantastic manner, many of which present a very strong resemblance, especially by moonlight, to old ruined castles. Amongst these wonderfully picturesque hills the wagon road winds for many miles ...'

I am looking at one of those majestic ruined castles as I sit at my desk and write, and I wonder, as I often do, if the wagon road wound through our land and if, perhaps, Selous was describing the brooding magic of these very hills of stone: the silent guardians of the past. Trees grow and die, and rivers change their course, but the shape of this ancient landscape remains the same, inspiring worship and wonder in the humans who have passed through it.

Chapter Twenty – Back To Earth

Honest Mpofu and Hanisi Dube have a couple of things in common. They share the Grade Seven classroom at Marula Junior School, and both are exceptionally talented wildlife artists. But that's about the extent of it. Honest is a day scholar. Although he started school late and is now 14 years old, he's intensely shy and interacts very little with the other kids. I don't think I've ever seen him laugh. Winter and summer, he walks to school barefoot, wearing a ragged blue jersey and pair of grey shorts that barely cover the tops of his spindly legs. His father, a veteran of Zimbabwe's Bush War, receives a monthly pension from the government, but instead of spending this on food for his five children, he's most often at the local store drinking beer with his friends.

When Honest leaves Marula in December, it will be the end of his school days. If he can't find a job on a farm, he will work in his father's fields.

Hanisi, on the other hand, became a boarder when his parents, both medical doctors, found work in Johannesburg. Polite and confident, he's always one of the first to answer questions in our weekly conservation class. Next year, he'll go onto Plumtree High School, where no doubt he will excel academically, artistically and on the football pitch, as he does at Marula.

Hanisi glows with health, hope and animation, while Honest's eyes are expressionless and seem far too large for his pinched face. There's a greyish pallor to his skin, partly from the ingrained dust he never manages to wash off with his daily splash in a bucket of cold water, but also because he is clearly malnourished.

The physical differences between the two boys, and even two animals in a similar condition, would be strikingly obvious to anyone. As humans (the nicer variety), we tend to be empathetic to our own kind, and to other living creatures to which we feel a connection. And yet we can pass through a piece of land that is virtually crying out from neglect and abuse and see nothing at all, blind to the fact that a healthy earth is the foundation of *all* life, and that without it, Honest, Hanisi, or any single one of us would not continue to exist.

Because we don't really understand or appreciate it, we tend to think of the land, if we think of it at all, as a slave – or an endlessly renewable resource. I used to feel the same, until Rich and Stone Hills taught me differently. Provided I could see a few trees and a bit of colour, I believed that all was well, and if there *was* a problem, someone far more knowledgeable than me would sort it out. And the modern Global Village concept doesn't help. Now that we are supposed to be a part of the amorphous whole, our lives have become increasingly controlled by others, and our individual responsibilities even more diluted. We may be citizens of the world, but we have become caretakers of nothing.

Rainforests are reckoned to be earth's richest gene pool. They are the lungs of the earth, breathing out oxygen and absorbing the carbon dioxide that would otherwise pollute the atmosphere even further. And yet, not long ago, the fragile forests that cling to the fringes of Australia were referred to as 'bastard scrub', to be hacked out to make way for crops and development. In the first 200 years of white settlement, three quarters of the rainforests were destroyed and, unbelievably, in this age of supposed environmental enlightenment, logging continues today.

Stone Hills has had its share of abuse, too, suffering permanent damage from the hooves of hundreds of cattle from all over the district that were regularly driven to the arsenic dip on the banks of the Matanje River. When we moved here in 1989, the land carried deep scars from decades of overgrazing and neglect. Then the cattle moved off, and Rich got to work on controlling the erosion, but no matter how much patching up we do, the damage can never be entirely reversed.

In his weekly conservation classes at Marula, Khanye always emphasises the importance of healthy land as habitat for both humans and other animals. The kids nod, yawn, and make notes in their books, then they go home and, like the rest of us, still don't notice the damage that is in their backyard.

So we decided to get them practically involved.

Every year in late November, the Grade Sevens arrive in the afternoon to do some hands-on erosion control, followed by a farewell dinner and the presentation of their conservation certificates. But now we wanted to do a regular project on a larger scale with both the Grade Sixes and Sevens, giving them knowledge and experience that they could really use.

Children aren't known for their love of manual labour, particularly on their days off school, so I was doubtful that we'd attract many volunteers. But once Khanye had explained what we were trying to do, dozens of hands shot up, and he had to select the first 30 from the keenest participants in class, with the promise that the others could participate the following week.

For the next few days, Ruthie and Anna were busy in the kitchen, cooking up huge pots of meat and vegetables on the wood stove, and on the Saturday morning, Johnson and Big Fight were called in to stir up mountains of sadza in two three-legged pots over an open fire outside the lodge.

The winter sun was shining benignly from a sky of cloudless blue when we picked up 30 wildly excited children from the school yard after breakfast on Saturday. With them came Janet Guvakuva, their art teacher, who had been assigned the job of keeping order in the ranks. Mafira was waiting at the main gate with the tractor, and they all clambered into the trailer and rattled off down the road to a spot at the edge of a vlei in the Pundamuka Valley that is so deeply scarred it makes you cringe to look at it.

For years, it's been a favourite camping place for herds of wildebeest with nothing better to do than to hang out under the trees, saying 'umm' to each other every now and then. Naturally, they ate all the grass, and by continually trampling the area, they created ideal conditions for the rainwater running off the vlei to gouge out channels that have become steadily deeper and longer every year. These days, the situation is made even worse by the wild fires that sweep through Stone Hills from the surrounding properties, removing the grass cover that helps to stabilise the soil.

'Oh, don't worry,' I've heard people say cheerfully, 'nature always bounces back.' Nothing could be further from the truth. Balls bounce, nature doesn't, and even the best football in the world won't last for long if you kick it to death. Unless we did something to intervene, those furrows would cut back further and further into the vlei, draining off its precious moisture, carrying away its soil and finally dumping it in the riverbed.

The children were an inspiration. First, they scoured the area for rocks, carting them back to load onto the trailer, many of them so large and heavy that the skinny little bearers staggered under their weight. And when that was done, they had to lift them all out again at the erosion site, making piles in various strategic places.

Then we all stood around while Khanye asked them to describe how the erosion came about and how it could be mended. The good little girls answered first, of course, shyly but with quiet authority, while the boys studied their feet; but once the real work began under Rich's instruction, it was the boys who swung the picks and dug their shovels into the hard, impacted soil, breaking it open and levelling off the steep sides of the furrows. When I arrived with their lunch, a couple of the worst areas were already buttressed with walls of rocks. Now, instead of the water rushing along the channels when the rains came, the rocks would control the flow, giving it a chance to spread out and sink into the ground. And behind them, the soil would slowly build; grass seeds would fall and sprout, and trees would take root as the healing process gathered momentum.

The next 30 volunteers came the following Saturday, along with six of the girls from the first group who begged to come again, and unbelievably, they worked even harder. 'It's a competition,' they told us. 'We want to be the best!'

And so, thanks to the enthusiasm of a bunch of rural kids, the land began to breathe again. By the time they left school at the end of November, the rains were well under way, and they could see for themselves the miracle they'd performed in bringing one exhausted little patch of Africa back to life.

I'm not trained in ecology, but I have discovered that when you get to know and respect a piece of land, it begins to speak to you – and so much more so when you see it through the eyes of a wild animal whose world it truly is. Although we walked, and sometimes ran, for miles after Badger, there were times when we sat for long hours watching him frogging in the river or trying to dig out an antbear – quiet, contemplative times when I really began to notice what was happening around me.

There's no shortage of things to enjoy when summer explodes into vibrant colour and life after the first rains – but it's in winter, when the dry leaves are thick underfoot and all you can hear is the wind in the bleak, bare hills, that the land is truly revealed, like the furrowed face of a very old person who has suffered but endured.

With Badger, we explored places that we never would have seen without him: cool green glades hidden deep in the shadows of the hills, and clear rock pools where he drank and dug and played. For as long as we could, we tried to keep him away from our boundaries, for once he crossed through our

224

fence, a hostile world awaited him: a world of new settlers, their dogs and snares – and hunters, to whom a honey badger is nothing better than vermin.

He spent his first night out alone after he had pulled a large leguaan from a hole in the bank of the Habhe Dam close to home. I called Rich out to film him, but at 10.30pm when Badge was thoroughly absorbed in his meal, we had to leave him to it, and luckily he wasn't discovered by other hungry predators.

A wild badger cub's bond with his mother never weakens; only when she next comes into season and he is forcibly evicted, does he reluctantly take off on his own. And so it was with Badger and me – very rarely did I come home at night without him, even if he did only catch me up much later. What a privilege it was to be the mother of such an incredible animal, and the object of such affection.

When Badge was just over a year old, I went away on one of my regular trips to Australia to see my parents. Three weeks later, Rich picked me up from the Bulawayo airport, and by the time we reached home at around 4.30pm, Badger was already on his afternoon walk. I didn't bother to change. We dropped the suitcases in the house, radioed Khanye and got their position – in some koppies on the other side of the Mathole River. And there we found Badge, totally absorbed in the persecution of his very first tortoise.

'He's been busy for a couple of hours,' Khanye told us. 'I've tried but I can't get it away from him.'

I watched from behind some trees for a moment before softly calling his name.

Immediately he stopped and turned towards me. And then I was kissing the top of his head as he squirmed in my arms, turning himself inside out with pleasure, the tortoise temporarily forgotten. Even when he returned to it a few minutes later, I only had to call him and back he would come for another exuberant welcome, giving Khanye the chance to whip the poor creature away to safety.

At 18 months old, Badger was reaching an age when most wild honey badger cubs are leaving home for good. It was the last thing that we wanted to do, but we knew it was time for us to start letting go. So when Khanye called in one night at 8.30pm to say that Badge was a-frogging in the Pundamuka River on our north-eastern boundary and refusing to leave, I said: 'Come home without him then,' sounding far more relaxed about it than I felt.

Rich was away, and I went to sleep with the telemetry receiver and aerial on his side of the bed, switching it on at midnight and then again at 2am, and getting no signal, only static. But at 3.30am there was a loud ticking – and loud means close. Badger! I leapt out of bed and dashed through the front door, just missing a large pile of steaming puke. And he'd been exercising his scent glands to the full, making quite sure that I knew he was home. A quick check of his enclosure confirmed that he'd finished his food, so he'd probably broken his personal record of 45 frogs in one sitting, gorged himself on a full plate of meat half an hour later, and completely overwhelmed his digestive capacity.

He didn't come to my calls, so I went back to bed, sure that he wouldn't go far. He didn't. After excavating a large hole in the garden for no particular reason, he'd moved up to the garage at the lodge, where he'd spent an industrious few hours ripping up the seats of one of the safari vehicles.

I don't think we'll be buried on Stone Hills after all, I wrote in my diary. *I don't fancy being exhumed by a badger.*

A month later, he disappeared.

I was watching through the sliding doors when Khanye opened the gate for him at 6.30am. Badge headed straight for the servals' enclosure, and having baited the young male Rafiki, who spat and clawed at his nose through the wire, he trotted off down the vlei, tail up and clearly in a wonderful mood.

Normally, I would peep at him through a tiny gap in the curtains, knowing that if he saw the slightest movement, he wouldn't leave the house until he had rooted me out. Now, there was no chance of looking in or out of the bedroom window, as it was draped on the outside with a towel and a sheet that were anchored onto the ledge with stones and rolls of wire. I'd started with just the sheet, which bathed the room in a rather nauseous pink light, but when that didn't work, I'd gradually added the entire contents of our linen cupboard plus a good number of items from the workshop – all because of a small, fanatical bird whose neck I should have wrung years ago.

The bird bath – an enormous, slightly concave piece of granite – is positioned right below the window where I sit and write, so I can watch them drinking and bathing all through the seasons. And until *he* arrives in November, our daily wake-up call is kindly provided by Gwendolyn and Archibald, the Kamikaze Kids, otherwise known as yellow-billed hornbills.

Bang! They launch themselves at the window and bash it with their banana-shaped beaks. *Bang! Bang!* At any moment we expect the glass to shatter and the birds to come hurtling onto the bed. And after each attack, they chuckle away delightedly to each other.

'Bravo, my darling – what a simply *stunning* performance!'

For the hornbills, knocking themselves senseless every

morning is clearly an indispensable way of stirring up the brain cells in the absence of a strong cup of coffee. But it's an amusing hobby, not a bloody crusade, as it is for the groundscraper thrush in his spotted sports coat, who is one minute collecting worms quite normally on the lawn, and the next hammering an ear-piercing rat-a-tat-tat on the glass in a furious flurry of feathers.

One rat-a-tat-tat would be fine, even two would be tolerable, but he goes at it for hours, glaring at me through the window like some deranged member of the US Temperance League.

Now the naturalists amongst you will be smiling condescendingly. Doesn't this poor twit of a woman know that the bird is merely attacking his own reflection? Well, you're wrong. Because he only does it when I am there, and the more I curse at him and flap my arms, the madder he gets. And when I first hung up the sheet thinking I was safe, he crept through a gap at the side, and with a triumphant burst of song (possibly a hymn), he was back on the attack. His personality is enshrined in his scientific name – *Turdus litsitsirupa*. Presumably Linnaeus had a similar problem with one of its relatives.

Anyway, as usual, I digress.

I had barely settled myself behind the pink sheet, when Khanye called to say that Badger had disappeared. All day he searched, climbing the larger features and listening for signal, but it was no good – either transmission was blocked because he was inside a hole or somewhere amongst the crowded koppies at the bottom of the farm, or he was already far away. Once again, Rich was in South Africa working on his film, and I phoned to tell him that Badger had gone, really gone, for the first time. If we couldn't pick up his signal, there was very little we could do. Our neighbours knew we had a honey badger, but there was nothing to distinguish him from a wild one, and Badge might well take it into his head to raid a chicken run or steal a hunter's bait.

I barely slept that night: every hour or so, I'd turn on the receiver, straining to hear the slightest peep, like an anxious mother waiting for the sound of a vehicle to reassure her that her child was safely home. Letting go was going to be harder than we had ever imagined.

Badge is fine, I wrote in my diary in the early hours of the morning. *He's been far away on the scent of a lady, but he'll be back. That's what I want to believe. But I can't help playing out all the possibilities in my head, and I am conscious of my face twitching as I experience every possible emotion – the joy of having him on my lap again, the anguish of losing him. It should have happened a long time ago, of course. We can't expect him to keep on being the good little baby badger when he's now a Badger with Balls. His behaviour has been strange for the past week or so: hanging around the house and refusing to go out on walks; the mumsy way he's preferred love to adventure; the absolute rapport we have had – stronger than ever. It's almost as if he's been preparing us for this, and although I know that's fanciful, with Badger the possibilities are limitless.*

Early the next day, Khanye took off once again with the receiver, while Mabhena patrolled the fence line with a radio, looking for spoor. And I paced around uselessly at home, waiting for a message but dreading what I might hear.

At 10am, I turned the radio up to full volume, and went

out to feed the three yellow-fronted canary chicks in the outside cage with seeds stuck to a dab of ProNutro on the end of matchstick. As usual they spattered the mixture over me and made a horrible mess of themselves.

'Main house, main house – come in.'

I dropped the matchstick, charged back into the house and grabbed the radio handset.

'Go, Khanye.'

'Good news. I've picked up his signal.'

'Fantastic! Where?'

A pause. 'On Marshlands.'

Good news – and bad news. On the map, Stone Hills is 6 500 acres, but if you include all the koppies, it's probably twice that. It sounds like a lot of land, but the wildlife that depend on it totally, need space, especially in thirsty country like the Matobo. Shortly after we bought the farm, we managed to negotiate a first option to purchase Marshlands – a very hilly but well-watered piece of land on our northern boundary, around the same size as Stone Hills. The Land Acquisition Act had just been passed, putting all commercial farmers at risk of eviction, but as we were classed under tourism rather than agriculture, we believed that we would be exempt. In any case, the opportunity was just too good to miss.

A year or so later, Marshlands came up for sale, and after some negotiations, Rich went into town to sign the papers. The appointment with the lawyer was scheduled for 10am. At 9.45am, I received a call from a friend in town.

'Government has put out the criteria for compulsory land acquisition,' she told me. 'It's in today's paper.' She began listing them: underutilised land, absentee landlord, amongst others. No surprises. And then, 'They stipulate that no one can own more than one farm.'

I caught Rich just as he was stepping out the lift at the lawyer's offices.

'Cancel everything. We can't buy Marshlands.'

If we had, we'd be drawing attention to ourselves and that could mean losing both pieces of land. We couldn't risk it.

Then another solution presented itself – in the person of Frank J Albright Jnr – a wealthy American hunter who wanted to buy a piece of Africa, not for hunting, he assured us, but as a conservation project. We couldn't enforce it legally, but we stipulated that in exchange for the option, Albright would appoint Rich as wildlife manager. And if all went according to plan, we could eventually take down our dividing game fence, giving us double the amount of land for our animals and theirs.

So much for wishful thinking. It wasn't long before Marshlands became the district base for leopard hunting with dogs, and the wild animals brought in to restock it were hunted as trophies or shot as bait.

Albright rarely visited, and nor did his manager who was hunting elsewhere in Africa. Things became even worse when half the farm was granted by the Lands Committee to a local businessman who introduced large herds of cattle. When the businessman's wife discovered that he was being unfaithful, she set their house in Plumtree alight and incinerated them both, leaving their two sons, who were even less interested in the land, to take over. Every year, wild fires swept through it, and the cattle competed with the animals for what little food was left.

Marshlands was a sad place, and Badger couldn't have chosen anywhere worse for his first solo excursion away from home.

Chapter Twenty-One – Going Solo

My friend Zoe moved to London years ago, but she left her heart buried under a musasa tree in her garden, along with a lifetime of little treasures she had gathered from the veld. She visited us one February, and we decided to spend a week just rambling around the farm, soothing the spirit and going where the mood took us.

Zoe is an artist and a potter. For her, true beauty lies in the small things that others may miss: like the shape of a leaf, and the colours and texture of the stone she holds in the palm of her hand. She has an eye that delights in detail. A colony of small black ants had built their nest amongst some bricks under the gate of her home in Harare, and every time people drove in and out, they'd squash it flat. Zoe inspected it daily to see how they were faring, and she has a series of photographs showing the workers rebuilding, undaunted, in exactly the same place every time it happened.

We stopped at the foot of a koppie one early morning soon after sunrise to watch a bull giraffe stripping the fresh green pods from a silky acacia. I scanned the rocks with my binoculars, and there at the very top of the koppie lay a huge male leopard, quite still, with his eyes half closed, as relaxed as if he had been poured out of a bottle. We stayed with him for an hour, passing the binoculars back and forth between us under the cool scrutiny of those yellow-green eyes. We were at just the right distance: close enough to take in the thickness of his neck, the great width of his head and the length of the elegant tail draped over the rock – and far enough to give him space if he wanted to slip away.

There were zebra grazing below him, and a couple of gemsbok a few hundred yards off, unaware of the eyes that followed them. The leopard was maybe seven years old and in his prime: a champion survivor with a huge price on his head that many would be longing to claim.

Next day, Zoe and I followed the spoor of a female past the house, heading for the same area. In our wanderings amongst the koppies, we picked up some shards of marked pottery and a blue trading bead that she added to the collection of feathers and pieces of driftwood soon to adorn the window sill of her flat overlooking the Barnes High Street.

The scouts found the male leopard's spoor almost every day for the next two weeks. We've noticed that around February to April every year, the males go in search of available females – and twice we picked up the tracks of a smaller cat travelling with him, and we heard them calling in the night.

Then he left for good, and his disappearance coincided with news of the killing of yet another large male leopard on Marshlands, lured there by the carcasses the hunters hang as bait, often along our boundary.

Marshlands was the last place on earth I wanted to visit. During the rains, from November to April, I try to pretend it doesn't exist, but that's impossible in the hunting season when the dull thump of rifle fire once again goes echoing through the hills, and lands like a fist in your chest. But Badge was there, and although he would respond to Khanye, he certainly wouldn't follow him home. Only Mother would do.

I made a couple of phone calls, first to the wife of the hunter who ran the place for Albright and then to the safari operator's office. They told us that there were American clients in camp, along with the South African dog handler and his pack, who are renowned (or so I read on his website) for taking out 'monster' leopards from Zimbabwe every year. A description, I feel, that is far more applicable to the pursuers than the pursued.

Hunting cougars with dogs has long been a favourite sport in America, and it was thanks to the American hunters' desire for a similar African experience that 'coon hounds' were introduced, first into South Africa and then into Zimbabwe. President Theodore Roosevelt was an aficionado, and it's interesting and rather ironic to hear that his hero Selous, who accompanied him on safari, was strongly opposed to this method of hunting.

I met Khanye and Mabhena at the koppie on the Marshlands boundary where they were picking up Badger's signal, maybe around a kilometre away. It would have been easy to slip through the fence, but with armed hunters (and poachers) in the vicinity, we didn't want to be caught wandering about unannounced. I took both of them with me so we could pick up as much information as possible.

When we arrived at the Marshlands main gate at around 11am, we found it padlocked. I hooted, we shouted, and eventually a man appeared out of the long grass and let us in. This was enemy territory – I couldn't think of it any other way – and as if to confirm it, the first thing we saw was a flock of vultures circling lazily in the distance.

The road sloped down through an open vlei, then cut a deep red channel through the koppies where the soil had washed away. We passed piles of firewood, and a couple of abandoned cattle pens ringed with rusty wire and broken wooden rails. In the 5 kilometres from the gate to the hunting camp, there were only emaciated cattle and their tracks, and not a sign of a single wild animal.

You can see the camp from miles away: a line of thatched buildings, painted green, sitting exposed on top of a *dwala* – a huge granite whaleback. It's at the mercy of the winds, but the view of the chaotic jumble of koppies spreading out below it is breathtaking.

After a steep climb over bare rock around the back of the camp, we rounded a corner, then pulled up suddenly to avoid plunging hundreds of feet over the edge of the *dwala*. A few yards away, a large beefy man, narrow of eye and thick of neck, was standing in front of the open bonnet of a Landcruiser, wiping his hands on a rag. His dog, a small terrier, came running over to greet us, and I noticed that he had injuries to his head and chest. The man himself didn't exactly wag his tail, but that's hardly surprising given our reputation as the bunny huggers from next door who, for some inexplicable reason, are concerned about our rapidly diminishing leopard population.

Khanye and Mabhena jumped out to join a couple of game scouts standing in front of the dining area, while I gave Mr Dog Handler a friendly smile. I explained that we'd come to find Badger, and that I thought he'd probably been tempted through the game fence by the smell of their leopard baits hanging in the trees.

He shook his head. 'That's not so; we're not hanging any baits here these days. You can go and look for your badger, if you like – the clients are hunting somewhere else.'

'Have you had much luck this year?' I asked, trying to sound as though I couldn't care less.

The man leaned against the door of his vehicle and lit up a cigarette.

'Luck?' he said. 'Hell, no. It's getting more and more difficult to find leopard. These land invaders have chased them away. Every year I come up from South Africa, it gets worse.'

So, why do you keep on hunting them, you bloody idiot? I wanted to say, but that would have been the end of the conversation. Instead, I kept on smiling and nodding sympathetically.

'That's too bad. So, how many have you managed to take from Marshlands this season?' (Politically correct hunters have their own little store of euphemisms. Rather than killing something, you either 'take' or even better, 'harvest' your trophy, conjuring up a picture of grateful animals dancing merrily around a maypole.)

'Only one.' He flicked his ash into the wind and took another long drag on his cigarette. 'There's another male around but he's not quite in his prime, so we'll leave him for the females. Anyway, we never take more than two a year from here; it wouldn't be sustainable.'

I'll bet.

I knew it was starting to sound like an interrogation, but I had to ask.

'I've heard that if you hunt with dogs you're pretty much guaranteed success. Is that right?'

'Let me tell you, lady,' he said slowly. 'That is complete *rubbish*. Hunting leopard with dogs is the same as hunting them any other way – sometimes you succeed, but more often than not you fail. Take my word for it.'

It was getting late and we didn't know how long it would take us to locate Badge. So after a few more casual questions, I signalled to Khanye and Mabhena and we climbed into the Landcruiser.

'You'd better take Philemon with you,' the man said. 'He'll show you the roads.'

One of the scouts got into the back, armed with a shotgun. I started the vehicle and wound down the window.

'By the way, do you often see honey badgers?'

He nodded. 'Ja, they're always stealing our baits. Those little buggers sure know how to climb.'

'Do you ever shoot them?'

'No.' He dropped his cigarette and ground it onto the rock with his heel. 'Not unless the client wants one.'

And what the client wants, the client must have. After all, he's the man with the bucks.

We managed to keep straight faces until we were halfway down the hill.

'So,' said Khanye, his face cracking into a wide smile. 'What did he say?'

I repeated the conversation.

He and Mabhena spluttered with laughter.

'That's not what we heard! Those scouts told us they're keeping 15 hunting dogs at the camp, and there's another *mukiwa* who hunts there as well. They've already killed six leopards in the district this season, and if they put up a female, sometimes they shoot her.'

'So how many have they taken from Marshlands?' I asked.

'Two so far this year, but they want more. They're still hanging baits all over the farm, plenty on the boundary with Stone Hills. And those guys say that if the dogs get on the spoor of a leopard before 10am, they hardly ever fail.'

'And that other *mukiwa*?' I asked. 'Has he also got dogs?'

'Oh yes,' said Mabhena. 'They are much worse than these ones. They chase everything – buck, servals, honey badgers, whatever they find, and the animals panic and sometimes break through the fence. But if a leopard crosses into Stone Hills, the hunters never follow it.' He chuckled. 'Everyone remembers what happened when they did that. Mr Peek *tuka'd* them big time!'

According to Philemon and his mate, the hunters use two types of dogs. One is the coon hound, bred especially for leopard hunting, and the other is the small and fearless terrier, used to flush out the cats that take cover in caves or holes. Not surprisingly, fatalities are commonplace. The little fellow we had met at the camp had been injured on a recent hunt, and Mr Dog Handler's other favourite terrier had been killed on Marshlands not long before. Jolly good sport – provided that you are on the right end of the gun.

It was more difficult to find Badger than we had imagined. We stopped near the place where Khanye had reckoned him to be, but now the signal was faint and intermittent, and it sounded as though he was moving back to the area below the camp. Khanye thought he might be following my scent. Leaving the scout in the back of the vehicle, we took off on foot through rough, scrubby country, scoured relentlessly by wind and fire and almost devoid of grass cover. Once, we heard the sound of hooves, as four wildebeest fled away from us through the trees. Badger kept moving – we'd pick up his signal, and lose it again when the koppies blocked it. We'd walked for almost an hour when finally the tick-tick-tick came through, loud and clear, like Captain Cook's alarm clock, which meant that either Badge was transmitting from inside the belly of a leopard or he was still in one piece. We followed him up the side of a koppie, I called, and a couple of minutes later, he trotted out into the open, very pleased to see us, but not nearly as relieved as I had expected him to be. I began to suspect that rather than following my scent, as we'd fondly imagined, he'd been trying to dodge his over-protective family.

I could read it in his face. *Of course, I'm fine, Mum. For goodness' sake, stop worrying*! It's the sort of thing they all say when they are at their most vulnerable and idiotic.

It was 1pm, and hot. Normally Badger would never emerge until at least 4.30pm, and even then he was always watchful and a little nervous until sundown. No one had chased him onto Marshlands – this was his first real adventure on his own, and we'd spoiled it. Would he follow me?

He did, and for the first hundred yards or so, he trotted along in front, looking very chirpy. Then the tail dropped, and he began to pant. By the time we reached a small stream, he had a long drink and lay with his belly flat against the damp sand, his paws twitching, as they always did unless he was in a deep sleep, in case they might locate something edible. Clearly, that was quite far enough, particularly for someone who had been living it up for the past 24 hours. Khanye left us to return to the vehicle, and I sat with Badge for a few minutes, splashing water over his back to cool him down. We couldn't stay for long. I wanted to get him away from that place.

'Come on, boy, that's enough.' I walked off, calling and he followed, reluctantly, sticking close to my heels. Nothing could be more intimidating for a secretive, nocturnal animal than wandering about in the middle of the day in a strange place. We had a long way to go, and I wondered what on earth I would do if he lost his nerve and ran away to hide. I'd have to wait with him until dusk and walk home in the dark without the torch I hadn't thought to bring. I had a radio in my backpack, but contact would be impossible from amongst the imposing barrier of koppies that stood between us and home.

We were close to the boundary with Stone Hills when the putrid stench of rotting flesh wafted our way. The carcasses of two cows lay a few yards apart in a dry riverbed, covered with the jostling bodies of white-backed vultures. As we appeared over the bank, they flew up en masse with a great flapping of wings and landed heavily on the surrounding trees. With full crops of flesh, they wouldn't be going far. While I held my nose, Badger did a thorough inspection and then fortunately came to my call.

Five minutes later, we were at the fence. I couldn't lift Badge over, nor could he squeeze through the wire, so we walked until I found a gap underneath it, marked with a pile of the chalky white dung of a well-fed hyaena. Badge went through, I climbed over, and as I jumped down onto the other side, the strap of my sandal broke. I swore and Badge looked up at me and whimpered. It was going to be a long, slow walk. I didn't know exactly (or in truth, even approximately) where we were, and Badger wasn't going to take the lead, but it didn't matter. We were back on Stone Hills, and I felt as relieved as if I'd just hopped over the Berlin Wall. In fact, I wish we had a 10-foot wall all around the farm to keep our animals in and the world out – something that might have presented a bit of a challenge, even to a brainy badger.

After following the stream for a while, we turned away and cut through the hills in what I hoped was the general direction of home. With any luck, we'd be there by four. Always early, the kudu would soon be gathering outside the garage, waiting for the rattle of cubes as Big Fight poured them into their dishes.

Visitors to Stone Hills often call it a piece of paradise because of the harmony they feel here and the ever-changing beauty of these enchanted hills. They're wrong of course: we live in uncertainty, and always have. Not just on the political front, but also from the constant menace of droughts, wild fires and poachers. Bountiful summers don't last for long; they are followed by harsh dry winters, with heavy frosts and biting cold, when all but our hardiest animals struggle to survive. But this land is loved and cared for, and I think that is what people sense when they are here; just as you can feel that life has drained away from Marshlands, and that its heart is broken.

From now on, we would be walking steadily uphill. Badger kept stopping in the shade, and calling me back with his baby whine, the one he used to beg for an apple at the end of a morning walk. He was dragging after me, and finally he lay down under a tree, rolled over on his back, and put his paws in the air, so the breeze would cool them. *I surrender*. It would have been cruel to push him any further, so I lay down next to him, and gently tickled his tummy. What a boy, and what incredible devotion and trust he had shown me. I think he really would have followed me to the ends of the earth, wherever they might be.

We lay there quietly for half an hour, and then I picked him up. He didn't move a muscle, just flopped into my arms, tummy up, as I hobbled off, cursing my blistered foot, bearing him before me like a hefty sacrificial lamb with anal glands and very large teeth. And so we proceeded: he'd walk for a bit, then wait under a tree asking me to carry him again. Until finally we came into sight of the Habhe River, only a few hundred yards from home. With a last burst of energy, Badger launched himself down the hill and dived into a large, shallow pool. And while I sat on the bank and dabbled my feet in the water, he went crazy, weaving around like an otter, and chasing his tail.

It was Badger's first visit to Marshlands, but not his last. He would be lured there time and again by the other badgers who congregated to feed on the leopard baits hung by the hunters.

They're still hunting leopard – but Mr Dog Handler had a nasty experience some time ago. He lost a lot of blood when he was badly mauled by a wounded tomcat, and it took a couple of operations to get him up and off after his hounds again.

Isikhuni sitshisa umkhwezeli, goes the Ndebele proverb – he who bites get bitten. Some people never learn.

Chapter Twenty-Two – Rain Dance

The water on Stone Hills runs deep and clear and cold. We pump it up from the rocks, 60 metres down, and everyone who visits us remarks on its sweetness and purity.

When we came to the land in 1989, at the height of a decade of drought, the sinking of a borehole was Rich's first priority. There was nothing else – no dams, no weirs – only two concrete reservoirs for the cattle, and both were empty.

Drilling a borehole is frighteningly expensive, and even more so when the equipment has to be brought 65 kilometres from town, so you have to be pretty sure of your site before you commit to it. But on 6 500 acres, crowded with koppies and criss-crossed by rivers that run dry in winter, where on earth do you start looking?

Rich's father would have known. Dick Peek had the gift of divining, using a flexible Y-shaped stick, freshly cut from the mulberry tree that grew in the garden of their Glendale Farm. With the point of the stick facing away from him, he would bend the prongs outwards and walk slowly along. And when there was water underground, the stick would move up or down, and twist in his hands, sometimes so strongly that the bark would peel away.

But Dick died many years ago, and although Rich is able to feel the presence of water, as many people can, using a piece of wire, this merely tells him that water is there, giving no indication of the strength or weakness of the flow.

Rich, too, could use the mulberry stick, but he couldn't do it alone. Only when his father was walking behind him, holding onto his arms and somehow connecting him to that special sensitivity, would it respond. But it stopped the moment Dick let him go, like the flicking on and off of a light switch.

Rich went to consult John Patterson, a well-respected diviner, particularly of mineral deposits, at his home in Bulawayo. But John was ill. The procedure totally drained him: even after one intensive session, he often had to take to his bed to recover. For the sake of his health, he told Rich, he had decided to give it up.

Instead, a Mr van der Riet came out from town one morning with his divining rod and plenty of guarantees of success. He quickly found what he said was a promising site, and made complicated measurements all around it, claiming that he was able to tell how many gallons each fissure would produce in an hour. But Rich was sceptical, and even more so when Van der Riet pinpointed at least 10 likely spots, as in this arid area we'd be lucky to find even one that was reasonably productive.

So he decided to do things his way, using aerial photographs and his own knowledge of the farm. By staring at the photos intently through a stereoscope, which gave a three-dimensional effect, he found he could pick up lines in the rocks, possibly indicating a split or a fissure. Some of these lines matched up perfectly with those on different rocks on adjacent hills until Rich was finally seeing patterns. And where the lines crossed over, and the fissures converged, he reckoned would be a likely place to find water. Rich stared at the photos till he was boss-eyed, then went out on the ground and tested his theory with a piece of wire, marking all the likely places with rocks, until the same patterns emerged, duplicating almost exactly the marks he had made on the photographs.

Rich went back to see John Patterson for a second opinion, but without disclosing his own findings. When the older man had spread the photographs out on his dining room table, he dangled a bottle of water on the end of a string over them, slowly moving it around until the bottle began to swing, slowly at first, and then picking up momentum until it was circling strongly, very strongly – right over the area that Rich had identified.

Not long afterwards, the massive drill went into action and bored a hole on the banks of the Matanje River that has been producing 500 gallons an hour consistently for the past 16 years. But we never take it for granted.

The rains are usually over by February or March, with a rare bonus of April showers. Winter begins in May with the first frosts in the vleis and along the rivers. 'There is forest in the veils', wrote one of the scouts in his daily report, making it sound far more poetic than it feels. June is mostly remembered as the dress rehearsal for July: the month when the sharp teeth of winter bite down hardest on the land. Then along come the wicked winds of August, and together they claim their share of the weak and sick. Spring begins in September, and with it comes the first herald of summer: the creamy-white blossoms of the wild pear, dazzling against a crisp blue sky. On a warm day, the air is alive with the whirr and hum of the insects lured from their winter torpor by its honey-scented blossom. But this is a temporary respite: rain is still far away, and when the flowers of the wild pear, the scarlet *Erythrina* and the golden *Cassia* lie bruised and scattered on the ground, we are face-to-face with October, the meanest month of all – the month when the waiting begins. We should be used to anxiety by now – our lives are never free of it – but the fear of drought never diminishes.

The wildebeest and impala very sensibly time their calving to coincide with the rain in November or December, but the eland give birth in September, or even earlier, when there is barely any nutrition to be found in the skeletal trees and the drifts of dry leaves in the koppies.

In the middle of September, the year after the witch-hunt next door, Mafira called to tell us that one of the domesticated eland was giving birth in the boma and that the calf's head was already exposed. We brought a herd of eight captive born young eland to Stone Hills in the early 1990s, and the scouts followed them as part of Rich's project to discover the species of trees on which they liked to browse in the different seasons, and those they would never touch. The project achieved something else too: at first the scouts would take Rich a twig from the tree and give him the Ndebele name, and then Rich would identify it and note it down. After a while, the scouts asked for a copy of his list, and within a few weeks, they knew all the scientific names too.

We rushed up to the boma. Two other eland cows were watching intently from the other side of the fence as the mother gave one last convulsive kick – and out came the baby: a slithery, slimy little thing, still gift-wrapped in the birth sac. The cow gave it a few half-hearted licks, and one ear sprang free of the membrane, sticking out at a right-angle, like the signalling arm of an old Morris Minor.

The calf shifted around a bit, trying to stand, then the mother rose and as she did so, the umbilical chord broke. She took a few more steps, so the last of the chord came away, then turned back and gazed with what seemed to be complete astonishment at the calf. Where on earth did you come from? She'd lost her calf the previous year, and judging by the strength of her maternal instincts, it was hardly surprising. We left one of the scouts watching them, and by the evening she'd finally licked her calf clean, perhaps on the advice of the other two cows, though she had not yet fed it. But by the next morning, the calf was feeding and all seemed well.

The domesticated herd stays out in the veld all day, but comes back to the boma at night, where they receive cubes and banna grass from the garden, so they are all in good condition. But although many of the wild eland come to the house for food in the winter, for the most part they rely on dry leaves, herbs and the new shoots on the trees for their sustenance; the constant search for food saps their energy at the time the breeding females need it most.

We didn't think that the rain dance would happen after Emily had been accused of witchcraft and her drums and potions destroyed by the so-called prophets. But she arrived at the house on a Tuesday afternoon, requesting permission for the dance to be held that Saturday. If the drought were to end, the ancestors would have to be appeased.

Normally she would have come with her helpers well in advance to clean the rain rock and sweep the area, but this time, none of the usual preparations were made. She agreed that, as before, we would be allowed to film the dance.

When we arrive at midday, the first person we see is Emily in her blue headscarf and beads. Never a smiler at the best of times, she now looks positively grim. Normally, a procession would have walked from the gate singing and beating drums; today there is a large disorganised group of around 50 people milling about, apparently without direction.

We sit in the vehicle, while Khanye and Mabhena go to find out what is happening.

We know four of the dancers, all dressed in the traditional black and white: the little gogo with the grasshopper legs, who never seems to change from year to year; MaNdlovu sporting a bunch of ostrich feathers on her head, and Gladys Mabechu, rake-thin but always prepared to dance when the drums begin. Along with Emily, all four have been accused of witchcraft. But today another woman has joined them: an Amazon, but fully endowed, with a head like an ox, and gigantic knockers heaving under a thin white T-shirt. 'She's from the other side of the railway line,' Khanye whispers. I should have guessed. And an old man, a Mr Ndlovu, with no teeth and a pleasantly wicked smile is holding a horse tail and chatting to the women.

The five women wrap the *amahlwayi* around their lower legs: these are the cocoons of mopane worms, strung into lines and filled with tiny stones that rattle when they dance. Normally, the dancers would approach on their knees, today they do not, and when they arrive at the rain rock they notice that it's full of dirt and leaves. Mr Ndlovu, who seems to have taken charge, sweeps it clean. Then one of the dancers brings a gourd of beer that she pours into the depression in the rock, and they drink, on their knees with their hands behind their backs, in the customary way.

Eventually, the drums start, the women begin to sway and stamp their feet, and the crowd begin to clap. It's good to see that despite her frailty, Gladys can still wiggle her hips like a girl. But the dancing is apathetic, only Heffalump gives it her considerable all, as she pounds the earth on great flat feet. We try to look elsewhere, but it's impossible to keep our eyes off her. Mr Ndlovu skips nimbly out of her way, and there's a loud rumble as an enormous boulder slips off the top of the nearest koppie. If Heffalump wins the favour of the ancestors, we'll have to start building an ark.

'My drums are crying, asking for rain ...' the songs begin.

'We need the rain to fill the Shashani River ...'

'Answer us when we sing, oh, Tobela. Come to us, rescue us, we need your help ...'

There are three drummers: a young man, a strapping young woman and a pretty girl with large expressive eyes, wearing a blue silk scarf on her head. She gives me a long, resentful stare that makes me feel a bit uncomfortable, until I notice that she looks at everyone the same way. After a few minutes, she gives up and moves off, and the dancing stops while they call in a young man as a replacement.

249

Gogo tires easily, and she's standing on the sidelines, flanked by a tall woman who keeps the old lady swaying and clapping, and a smaller one who is showing the crowd how to clap in rhythm with the drums. A pretty girl in an orange blouse and a straw hat gives me a shy wave from the crowd – it's Lydia, the Grade Three teacher from Marula School. Next to her is MaNdebele, dressed in pink with a white shawl over her shoulders. She's another witch, but if she's worried about it, it doesn't show.

Once more the drummers stop and so does the dancing, as the young man is again replaced. The crowd looks restless and unhappy. Mr Ndlovu takes the stage, turning in slow circles and waving his horse tail over his head. Despite being old and bent, he manages to keep to the rhythm of the drums. Then a young man bursts through the crowd, half crouching and leaping forward, his feet slamming into the dust.

'If you don't sing hard, the rains won't come!' he shouts.

Now this is all wrong. Custom dictates that the dancers should be only very young women or those past childbearing. Never a man.

A scowling Emily leaves the other dancers and goes over to the latest drummer to give him some instruction: first, peck with bent fingertips, and then beat with a flat hand. Not very difficult, but the man looks sulky and won't meet her eyes. After a few minutes, he too gives up, and she takes his place.

The Amazon, who never seems to tire, leans on her dancing stick and begins to hyperventilate. She grabs the arm of the small woman next to Gogo, and drags her wildly around the arena. Then she stomps about, spitting out incoherent words that sound very much like 'shit!'. No one is taking much notice, so she falls onto the ground and rolls about in a supposed trance. The crowd is unimpressed.

Another surprise. Emily's brother, Madliwayidonki, appears and began to dance, immediately below where Rich is filming. MaNdlovu, adorned in her nodding ostrich feathers, starts to back up towards him, speaking angrily, her eyes rolling.

'If someone is stronger than me, then let him come here and take the stage!'

The drummers keep going, but the dancers retreat. Amongst the crowd, the atmosphere has changed from apathy to hostility.

MaNdlovu edges Madliwayidonki back into the crowd of men, then flings her stick at them. It misses, but lands right below the rock on which we are sitting.

'Don't take away my shadow!' she shouts.

'I don't think you should film any more.' Khanye whispers to Rich.

MaNdlovu marches off stage, and the other women crowd around her.

Everyone is silent – waiting. She returns, her eyes wild as if possessed; she circles the old man, and once again throws her stick. Neither time has it made contact, but it is very close. The drummers begin, and MaNdlovu stomps over to Emily, her stick raised as if she is about to hit her. Emily takes no notice, and continues drumming looking straight ahead, as if nothing is happening.

'You should be dancing, not drumming,' she shouts in her face. Emily carries on.

We collect our stuff and leave quietly. Something is going on that we can't understand, and we don't belong here.

Khanye and Mabhena stayed on for the rest of the dance, and Khanye told us the following morning that after we left,

MaNdlovu turned on Emily's brother demanding that he show her what was in his pocket. He refused, but then Mr Ndlovu led him away and searched him. He was carrying a brown paper packet of *nyatela* – a powder that has the power to make animals weak and easily hunted, and affects humans in the same way. Mr Ndlovu held it up to show the crowd.

'You,' he ordered Madliwayidonki, 'will stay here where we can see you so you can do no more harm.'

'And you,' pointing at Emily, 'will stop drumming. Together, you have been plotting to ruin our dance.'

And from that moment, everything was back on course. The people cheered up, the drummers did their job and the dancers danced with vigour. The spell had been lifted, the troublemakers removed.

MaNdlovu had apparently been speaking in the voices of the spirits. Her demand that Emily should dance was a test; she knew the *nyatela* would also have affected her, and that she would refuse. And there was another problem: Emily should not have joined in the ceremony at all, as her husband had died a month before, and therefore she was still 'defiled' and would be until his spirit had been brought back home after a year by the *umbuyiso* ceremony.

'But Khanye,' I said, 'I didn't know there was a husband. I thought that Kephas was living with Emily?'

'Well, he is sort of,' Khanye replied. 'But the husband was nearly 90, and even blinder than Kephas, so he probably didn't realise what was going on.'

So dear old Kephas, the octogenarian herbalist with the celestial smile, was a toy boy. And somewhere in his hut, perhaps hidden in his pile of marula nuts, is the magic potion that keeps Emily sweet.

Chapter Twenty-Three – Jongwe's Lucky Day

I wake at 5am to a fiery red sky – we've left the windows and curtains open for the heat – and a line of zebra are walking slowly away from the waterhole, their hooves kicking up puffs of dust.

Rich leaves with Badger, and when I'm sure that they are safely on the other side of the river, I pour myself a cup of tea and sit on the back veranda looking up at Dibe Hill. The wind has stilled and apart from a few ragged snatches of birdsong, everything is quiet. Then suddenly a posse of baboons appears silently over the top of the rocks. They sit yawning and scratching themselves for a while, but by the time I come back from fetching my second cup of tea they've gone: our local biker gang, off to spend the day swaggering about in search of naked chicks and other delights – all of which are becoming harder and harder to find.

Another eland cow went into labour in the boma – one of the two that had been watching the first cow give birth from the other side of the fence. Wide-eyed, she kept swinging her head towards her belly, the source of her pain. Finally, her waters broke, but nothing further was happening, so we left her. During the night, she gave birth to a stillborn calf, very premature, its tiny body wet and black, with hooves like jellied aspic. Her calf from the previous year had only lasted for a few hours, and I'd seen her going back and forth to the place where it had died, calling in that strange way they seem to reserve for their sorrow.

A few days later, Mafira reported that the first calf had begun suckling from both her own mother and from the bereaved cow. It was an odd scenario, but the two females had lived together for 10 years, and perhaps it suited both the awkwardly reluctant mother and the other, with her bursting udders yet no baby to feed.

Their compromise didn't last for long – no more than a couple of weeks later, the foster cow killed the real mother. We found her lying up against the gate of the boma, where she had been trapped and killed by a horn rammed straight into her chest. Only then did we discover that there had been aggression between the two of them from the start, and that they had been separated at night in the boma, until someone had accidentally left the interleading gate unlatched.

Her eyes, so deep and calm in life, were wide open and covered with an opaque greenish film. She was already bloated, but still warm, and as I stroked her neck and chatted to our young manager, he kicked carelessly at her horns. He probably wasn't aware of it, but it showed how he felt. She'd been just another animal in life, and now she was a lump of *nyama* – meat – no more than that. It was disrespectful but I said nothing; he wouldn't have understood.

The murderer was unrepentant. She went out with the herd that morning, the calf running at her heels, and turned into an exemplary mother.

October dragged on. I glared at the sun, and it glared back at me. What was left of the grass was as brittle as a biscuit, and the cicadas had begun their dry, rasping screech that pierces your eardrums at midday when it reaches its crescendo.

I began taking a bottle of water for Badger on our walks, which were becoming later and later, as we tried to avoid the worst of the heat. The first time I did it, he drank it gratefully out of my cupped hands, but with his eye fixed firmly on the plastic bottle. I hung it on the end of a branch and the moment I turned my back, he was after it, as quick as a Fijian up a coconut tree.

It was too hot to go far in the mornings, so Badger amused himself by making the acquaintance of the Bandits – a troop of around 25 banded mongooses he found foraging on the side of a koppie. I hung back, and ducked behind a bush to watch – not that the Bandits were in the least bit interested in me. They were circling Badger at a safe distance, spreading the alarm with high-pitched growls. Then a couple of the braver ones came in closer – and closer. But when Badger turned to look at them, they lost their nerve and rushed off, making a noise like a series of exploding farts and scattering the troop.

Badger was only mildly interested; he galloped after them in an amiable sort of way, but soon became tired of the game and came to find me crouched behind my bush. He climbed into my lap and lay there whining – a sight that flabbergasted the spectators. With little chitters of amazement, they came down off the rocks and surrounded us, standing up on their hind legs, and holding up their dainty front feet sheathed in black gloves, their pink noses twitching with horror.

On one early morning walk along the Matanje River, I spied another local resident on the opposite bank. Badger fortunately didn't notice him: a swiftly moving black mamba, lured from his winter hideout by the warmer weather. Whatever Badger's level of tolerance, I didn't want to risk him tangling with a snake from which two drops of venom are enough to kill a man.

Only a week before, I'd heard some strange noises outside the kitchen. Everyone was gathered there – squirrels, dassies, birds – all staring at the same spot. And apart from the dassie, who was making a sort of choking sound and a couple of subdued clucks from the francolin, they were absolutely silent.

I stood and stared with them, and then I saw it: a length of dark grey tail disappearing unhurriedly up the koppie. My eye followed the flow of it, up and up, until I caught sight of the head of the biggest black mamba I had ever seen, its body as thick as a man's forearm. One metre, two, three, four and counting; it didn't seem possible that that head could possibly belong to the tail, and I reckon all the animals around me felt just the same way.

We do tend to dispose of dangerous snakes that venture into the house, or very close to it, but I wouldn't have dreamed of fetching the shotgun. Not only because I was transfixed and totally intimidated by this reptilian leviathan, but because it would have been like killing an elephant. Mambas are territorial; that snake was where it should have been, and it had kept out of our way for many, many years (and laid hundreds of eggs, as Rich reminded me, somewhat tetchily, when he came home later that afternoon).

At last it seems that the weather is changing. The sky is a deep, smudgy blue with fluffy white cumulus clouds building into their familiar cauliflower heads. We can hear the distant thunder, see the mist of rain blurring the horizon, but then it's gone, after spitting a few fat drops at us that leave a pattern of spots in the dust. It's tantalising: like chocolates that are meant for someone else. You can see them, you can smell them – you can drive yourself mad imagining how they would taste, but in the end all you are left with is the pretty wrapping paper in the form of a spectacular sunset – the aftermath of somebody else's faraway storm.

Some of the more optimistic trees have already decked themselves out in green, but they look rather forlorn standing out there on their own, like kids dressed up for a birthday party that's just been cancelled.

Once again, Zimbabwe is hungry. When maize does arrive in the country it is distributed to the party faithful, while others go without.

We are in the office when a battered white truck pulls up at the garage, with a strident blast of its horn. A government official has arrived, his shirt collar straining against the folds of fat around his sweaty neck. Cursing, Rich goes to intercept him, and I can hear their conversation from my desk under the office window.

'Why don't you give us meat?' demands the man, in the

hectoring tone he uses to bully the locals.

Rich doesn't hesitate. 'Why does it always have to be me – *my* animals? They're starving but I must give you meat! Why don't you eat your own cows and leave mine alone?'

'If you don't give us meat, I might have to come and poach!'

Rich informs him, at full volume, that if he wants to do time in prison, he's very welcome (even though they both know that this would never happen).

'If I come and poach, will you shoot me?'

'Yes, I will!'

Standing up for yourself is not encouraged in Zimbabwe. Farmers are still being evicted, arrested or presented with so-called partners, but what the hell? Rich has been very quiet recently, and I know he's worried sick about it, but he has done the right thing. If they are going to take the land away they will do so whether he speaks his mind or not. Better that than be walked over.

Rich is away a couple of weeks later when I hear from Rob Rosenfels on neighbouring Good Luck Farm, that a consignment of mealiemeal is due to arrive at the depot in Plumtree the following morning. Not long before, I'd driven to a private milling company close to the Botswana border, queuing in the broiling heat behind a long line of dilapidated taxis and cars, in an inferno of exhaust fumes, noise and white dust. I'd given up after a couple of hours, and gone home with nothing.

We plan to meet at the gate at 4.15am. I'm in the pick-up with a trailer, and Precious the handyman is driving the Toyota, but halfway there, I realise that I have locked Nandi in the house and that the key is in my pocket. I turn around and roar back to hide it for Ruthie. We have never yet had a problem with theft, but these are hard times. When I get back

258

to the gate, I can see the lights of Rob's car, and the sound of my horn brings Mabhena stumbling out of the guardhouse.

We arrive outside the locked gates of National Foods at 5am. Only one person is in front of us, another local farmer. We climb out with our thermoses of tea and catch up with a bit of gossip till 7am, by which time there's a crowd of people and a line of cars behind us. Word filters through that the truck is still in Gwanda, three hours away at least. At 10.30am, the gates open, and we drive into the narrow strip of shade alongside the National Foods building.

There aren't enough neighbours left to provide any more scandal, so I sit in the vehicle with the door open, revising an magazine article that sounds worse and worse the more I work on it. There's a tap on the passenger window. A middle-aged man holds up Jongwe, a handsome cockerel, the emblem of Zimbabwe's ruling party. The bird's head is hanging limply over his arm – it's almost expired from heat exhaustion. I pour water into the top of the flask and he drinks till he's fit to burst. Then I splash his feathers, and for the next few hours, he sits gratefully in a pool in the back of the Toyota. People keep arriving on foot, and with vehicles – but we were the first, and we've been given numbers to prove it. I practise my death stare on anyone who dares to sidle up hoping to jump the queue.

At 1pm, we can hear the distant roar and see the dust of the truck coming down the road towards the depot. People start laughing and shouting with excitement, and it gets even better when we see that it's a 30 tonner, fully loaded with bags of mealiemeal.

'We're bound to get a ton each,' says Rob, rubbing his hands together. 'Maybe even more.'

It's going to be worth the wait.

The huge truck draws up in front of me with its engine still running. We are palpitating, ready to rush into the building the moment we are called. There's jostling from behind, and I'm beginning to feel that we are in the starting stalls at a race. Then a fleet of small pickups arrive next to the truck, and the workers start slinging bags onto them. Someone says they belong to the local storekeepers.

We wait for another hour, muttering along with the rest of the crowd.

Finally, the loaded pickups leave, and the workers dump a pile of bags onto the forecourt of the building. The truck revs up, enveloping us in a choking cloud of black smoke, and drives away.

'That's it,' the cockerel's owner says bitterly. 'Now they'll go to the same storekeepers to make another delivery.'

'You should start a riot,' says Rob angrily. 'On second thoughts, don't,' he said hastily, imagining us getting caught up in the mayhem.

We stand in a queue for another half an hour before we are called. The heat is beating up from the tarmac. I am number one, first off the rank, but when I skid to a stop at the pay desk, there's a crowd in front of me.

'I'm first!' I yell, holding up my number and elbowing my way to the front.

'No you're not!' a tall man wearing sunglasses shouts back at me. 'I've been here since 4am!'

The gloves are off.

Rob is puce with fury, and he's ready to kill. He's a large man. I'll be right behind him.

'Bloody liar!' we yell in unison.

The cockerel man steps forward. 'These people were first,' he says firmly. 'I saw them with my own eyes.'

For some reason, his words get through to the shady character. Grumbling, he steps back, and at last, I present my ticket and my cash to the man behind the desk.

It is done. I smile and give the thumbs up to Mr Cockerel and he smiles back. Quid pro quo – it's the same in any language. I drive around to the loading zone and sit in the cab, feeling the vehicle give a satisfactory shudder with every 50 kilogram bag that lands in the back.

Strictly speaking, we are only allowed one load, but we have a staff of 20 to feed so we don't care about the rules. I pretend I don't know Precious who is four numbers behind me. When he's told how much he owes, he comes out to me to collect a cheque and then strolls back chewing the end of a matchstick and looking bored. He's a whizz at picking locks and finding his way through closed windows, and I can see now that he'd also be a pretty good crook or poker player.

We drive off, windows down, with the fan blasting air into the cab, looking out for people that might jump the vehicle and steal some bags as they've been doing in Bulawayo recently.

We reach home 12 hours after we left it with a total of 740 kilograms of mealiemeal. It's enough for each of our workers for two months, but there's nothing for their families, most of whom live far away.

I was dead right about Precious. Not long after, he was rumbled with four pairs of double sheets and a couple of towels, having helped himself to the keys of the storeroom that are kept locked in our office.

That evening, we find Badger at the Habhe River. He's discovered a hole in the sand, and after digging for a while, a little water starts to seep in. He keeps dipping his paw into it, fascinated. Then we move on to Coucal Spring, a tiny stagnant pool surrounded by thick clumps of sedge. Badge wades in up to his belly and begins puddling up the mud on the bottom, an activity that won't endear him to the other animals coming to drink later that evening. Up jumps a slippery platanna, and lands on a rock. Badger leaps at it, jaws snapping, but the frog springs back in the water with a splash, taking refuge in a crevice between two rocks. Frogs are hard to find these days, and Badger isn't going to let this one go in a hurry. For the next half hour, he uses his feet to stuff debris into the gap, but it keeps floating out again, and the frog refuses to shift. Totally frustrated, Badge abandons the frog and goes into overdrive – zipping in and out of the sedges and nipping my feet. I give chase, growling, and when he ambushes me, I wave the strands in his face, sending him haring off again. Just like him to choose the hottest, most miserable day of the year for his most strenuous games.

'I give up!' I begin to walk away, but five minutes later, he's trotting towards me with a *Boophane* bulb swinging in his jaws. He rolls around with it, clutches it to his stomach, shreds off layers with his claws, and I haven't the heart to ignore him. I score only once, grabbing it from his mouth and hurling it away, but he's back in a flash, and this time he sits on my foot so I can go no further. Finally, I escape and head for Hongwe Tengana Hill, making a wide detour around some giraffe. And out of the grass comes Badger carrying a piece of driftwood, taunting me, demanding another game. We play till it's dark, and end up right in the middle of the herd of giraffe, causing a stampede.

I arrive home at 8pm, and as I walk into the house, the mobile phone rings. A man calling himself Leonard is coming to see us in the morning. We've heard about him – he's a highly placed government official, a powerful man.

We eat in silence: there's nothing to say. Although we share our fears, they isolate us. It's as if we are standing on opposite sides of a deep hole filled with churning black water, waiting for a monster to emerge.

A new black Pajero drives slowly through the open gate at 9am the next morning. We lock the office, and follow it up the driveway together. How many times have we done this? And yet the anxiety never lessens. Leonard Mungara and his colleague, both wearing dark suits, greet us pleasantly enough, but that means nothing.

'How are your animals?'

'How is business at the lodge?'

The usual questions with the usual answers. The animals are dying in the drought, not many of them left now (for God's sake, someone chase that herd of wildebeest away from the waterhole); tourists don't come to Zimbabwe any more (they are worried by the politics and the reports of violence) the lodge is falling to pieces (witness if you will the great green greasy swimming pool and the holes in the thatch).

We go inside for tea and after half an hour of small talk, Rich's small fund of patience is at an end. He turns the conversation to the farm invasions and I can see he's winding up, starting to gesticulate, wagging his finger at the two men. But they don't take the bait – in fact they say they agree with him, and Leonard looks so mild and unthreatening, that I leave them to it. He certainly wants something, but I'm pretty certain it's not the land.

As I turn to say goodbye at the door, Rich has taken off his glasses and is rubbing them furiously with his handkerchief. Now they're in for it. Two hours later, off they go in their black Pajero, slightly faster than when they arrived. I don't need to ask: I know that Leonard has two burning ears and a migraine and that he won't be back in a hurry.

He never did say what he had come for. But we heard from the front gate that Mabhena had turned him away a few days earlier when he'd arrived with one of the local tarts looking for accommodation.

I told Khanye about the visit the next morning on our walk with Badger, and I asked him something that Rich and I could never bring ourselves to discuss.

'What would *you* do about Badger if the land was taken over?'

'I think I would let him rest,' said Khanye softly. 'What else could we do?'

Chapter Twenty-Four –
Grand Ole Opry

Is there anything more wonderful than an African river?

Everything on Stone Hills begins and ends there – Mathole, Matanje, Hable and Pundamuka; our rivers are the blood of the land, the veins that run through it.

In winter, the river sand is clean and soft, and the long brown grass is crushed by the hooves of animals that come to drink from its still pools. As the leaves fall and the sap retreats, you can smell the spicy fragrance of pot-pourri and the muskiness of curing tobacco.

And when the good spirits of summer arrive and bring the

rain, where else but the river can you go, now that the silence of winter has been broken by a tide of birdsong, and the air is vibrating with the sound of the River Band, tuning up for its first gala performance?

They're making frog music: percussion, brass and strings. There's the clicking of castanets; the sound of bubbles that pop on the surface of the water; the smoker's croak of the guttural toad, and the squeak of a door on rusty hinges – the love song of the common river frog.

Rich calls it the Grand Ole Opry – a parade of baritones and tenors; sopranos and altos; with a pretty flutter of trills from the chorus girls – and look, isn't that Dolly Parton in full cry, puffed right up and singing her heart out?

In fact, it's the males who are calling in fervent courtship, their vocal sacs ballooning out under their throats, and they will kick, wrestle and push for the best position, the one that will make their voices carry the furthest to the waiting females. To us, it sounds chaotic, as though a reggae band has gate crashed the first night at the Proms, but actually it's pretty well organised. Males of some species will sing in chorus, making sure the females can't miss them, while others will considerately call in turn, giving each other a chance to be heard.

When one Bocage's tree frog says 'Ow!' it sounds as though he's been dug in the ribs, but when they start up in an agonised chorus, it's really disturbing, as if they're being subjected to a mass amputation in a French field hospital.

The basso profundo of the red toad is simply mournful. 'Whoo-oom! Whoo-oom!' he calls, and there's a swirl of water as he grabs his female and climbs aboard, grasping her tightly with the rubbery nuptial pads on his fingers. She submits because she has to, but you can see from the morose look on her face that it's no more than an unpleasant duty, and if there was some polish handy, she'd far rather be painting her nails. Amplexus, they call it in toad-speak, where the male deposits his sperm onto the eggs as she lays them. Amplexus! I ask you. We make it sound like a tummy exercise.

Dragonflies zip and zap past us at high speed in their anxiety to lay and get laid while the water lasts. Their mating begins in flight, and in drily scientific terms, they are 'in cop', despite the fact that the female is having the ride of her life in a fashion that consigns the proud members of the Mile High Club to fumbling amateurs.

The red toads stay stuck together for ages, not because the female is enjoying it but because she doesn't have a choice, and where there is fierce competition, she sometimes drowns as other males try to force her paramour off her back.

Trouble is, there's nothing about amplexus that makes a lady frog feel special. Males aren't choosy. In fact, some species will grab anything that remotely looks like a frog. A male so accosted will let out an indignant squawk – *Hands off, you idiot!* – which apparently sorts out the confusion.

When I first came back to Zimbabwe from Australia in 1984, I suffered from a bout of insomnia. Sleeping pills, hot baths, Milo and deep breathing didn't help. Only when Rich had the idea of playing me a recording of frog calls did I pass out peacefully for my first good night's sleep in months.

For a country boy, some of Badger's tastes were sometimes gratifyingly sophisticated: frogs' legs, tiny freshwater shrimps, crunchy crabs were all on the menu, and although I applauded his connoisseurship, I would rather that they hadn't been quite so *alive* when he tucked into them. The red toads in particular always looked rather sad and resigned throughout the whole performance, as though they'd always suspected it was going to end like this.

For Badger, they were fast food, gulped down in a few minutes, whereas other species carrying cardiotoxic secretions under their skin, like the guttural toad, required a lot more work to make them palatable. If he caught them away from water, Badger would rake at their backs, then rub them in the dirt, presumably to disperse the toxins, while wrinkling his nose, lifting his lip and turning his head away with an expression of utter revulsion. But if he was close to the river or a convenient puddle, he'd kill the toad (or so I liked to believe), dunk it and then rake at it under the water, giving it a good scrub so he ended up with a nice clean meal.

A wriggling ball of tadpoles looked like an easy catch, but as soon as Badger plunged his head in after them, they'd disperse, causing him endless exasperation. But when he did manage to land one, he'd keep it clean by eating it off the back of his foot.

Sexily sheathed in shiny red and black, rubber frogs look very suave as they waddle along in the torchlight with their spindly legs wide apart, as if they've just wet their pants. Their long trills, often heard far away from water, are some of the most melodious and evocative of all the summer serenades, and when Badger tracked one down and dug it up, he thought he was in for a real treat. But the rubber frog carries one of the most potent toxins under his skin, and within moments, he was shaking his head and foaming at the mouth. From then on, he ignored them.

Even in the dark, we could tell what Badger was eating. Frogs sounded wet and squishy, corn crickets were crisp and toothy, grasshoppers a mere smack of the lips.

Wandering along the river at night, the full moon rides

along next to us in the water, its face blurred with ripples. Our torchlight picks up countless emerald eyes of spiders in the grass, and I feel as though I'm in an aeroplane, looking down at the tiny twinkling lights of a city.

A ball of pure white foam, glistening like ice in the moonlight, hangs over the water at the end of a branch. At night, the female *Chiromantis*, the foam nest frog, secretes a fluid that she and her mate whisk into a bubbly froth with their hind legs. She lays her eggs in it; her mate and other keen hangers-on fertilise them, and in the morning, when the sun dries the outside of the nest, it forms a protective crust with the consistency of meringue, which keeps the inside cool and moist. A few days later, the partly developed tadpoles wriggle down and drop into the water, having had a head start over all the others. It's a brilliant strategy – until it rains, when the whole nest may be swept into the water like ice cream that's slipped off the cone.

An inch of rain! It begins with a few fat drops, and although it looks promising, we've been fooled once too often. 'Don't look at it,' we always tell each other. 'You might chase it away.' But this time it is for real. I run to the garage and stand under the corrugated roof, where the loud staccato of drops over my head gradually builds into a deafening hail of bullets.

The house still leaks. It was fixed in the winter, but the squirrels can't be bothered to come in through the windows, so they keep making holes in the thatch. Half an hour later, the downpour subsides and from the veranda, we watch a tremendous emergence of termites all over the vlei, with the birds diving through a light mist of rain to catch them on the wing.

After the storm, everything takes on a deeper, richer

colour. Dark clouds race across a deep red sky streaked with golden light; new leaves flutter and whisper in the wind, and somewhere out of sight, the impala call in their young with loud burps like satisfied customers at a beerfest. All over the veld, the ink flowers, carpets of tiny moles' spectacles and clusters of ferns are uncurling, stretching, pushing free of their winter prison. The air is perfumed with flowers and the fruity, loamy smell of damp, black earth.

Even the moody wind has changed its tune. It can be playful or vindictive, soft or sharp, as ready with a bite as a caress. But in summer, when it is at its most genial, it seems to awaken history in the hills, putting life into the forgotten souls who rest there. No longer is it a curse, squeezing itself cunningly through the cracks in the sliding doors – now we fling open all the windows and doors and welcome it in.

The whole dynamic of summer is intoxicating: you want to shout, 'Take me with you!' It's crazy but you feel as though you'd even be willing to die if it meant that you could be lost in this moment forever, knowing that no words or pictures can ever recapture it. Now there are tiny shoots of green on our bare back lawn, and soon the long grass will cover the scars of winter and the bleached white bones lying scattered in the veld.

I remember the first time that Badge felt rain on his fat little body. He ran all over the place trying to get away, even up a tree, shouting at me to do something about it. He'd roll around in the sand, and tunnel into the long grass to dry himself off, until he discovered that he could stay warm and dry simply by sheltering under Khanye's green poncho.

He was always frightened of deep water, but he'd stand

by the little waterfalls along the river, trying to stop them with his feet and nose, and to catch the water as it ran by.

When our streams are transformed into rushing torrents, crossing them is not always easy. I was out with Badger early one rainy evening when he began trying to dig a hole in the side of a rock-solid termite mound. He'd been stuffing himself with crickets, tadpoles and frogs, and his tummy was full, but typically, once he had started, he intended to persevere.

I sat on the top of the mound, feeling hungry and getting a wet bottom, until he finally gave up and trotted down to the water's edge. He watched it sweeping by for a few seconds, and then came back and looked hopefully up at me. Message received. I picked him up, cold, wet and dirty, and carried him across in my arms, while he sucked gratefully at my earlobe – which may not sound very pleasant but is an awful lot nicer than having a squirrel drag its anal glands across your head, or an owl rub half a dead rat into your hair – all of which I have suffered in the name of love.

We were nearly home and Badger was thumping along the road behind me, hiccupping madly, when he stopped to inspect an interesting hole. I turned to check it out, and at that moment, there was a loud hiss directly behind me, terrifyingly close. I spun around, swiping the whip in all directions; it sounded as though the snake was right at my feet. Being well away from the river, it was likely to be a spitting cobra or a puff adder, and if I so much as moved I could step on it. Suddenly my feet and bare legs felt very vulnerable. I stood rigid with fear, wildly swishing the whip like some crackpot lion tamer. (Actually it wasn't much of a whip, just a long tapering rod bound with melted plastic that we carried for just such occasions, but was more useful as a bum-beater for a recalcitrant badger.)

'Bookey, Bookey, do you read?' came Rich's voice over the static hiss of the radio that was strapped to my back. Not a snake after all, but my husband telling me to come home for dinner.

Despite the healthy population of snakes on Stone Hills, our encounters were relatively rare, until Badger grew up and began to pursue them actively. We'd just arrived home from collecting David from boarding school when the first real drama occurred. Luckily for all of us, the year was divided into four terms and four half terms – so the gaps between trips home were not too long. It was always the same: when we pulled up at the gate of the farm, Rich would stop the car, David would throw his school shirt, shoes and socks in the back and run the three and half kilometres to the house, reconnecting with everything he had missed.

The radio was chirping as we walked through the front door. It was Khanye and he sounded very stressed indeed.

'It's Badger – he's been bitten on the head by a cobra. You'd better come quickly.'

By the time we had dumped our bags and collected up towels, water and torches, David had arrived, and we all jumped into the cruiser and took off down the long vlei in front of the house.

We'd heard the stories, read the books and seen the film – honey badgers have a high resistance to venom – no doubt about it. But Badger was young and well under adult weight. Would his body be able to handle a full squirt from a potentially lethal spitting cobra?

Khanye waved to us from some trees down one side of the vlei. We stopped, and as we climbed out of the vehicle, a

272

black and white tornado came hurtling out of the grass and hit David in the knees.

'Whoa, Badger!'

David grabbed him by the scruff of the neck and lifted him off the ground, trying to hold him at bay.

In the car, I'd been working out how we could possibly keep Badger's legs higher than his heart to slow down the poison during the drive to the vet in Bulawayo. Higher or lower? But hang on, the bite was in the head. What were we supposed to do about that? I'd always found first aid a trifle confusing. But I did remember one thing.

'Keep him quiet!' I shouted.

'Keep him *what*?' my son yelled back, while Badger went berserk, running circles around him and grabbing frenziedly onto feet, arms and legs as he tried to wrestle him to the ground. The two of them had always played strenuous games, particularly when David had been away, but this was getting far too rough. Picking a switch from a tree, Rich began swatting Badge's backside, but mostly missing it and belabouring David instead. Then somehow David broke free and took off towards the vehicle parked about 25 metres away, with Badger at full gallop, right behind him.

'Run, David!'

Badger's snapping jaws were inches from his feet as he flung open the vehicle door and leapt inside, slamming it shut behind him. But Badge wasn't conceding defeat. Up the front wheel he climbed and onto the bonnet, where he peered at David through the glass while busily removing the windscreen wipers. What on earth had got into him?

Khanye had been following him on the trail of a mouse, when they suddenly bumped into the cobra, which appeared to be as surprised as they were. It reared up, hood extended and wagged the end of its tail, using it as a decoy to distract Badger, just as the Bibron's and the puff adder had done when threatened. Badge fell for the trick, and the snake struck down and bit him on the head. Then it waited, head up and weaving slowly from side to side, anticipating another attack. But Badge was in pain, and for 10 minutes or so, he kept rubbing his head on the ground. When the snake slid away, he tracked it up cautiously and at a safe distance.

This was Badger's first confirmed bite from a potentially lethal snake, and yet other than hyping him up with a burst of adrenalin, it had had no effect on him at all. Of course, we had no idea how much venom he'd received – it may have been very little – but from the way he'd been rubbing his head, we were pretty certain it hadn't been a dry bite.

When Rich opened the gate of his house the next morning, he greeted us all in his usual jaunty fashion, then he was off down the vlei for another bout with his adversary, who had very wisely disappeared – though perhaps not far enough.

A couple of days later, Badge went back to the area and hunted down a cobra – probably the very same one. Having chased it down a hole, he dug till he found the tail and immediately tucked in. Then, when he'd eaten about a third of its body, he pulled it right out and bit it behind the head.

By this time, the snake was dead, or at least paralysed, but already it had managed to give Badger a bite on the cheek. He began frothing at the mouth, rolling around and rubbing his face and the back of his head on the ground. For a while, it sounded as though he was experiencing some difficulty breathing, but the symptoms didn't last long. Half an hour later, Badge – never modest about his achievements – was back with his victim, revelling in victory. He flung the cobra around, inviting Rich and Khanye to play, and when they wouldn't join in, he lay on his back and flicked it with a perfect aim, straight at Rich, who up until that moment had been filming. The cobra flew through the air and curled around his left leg, causing as Rich puts it: 'a little automatic survival reaction', involving much dancing about and yelling, which must have pleased Badger no end.

Strangely enough, he didn't return the following day to finish off his meal. Perhaps revenge had been sweet enough.

In summer, Badger's morning walks started much earlier and, since there was so much to occupy him close to home, these were far more leisurely. Friends visited more often and for longer in the warmer weather; not because they wanted to see us, of course, but in order to spend time with Badger.

Marina Jackson and her husband Dave were his most devoted admirers; Marina had even wiped family and friends from her computer screen in favour of a Badger slideshow, from his rather timid babyhood to the cocky little character he had become in his second year.

At the end of one November morning walk with the Jacksons and their friends the Brebners, Badger chose Aloe Koppie for his day retreat, accepted his apple and retired. And we went home for a late breakfast.

I was pouring coffee at the sideboard when the talk, unavoidably, turned to politics.

'So how do you feel about the nationalisation of the land?' John Brebner asked Rich.

'Well, they keep talking about it, but nothing's happened, so we are not letting it worry us.'

John sounded puzzled. 'But didn't you see the notice in the *Bulawayo Chronicle*?'

'What notice? We don't get the paper.'

'I saw it months ago. Stone Hills has been nationalised, I'm sure of it.'

Rich was shaking his head. 'You must be making a mistake. Someone would have mentioned it at one of the farmers' meetings.'

But John was adamant. And on the following morning, he phoned.

'I've got the cutting here, taken from the *Government Gazette* and dated the 19th of May 2006. Stone Hills is number six on the list. You've been "acquired for the State by the minister responsible for lands under a section of the constitution". Sorry to have been the bearer of such bad news.'

He put the phone down.

I called our lawyer in Harare, who had been inundated with unwinnable land cases since the year 2000. He was out and they didn't know when he'd be back in the office. I must have left 10 messages with his wearily polite secretary until he phoned back in the late afternoon.

'I'm not sure how this is all going to work itself out,' he told me. 'There have already been some letters of offer given out to the Big Wigs who have their eye on specific farms, but no Notices to Vacate have been served yet. As far as I am concerned,' (and I wondered if I detected a note of relief in his voice), 'this has got to be the last nail in the white farmers' coffin.'

Chapter Twenty-Five – In The Spotlight

For years, we had believed that we were off stage, standing unnoticed in the wings. Violent invasions, murders, imprisonment – all the horrific events that had destroyed farmers throughout the country since the year 2000 had somehow passed us by. We knew we couldn't escape forever, but maybe – if we kept our heads down ... We wouldn't have dared to put words to it, but that tiny whisper of hope was always there.

What fools we had been. In Africa, the wheel turns slowly, inexorably. 'You have the watches,' the war vets had told the farmers, 'but *we* have the time.' Stone Hills had been sidelined, never forgotten, and now we had been hauled out from the shadows and onto centre stage, blinking our eyes in the glare of the spotlight.

Rich called Gibson Sibanda, chief lands officer, and made an appointment for the following day at 9.30am.

Sitting on a small bulge off the main road some 10 kilometres from the Botswana border, Plumtree town is the administrative centre for the Bulalimamangwe District, which sounds grand but isn't. Once upon a time, it was a sedate little place, with a row of neat shops – the butcher, the baker, the grocer, the garage and the hardware man. And a café on the station platform, which sold the best meat pies in the world, according to the eternally starving boarders of Plumtree High School, founded in 1903, and for years the finest boys' school in the country.

Nowadays Plumtree is the seedy capital of the Wild West: the border town that's a centre for foreign exchange, and a haven for the wheeler dealers who ply their trade back and forth between the two countries.

A goat was tethered to a mango tree in the yard of the Lands Office, and a young man in dreadlocks sat slumped in the sun, his head in his hands. There were a couple of empty beer bottles under his chair. The office door was shut.

'He's out,' said the man without bothering to look up.

'Any idea how long he'll be?'

'Maybe two hours. Can you spare me some money for a drink?'

'Sorry, we need it to buy fuel. Please tell Mr Sibanda we'll be back later.'

We drove to the fuel station, and stopped at the end of a long, haphazard line of vehicles interspersed with large rocks left there by customers who had driven away but wanted to keep their place in the queue. I'd brought a book with me, anticipating a delay, but after I'd read one page four times, I put it away and stared out of the window, my thoughts in turmoil.

Were they planning on taking us over completely, or would we be allowed to stay? And, if so, how would we protect our animals? Tourists had long since abandoned Zimbabwe, so hunting was considered the only way to make money out of wildlife. Was this what they had in mind for Stone Hills?

Soon after the invasions started, a local businessman and his family had visited the lodge.

'The trouble with you white people,' Themba Ncube told us over lunch, when the talk had as usual turned to politics, 'is that you just don't understand. Your support of the opposition, and your legal cases against the government make sense to you, but in our culture, you have accused the king, and that can't be tolerated.'

'But how else can we defend ourselves?' we protested.

'There are other ways of getting to the king. Maybe you should have sought some help from those with experience, who could have interpreted and guided you through the right channels. You've relied on white lawyers, when you should have been looking at the bigger picture.'

And what was that? Witch doctors, tribal customs, following the shadowy, obscure labyrinths that lead to the ears of the all-powerful? We wouldn't have known where to start.

The sun is high and hot, so I open the car window, and Plumtree town comes swinging in to the rhythm of the music that blares from every shop along its dusty streets.

280

An old man is sitting on the greasy steps of a general store next to a couple of bags of empty plastic bottles. He's having an animated conversation with himself, pointing and gesturing, and smiling, presumably when agreement has been reached.

Vendors sit under their faded beach umbrellas; little groups of people laugh and chat, and strangers join in. Fingers linked, couples stroll amongst pyramids of polished tomatoes and the lengths of coloured cloth hanging on wooden rods, blindingly bright in the sunshine.

The fuel queue crawls forward, and we are now beside an oleander tree, its fallen white flowers lying crushed on the pavement. A woman sits outside the dark green door of Sandy's Hair Salon, polishing her nails. Business is slow. There are deep cracks in its walls, and red paint flaking off its corrugated iron roof.

Police and soldiers in uniform wander by – people don't stop talking, but they turn their heads to watch them when they have passed.

At one stall, a lady wearing an upended felt fruit bowl decorated with a Christmas ribbon is guarding a bag of bread rolls. Thanks to the proximity of the border, there's more to buy in Plumtree than in Bulawayo, particularly for those who dabble in foreign exchange. This is the millinery capital of Matabeleland: flower pots are the current fashion, studded with sparkling stars in red, blue and black. I glance back and the old man on the steps is giving himself a lecture, and he's getting angry. He wags his finger and sticks out a pink tongue as he talks.

The cars begin to move, and we hastily wind up our windows to stop the diesel fumes from flooding the cab. Beside us, in the deep pool of shade of a mango tree, an old woman sits on the broken pavement next to her stall, her legs outstretched. Two fat, well-dressed girls approach with a wad of cash. After a bit of half-hearted haggling, they buy a roll of white lace. Gogo smiles, revealing a crooked row of brown teeth, and tucks the money down the front of her blouse.

A bus roars by crabwise on a misaligned axle, its back end halfway across the other side of the road, and I can see children's faces pressed up against its grubby windows. Then three little girls, scrubbed clean in green and white cotton uniforms, run across the street in front of us. They are so small that I can barely see their heads over the bull bars of the Toyota. They look up at me, and all three squeak, 'Hi!' and give me toothy smiles.

We are back at the Lands Office an hour and a half later, with a tank full of fuel. The goat is bleating, the young man has gone, and a sudden whirlwind sucks up the plastic bags lying in the yard and blows them against the fence. The door is open and there is the lands officer, Rich's old adversary, peering at us through his thick glasses over a pile of important looking papers.

'Ah, Mr Sibanda!' says my husband. 'I think you've been avoiding us.'

'No, no, Mr Peek,' he replies hurriedly. 'A little business to attend to, that's all.'

Greetings commence. We enquire after each other's health, our families. Mr Sibanda wants to know how the farm is doing, and how the animals are. How much rain have you had? Are your dams full? Any visitors to the lodge? I look at the maps on the wall, and there's Stone Hills, amongst many other farms, ringed in red.

The young man with the dreadlocks comes in and holds out a languid hand. Mr Sibanda introduces him as the new

District Administrator. He sits down next to me and his breath is rancid with the smell of stale beer and cigarettes. Surreptitiously, I lean away from him.

There's a pause.

'Mr Sibanda, we are here because we believe that Stone Hills has been nationalised.'

'Yes' he replies carefully. 'Technically speaking, that is correct.'

'So does that mean that the government are going to take our land away?'

The lands officer scratches his chin, hesitates.

'No-o-o, not necessarily.'

'Then what?'

'Well, from a technical point of view, you might be required to take a partner.'

'A partner?' My husband raises his voice, and Sibanda flinches, probably wishing his little business had taken him right out of town for the next three weeks.

'But you know we don't make any money out of the place,' Rich spreads his hands, empty. 'No tourism – no profits. There's nothing for a partner to take.'

Except for two thousand head of game – but Mr Sibanda knows that as well as we do.

He looks across at the DA for support, but he's asleep, or comatose. Or maybe he is dead. It's hard to tell.

Rich stands up and glares at Sibanda over the pile of papers.

'You obviously know who this partner is. What's his name?'

'Well, actually, it's a lady. She is interested in the land, but I'm afraid I cannot tell you who it is'.

'A lady. A member of the government, I suppose?'

Sibanda nods unhappily.

'And if we want to nominate our own partner? Technically speaking, of course.'

'Oh yes!' Sibanda brightens, sensing escape. 'That is a *very* good idea. You can submit a letter to the Ministry of Lands.'

I groan and they both turn and look at me. Another waste of time concocting a letter to the Ministry – one of the hundreds we have already sent – never to be opened or acknowledged. The DA's arms are folded and he's slipped even further down his chair. Any minute now, he'll be sitting on the floor.

Rich's phone goes, and he steps out of the office. I sit there dumbly, while Sibanda riffles around with his papers, looking quite cheerful.

'Mrs Peek,' he says suddenly. 'Could you find me a job in Australia?'

Rich's voice comes from behind me before I can reply. 'Forget it, Mr Sibanda, you're not going anywhere. If I'm staying in this bloody country, so are you!'

We drive back into Plumtree to see if we can buy some sugar. The music hasn't let up – jerky, repetitive rhythms, rolling drum beats. The music and words seem somehow disconnected.

The old man on the steps has gone to sleep, his head is resting on the bag of empty bottles.

Everything has changed, yet everything remains the same. And there is no sugar.

You whites, you don't understand ...

Only Africans know how to live in Africa; we need the pills.

There was nothing more we could do, except wait. Just as we had always done. We could write another hundred letters to the Ministry, but we knew that the decision had been made and nothing would change. It only remained to be seen who our 'partner' was and what she wanted. She certainly wouldn't be looking for a country retreat, and we guessed it wouldn't be too long before she made her first move.

Thank God for the rain. It kept coming, and our politically correct pied poodle was in his element. Now there was more prey around, he had the chance of honing some of the skills he had learned in the last rainy season. Like dealing with tortoises – those tricky little blighters wedged into their shells, as grimly determined to hang on as Badger was to extract them. He dragged them over the rocks, spent hours trying to winkle them out with claws and teeth, until in utter exasperation, he would drop them at our feet, demanding help.

But now there were pools in the river, and he hit on another plan. When he had located his victim, Badger carried it down to the water and dropped it on the bank, where he sat on it for a few seconds, pondering. Then he got up, tested the depth of the water, and pushed the tortoise in. And when it came up to the surface, he pushed it down again with his paws and held it under water. If he'd left it a bit longer, it would have drowned, as was no doubt his intention, but being Badger, he couldn't wait. He kept scooping it up to check if it was dead, and when the poor creature hadn't cooperated, he grabbed it by the edge of the shell and trotted off back into the bush, there to work on other means of finding his way into Pandora's box.

At two years old, he was a competent hunter, and although he normally came home at night for a meal, he was quite capable of feeding himself, just as any wild young badger would have been at that age. It was quite an achievement for the motherless cub who had arrived in a shoebox, traumatised, malnourished and close to death.

The only serious gap in his education was etiquette: Badger style – and for all of us, manners aren't instinctive. They must be learned. If I hadn't disciplined my son at an early age, for instance, he'd still be spitting at guests, biting old ladies and putting sausages up his nose.

The fact is, we all need to mix with our own kind, if only to maintain a semblance of normality. Rich and I are happy hermits, quite content to bumble about on what feels like our own, peaceful little island: an impression that is only strengthened by the luxuriance of my husband's Robinson Crusoe beard.

Our neighbours are not the usual hotchpotch of people who make up a farming community. With very few exceptions, they are members of the Rosenfels family (hereinafter referred to as 'The Family' – any resemblance to any other family, living or dead, being purely coincidental). Their forebears trekked up to Rhodesia by ox wagon in 1894, just over 40 years after the conquering Matabele army arrived under King Mzilikazi.

They all stayed: Matabele warriors and Rosenfels alike, and thanks to the very considerable fruit of their loins, you have to be pretty careful of what you say about The Family anywhere around Bulawayo in case you are speaking to a relative. Of course, they slander each other with impunity, but as one wife told a newcomer to the clan: let one outsider criticise them, and they stand together, shoulder to shoulder, like a herd of buffalo.

I was quite sure that the neighbours had written us off as relatively harmless loonies long before, until I had a conversation with Yvonne Rosenfels, who has lived with her husband on an adjoining farm for the past 51 years, and who I had hitherto regarded as a central figure in Marula's vibrant social scene.

'You know,' she said, patting my arm confidentially, 'We're quite happy alone on the farm. I wouldn't care if I never saw another soul.'

That's what we think, but when an invitation came to a party at Val and Charlie Ross's farm at Figtree to celebrate the spilling of the Mananda Dam, we were absolutely delighted. I didn't own a dress, but it was a chance to air my newly purchased straw hat, and Rich could dig out his blue shirt and khaki longs – à la Sir David Attenborough.

We sat in the car for a while after we arrived, surrounded by other vehicles, listening to the hubbub of voices from the lawn and feeling a bit daunted. But then someone spied us and yelled: 'Come on, the Peeks, what are you doing out there?' and we could hide no longer.

Within minutes, drinks in our hands, we had lost each other in the crowd, and for the first time in months, maybe years, we felt as though we were part of a community. No one spoke about politics. No one wanted to: this was a celebration, a time of bad jokes and good humour and, yes, thankfulness, for those few amongst us who were lucky enough still to be on our farms in the country that we loved.

While we were having lunch, a huge bolt of lightning struck very close by, and we all ducked instinctively, hoping – at least on our part – that it would be anywhere but in the dining room, where Val had laid out mountains of spectacular food. We all agreed it had been the best party ever, and we swore to do it again, often, although of course we haven't.

It has struck me occasionally that some of our neighbours'

earlier reticence about the Peeks might have had something to do with the last meeting of the Marula Farmers' Association (MFA), held a couple of years before.

Rich had been chairman for the past three years, not because he was the people's choice as such, but more because no one in The Family wanted the job. Before the land invasions and the collapse of commercial farming, meetings were a pleasant social event; now there was rarely anything positive on the agenda – only more time-wasting forms to be filled out, and depressing reports of land invasions, eviction notices and legal proceedings.

The ladies of the district took it in turns to act as secretary, quietly taking the minutes and occasionally putting in their two bobs' worth if the occasion arose. I did turn up at a couple of meetings to lend my support to the new chairman when he was first elected, but thereafter the pressure of work and my responsibilities to Badger, particularly at that time of the month, always conspired to keep me at home. My only contribution was 'something for tea', which was usually a plate of biscuits that Rich invariably brought back untouched, ignored by The Family in favour of their own expertly baked chocolate cakes, cream scones and savoury quiches, which they still miraculously produced even when there was nothing in the shops.

I managed to duck out of my responsibilities until 2006, when almost all the other ladies had decamped to town. Besides the gardener, who didn't want the job, there was no other choice. Rich came back from the meeting bearing the plate of biscuits and gave me the news. Like it or not, I was the chairman's moll, and the time had come to stand by my man.

So here we are at 2pm on a winter afternoon, sitting side by side at the long table facing The Family, plus a few hangers-on who are regarded with suspicion by all of us in case they are informers. Everyone is watching me, but mostly because they're fed up with looking at Rich, and there's nothing behind me but an empty stage.

First up is the veterinary report; a long discussion ensues about foot and mouth disease, and although I do try and take notes, after 10 minutes I can feel myself slipping away. I don't know what it is about meetings, but they make me terribly tired particularly after lunch. Frequent sips of water don't help. I rest my chin in my hand, staring fixedly ahead. Then I suddenly wake with a start, to the sound of snickering. All eyes are on the new secretary. Thank God I didn't drool.

Peter Rosenfels has acquired a mule from Mike Woods. But the mule has attacked and injured two handlers, bitten the tail off a dairy cow, declared war on a drum full of toxic gas and destroyed a 20-litre water container.

'Any comment on that, Mike?' asks the chairman.

'I'm not really surprised,' comes the laconic reply. 'Mules do have their bad days.'

For some reason, I note down that conversation in detail.

Time for tea. Someone has left our biscuits in the kitchen, still in their tin. I gorge myself on Betty Rosenfels' carrot cake, hoping that the sugar will help me stay awake for the rest of the afternoon.

Afterwards, Rich tries to persuade everyone to join a new association, set up to protect farmers' rights in Matabeleland. All the members of the MFA already belong to the Harare-based Commercial Farmers' Union but there's a general feeling that they are not paying proper attention to their members, so now some of our farmers want to do the job themselves. It's a hard one to sell: everyone is fed up with papers, forms and paying up, when there are no results to show for it. Rich explains in detail, and hands around the application forms.

'What's this?' asks Ernest Rosenfels.

'An application form for SACFA,' says Rich

'What's that?'

I'm very glad I'm not the only one who's been asleep.

Mr Ncube, the new boy at the district council, arrives dressed in a tight leather jacket. He obviously hadn't been told about the tea. Rather unwisely, he has come in search of levies. Although we all pay the council exorbitant annual rates to fix our roads, they haven't touched them for years, so we grade them ourselves. We can't refuse to pay, or it will give them another excuse to take the land. But our money has not gone to waste: council has just erected a lovely shade cloth shelter for their vehicles at their offices in Plumtree, a fact that is not lost on the members of the Marula Farmers' Association.

'And what has happened to the investigation into the millions of dollars that are missing from your funds?' asks Ernest, leaning forward with his hand cupped around his ear. He's a long time member of council and no pussycat when it comes to facing down officialdom.

There's a light sweat on Mr Ncube's brow, and his eyes are bulging, but he has come prepared. He launches into his response: 'Councilinfrastructuremovingforward minutestabledworkinprogressworkingagenda,' he gabbles.

Heartened by the stunned look on the faces of his audience, he shouts, he gesticulates, he spits with emotion, his voice rising higher as questions are fired at him.

'Insofarasworkingpapersbudgetsapprovedallstakeholders ratifications I am not the one ...'

The vibrations of his voice bounce off the walls and make him even less coherent.

Ernest sits and glares at him.

In the end, Mr Ncube is forced to admit that there is no money. But he has an innovative solution to the problem. The Marula Farmers' Association must write a letter to the council. That'll fix it!

He takes off towards the door: 'Okaythankyouverymuch,' mopping his face with a handkerchief.

'Go well,' growls Ernest, then mutters something derogatory under his breath.

We hear Mr Ncube's motorbike putt-putt-puttering away from the Farmers' Hall in the direction of the local store and the bar.

Now it's time for the report on roads. This is going to be a struggle. The mule and Mr Ncube were at least a humorous diversion, but there's not much in corrugations and maintenance to bring a smile to your face.

The voices drone on. I can feel myself floating away. I try to force my eyes open, take a few notes, look alert, but a few minutes later I have slipped back into la-la-land. Then the sound of Rich's fist thumping the table has me wide awake; there are raised voices, hands being waved about. Confrontation. Something to write about in my next book.

Rich and Rob Rosenfels are hard at it. The chairman's eyes are glittering; Rob is on his feet, brick-red with emotion. What's going on? Rich says that we must stop fixing our own roads. That's what we pay council for and if we keep doing it, they never will.

Rob disagrees. They are never going to do anything, however much we hound them. We must fix the roads ourselves.

I can't see what all the fuss is about. Might as well have another little snooze while everyone else is occupied. But suddenly, there's a loud scraping of the chair next to me. The chairman is on his feet, his beard bristling. He's had four years of this – he's sick to death of politics, foot and mouth disease, district councils, letters, papers, infrastructuresminutesagendasramificationsratifications and Iamnottheone.

'No one,' he declares, '*ever* listens to my suggestions. So, as far as I am concerned,' he glares around him, 'you can all fuck off.'

And those were the last words ever spoken at a Marula Farmers' Meeting. Not being sure of the correct procedure, but ever loyal, the new secretary writes, 'Fuck Off' in her notepad, puts it in her bag and slips out of the back door. I get home just in time to join Khanye on the afternoon Badger walk.

And I never did get around to writing up those minutes.

Chapter Twenty-Six – On The Wagon

The Rosenfels family has been a part of the Marula district for almost 120 years.

Their story began sometime in the early 1890s, when a peddler arrived at the Gibson farmhouse near Nylstroom in what is now South Africa's Limpopo province. His name was Max Rosenfels, and he was a German Jew who had arrived in South Africa some years before to work with his uncles in their trading stores. Max began to pay regular visits to the farm, not just for business, but also because young Jessie Gibson, who at over 6 feet tall towered above his diminutive

5 feet 2 inches, had taken his fancy.

Young Rosenfels was pretty direct. Instead of wasting time on courtship, he went straight to Jessie's parents.

'I like the look of your daughter,' he said. 'She seems like a hard-working girl. May I have her hand in marriage?'

Her parents consented, but when Max proposed, Jessie was very dubious.

'I hardly know you!' she protested, to which Max replied: 'Well, we'll soon sort *that* out.'

Which was far from a romantic start to a marriage that was eventually to spawn a tribe and to lead young Jessie into the wild interior of Africa, far from the safety of home and family.

'I can still see her sitting by candlelight, her grey head bent over some sewing,' begins a lovely piece entitled *Things My Grandmother Told Me*, penned by Rosa York, the eldest of Jessie and Max's nine grandchildren.

' "Just the coincidence of your Grandfather's meeting Mr Tom Meikle in Blauberg altered the whole course of my life," she told me. "Grandfather came home excited. Matabeleland was the country of the future, and carried away by his enthusiasm, we forthwith packed up our farm, and the country store we had in the Transvaal, and set off on our long journey of two and a half months to the 'Promised Land'.

"A span of 18 oxen drew our wagon, which was loaded to capacity with requirements for the journey, and with essentials we would need to set up home in wild and little-known country. We took with us some spare oxen, cows and calves, nine donkeys, and three native servants. On the coir mattress inside the wagon tent was the wicker basket that held our baby daughter, Rosa, not yet one month old.

"At the wide Limpopo River, a Mr Lee had a pont and it took him all day with repeated trips to row our stock and belongings across. Only the top of the tent wagon was above water when it was towed across. The next morning we found that our servants had deserted, as they were afraid of the Matabele.

"Then started a gruelling two-month journey. Grandfather drove the ox wagon over a road that was little more than a track, and I led the oxen and tried to herd the cows and donkeys ahead of me on the road at the same time. When they wandered off the road we had to stop the wagon to fetch them back.

"To add to our difficulties, watering places were few and far between and when we did arrive at a suitable stream, we generally camped, bathed and did our washing. I fried doughnuts, pumpkin fritters or pancakes. I had also packed home-made rusks, biltong (dried meat) and dried fruits. Occasionally, we managed to shoot a buck or a guinea fowl. How we enjoyed the fresh meat, the pot-baked beans, stamped mealies or mealie porridge and gravy! Afterwards we would sit by the fire, sipping our coffee with the starry autumnal night around us, and only a slight chill in the air. The fire had to be kept up all night as there was a real danger of marauding animals.

"Once the 'longwagon' broke, and Grandfather and I spent days making and fitting a new one from tree trunk we had chopped down. This was no easy task.

"Sometimes when we had outspanned, our wagon would be visited by curious but unaggressive natives, who would stand around the outspan, or squat on their haunches, quite uncivilised, barely covered by two small aprons of tanned skin, fore and aft. Some carried spears and knobbed sticks, their hunting weapons.

"We mostly travelled alone, but occasionally other wagons would catch up, travel with us for a day or so, then go on ahead or lag behind. These fellow travellers were always very kind.

"Fortunately, my baby, Rosa, was very good and slept most of the time, but one day I had a frightening experience. In a wagon pocket, I kept medicines, including a bottle of brandy. The constant jogging of the wagon caused the brandy to leak onto baby's pillow, and the fumes anaesthetised her for about 24 hours. I cried, but Grandfather kept feeling her pulse and assuring me that she would recover once she had slept it off.

"At the end of July, we arrived in Bulawayo. This mushroom township, consisting mostly of mud huts, tin shanties and tents had sprung up within a few months. At the end of the Matabele War (in 1893), Lobengula, King of the Matabele, had fled north, leaving his royal village a heap of ashes. The settlers then promptly put up their own habitations on the site of the ruins.

"We had little money so we pawned our jewellery. Mr Peters looked suspiciously at Grandfather asking whether he had acquired it honestly, and Grandfather, who had once lost £50 000 overnight in a Johannesburg gold mining venture, smilingly reassured Mr Peters. They often had a good laugh about their first meeting.

"Grandfather was one of the first traders to cross the Zambezi River, trading beads, copper wire, cotton prints and blankets for goats, fowls, grain and native cattle. That trip took two months.

"I started a laundry, and was kept very busy supervising and doing the ironing myself of all the starched clothes commonly worn in those days. From my savings, we bought a farm for £80.

"Unfortunately, the warlike Matabele warriors had not been finally subdued, and in the outside districts were massing for an attack on the handful of white settlers. One morning in March 1896, we found that our natives including the native police had deserted. Exhausted messengers galloped in from outlying places to tell of families being cruelly murdered. My brother who had been mining was amongst the casualties.

"In Bulawayo itself, a laager of wagons drawn up to form a circle and fortified with sandbags and barbed wire, was hastily constructed around the brick and iron market building. All the inhabitants were ordered to gather there without delay. We hastily packed a few essentials and moved into the laager. It was fortunate that we did, for that night bands of marauders burned our house and killed every living thing on the place, including our bitch with her pups.

"For six months, we lived in the laager, and cooked on open fires next to our wagons. The weekly washing was done at the Matsheumhlope River, a few hundred yards away. Sometimes while we were busy, the alarm would be given, and a fantastic flight of women would rush up the hill, their arms full of washing, their skirts hitched up for speedier travel, and their wide knicker-laces flapping in the wind.

"On our eighth day in the laager, your father (Sigmund Julius, but always known as 'Boet') was born, the Market Hall bar having been converted into a maternity ward. Grandfather was in the Town Guard, and one day whilst on patrol he found a deserted native baby crying in a derelict kraal. Grandfather brought him to me, and I took him into our wagon, and nursed him and brought him up with my own baby, otherwise he would certainly have died. He grew up on our farm as a trustworthy servant.

"After the Rebellion, we opened a second-hand store, and

I not only ran it, but also took in dressmaking and cared for my home and family.

"Some time later, we bought our present farm and I farmed while Grandfather carried on the business in town, and the children went to school there. The new railway line from the Union of South Africa had now been built as far as Bulawayo, so on Mondays I travelled out by train the 45 miles to the siding nearest to our farm. There was usually a servant and horse to meet me, but failing that, I walked the 10 miles to our farm. I did this once carrying a bag of silver to the value of £150 ... The further I walked, the heavier the bag became!

"During the week, I farmed or personally supervised the ploughing, the cattle, the erection of fences and so on. At weekends I returned to Bulawayo to be with, and give attention to my family. In 1907, we sold the shop and settled permanently on the farm.

"Times have changed since those days when people travelled by cart! Ours used to be the 'halfway house' where travellers stopped for the night, or for some hours to rest their oxen and horses. When your father celebrated his 21st birthday, friends came from far and near, and stayed for three days, feasting, dancing and merrymaking, some climbing into their wagons only for a few hours of sleep. When the meat for the barbeque ran short, we simply killed another ox. Today everyone is in a hurry, and there is hardly time for a cup of tea and a chat ..."

'Grandmother was a foundation member of the local WI and one of its staunchest members. When she passed on, she was nearly 80, but the impact of her personality was felt by the whole district. I have heard one woman say: "She was the most real person I ever met."

'Now she is at peace, buried amongst the blue hills of the farm she loved and worked for.'

Sadly, young Rosa died in her teens from blackwater fever. Boet, a tall and rather shy young man, lived and worked on the farm with his parents after he left school. In 1922, he married Lois Shone, whose family had arrived in grand style at Marula siding in 1909 from the Orange Free State. They chartered a train and packed it with family members, servants, all their possessions, their furniture, cattle, sheep and fowls. And as if that wasn't enough, there were two cart horses named Charlie and Moscow, together with a four-wheeled phaeton carriage; their beloved Collie dog Rover; and a few ostriches, 'which in the melee of getting housed and settled escaped, and for years afterwards could occasionally be glimpsed in the bush,' wrote Lois. The family lived on Wilfred's Hope Farm on Stone Hills' northern boundary, opposite the present Marula School.

'Of this little home ...' Lois continued, 'I have the clearest recollection and such loving nostalgia. Dad and a couple of labourers built the house of pole and dagha (mud) in much the same manner in which the native huts were built, except that it was oblong in shape, about 12 feet wide and 30 feet long, having a dividing wall across the centre.'

All but the last of their nine children were born on Stokestown Farm with only a midwife in attendance. And at the time of writing in 2010, eight of them, four boys and four girls, still survive. Rosa, the eldest is nearly 90, and John, the youngest is 62. Charlie, the fourth son, died in 1979 during Rhodesia's Bush War, when the vehicle in which he was travelling was blown up by a landmine.

When James and Vicky Rosenfels were married on Stokestown in 2004, it marked 100 years since the farm had been purchased by Jessie and Max, and I think it's safe to say that they would have been flabbergasted to know that their somewhat antisocial son had been responsible for 35 grandchildren, 62 great-grandchildren and, to date, six great-great-grandchildren.

All five grandsons were members of the Rhodesian Bisley team (long-range target shooting), and in 1965, Ernest won the Elkington Trophy for the finest shots in the Commonwealth. Max Snr (the eldest son) served in the Second World War, and became a senator in the newly independent Zimbabwe government in 1980.

Rich and I wanted to start gathering some of the family stories, so a couple of years ago, we picked up Julius Rosenfels from his house on Good Luck and took him down to Ernest and Betty's Glenmore Farm (or what is left of it), some 13 kilometres down the Mangwe Road.

We found Ernest in his workshop, in an apron and floppy hat, frowning through his spectacles at a broken part for the mill operated by some of the squatters on their farm. Ernest is no longer a cattle farmer. The squatters have occupied all but 1 500 hectares of his land – far too little for a commercial herd. And they've left him one small dam, from which water cannot be pumped. Yet they always bring their problems to him, and they'd be astonished if he refused to help. War veterans, invaders, squatters, settlers – whatever you choose to call them doesn't really matter, because they are here to stay. They are subsistence farmers, used to keeping a few cattle and growing a patch of mealies in their backyard in the traditional way. They have no experience, no money, no training, and no support from government. So the land lies idle, and with people like the Rosenfels out of business, the beef industry has collapsed, as has the rest of Zimbabwean agriculture.

Julius is Mr Greenfingers, the man who grew prize-winning Turkish tobacco, until sanctions against Ian Smith's Rhodesian government put an end to the country's exports. Ernest's son Neville has either built, rehabilitated or repaired at least 150 dams in Matabeleland, either for commercial farmers or for rural development. And Ernest is the craftsman. His love is for hardwoods – the fallen mukwa, olives and rosewood trees, which he turns into exquisite pieces of furniture: tables, chairs, lamps and yokes, and even a cot for a new member of the clan. But his pièce de résistance is a trek wagon, lovingly and perfectly restored by himself and Neville, and very like the one that carried his grandparents to this country in 1894.

Ernest leads us out to what he calls their scrap heap, but this is no ordinary pile of discarded metal. He picks up an axle inscribed with the words Gilpin 1896; these are the parts of old wagons they've been collecting for years.

Everything has been done as it used to be, and no detail has been overlooked. Like all the old wagons, it is constructed of individual parts that could be dismantled and carried across a river. The main structure is made of knobby thorn, and the soft, flexible wood of the cabbage tree is used for the brakes. The chickens were carried in a cage that hung from a large metal hook underneath. They'd all jump out when the wagon outspanned at the end of the day, then rush back to the cage in a fluster the next morning when they heard the crack of the whip and the lowing of the oxen – terrified of being left behind.

Ernest is a hard man, but he has the soul of a poet. 'This is my life,' he says, bending down to replace the axle on the heap. 'My brothers think I'm mad, but I love it.'

We have tea on the veranda of their homestead, looking out over the cool oasis of colour that is Betty's garden. She is a soft-spoken lady with kind brown eyes – everyone's favourite granny, at her happiest when she is tending her roses. From their veranda, the distant sky is white with smoke from a fire that's been burning for days. The settlers torch the dry veld early to bring on green grass for their cattle, and with no firebreaks and unpredictable winter winds, their fires often run out of control. There are four zebra standing in the adjoining paddock in the shade of one of the only trees left in a wide expanse of brown grass – one of them has a snare hanging loosely around its neck. Ernest has found hundreds of them in the bush, and the back of his trailer is full of rusty wire. A few days ago, he tells us, a herd of 16 exhausted impala passed by the house, having been chased there by dogs.

Betty brings the tea tray, the stories begin and, just as we had hoped, the two old boys fire each other up. They are both a bit deaf, so there are plenty of contradictions and raised voices. Chawl and Solly they call each other – nicknames they have used since childhood.

As soon as the children were six, they were packed off by donkey cart to board at Marula School, which had been started by Lois's mother, a qualified teacher, soon after they arrived in the country. They were carefree days. After Sunday school and tea, when the unfortunate girls were put to darning socks and other good works, old man Walton, the headmaster, would chase the boys, about 30 of them, away for the day. Off you go,' he'd say, 'I don't want to see your faces till 5pm.'

'We used to run those koppies on Stone Hills flat,' recalls Ernest. 'We were naughty little buggers. Often we used to pinch old man Unwin's donkeys from the pound, but when we got back, he'd be waiting for us with a sjambok. Then we got clever, and we'd let them go halfway back and run home.'

He holds out his cup for Betty to get him another cup of rooibos tea.

'In the rainy season, we used to go north of the railway line to Hopps Pool on the Mananda River, about 5 kilometres from the school. We'd be alone, no supervision, and after the rains the river would be a raging torrent. I couldn't swim – I still can't – but we'd slide down the rocks on slippery *sekuku* (soap nettle) leaves, leap in and see if we could get to the other side. A bit different from today when everyone is *kangela*-ing (watching) their kids,' he says rather scornfully, moving his head from side to side as if he's following a tennis match.

'Well,' says Rich, 'your folks had nine of you – they could afford to lose half!'

Lois Rosenfels was another extraordinary woman.

'She brought us all up with no electricity, no telephone, no running water, no shop around the corner,' says Julius. 'If one of us felt sick, she'd line us all up, hold our noses, and give us a dose of castor oil. The only time one of us was really ill was when Mary Lois got appendicitis in her teens. Mom made all our clothes, and when she heard about some really poor kids at the school, she'd tell the headmaster to give them ours and she'd make some more. On long weekends, Dad used to send a wagon to the school to pick up all the kids who had been left behind, often around 20 of them. They'd bring their mattresses and blankets, and the boys would sleep in the storeroom, the girls on the veranda of the house.'

The stories go on: an encounter with an infuriated Egyptian cobra that Ernest pulled out of its hole; Julius' crawling into a cave after a drag mark and finding himself face-to-face with a leopard; Ernest, at 21 years old, seeing Betty for the first time up a tree with her seven sisters: 'We had to shake the tree to get them out!' he says.

Only three of the brothers now live permanently in the district. As we drive out, Betty is sitting on a wall under an old fig tree outside their house, wearing a straw hat with a red ribbon. An enormous flowering leopard orchid tumbles down from a hollow in the trunk. Her arm is around her black Staffordshire terrier, and I sense her loneliness. She says she never wants to leave, but Glenmore is far down the Mangwe Road, her family is gone and visitors are rare.

On the way home, we drive up to the Pioneer Memorial on the summit of the Mangwe Pass. Made from great flat slabs of dressed granite, it was erected by Boet Rosenfels in 1954 – to 'honour their memory': a hundred years after the first wagon, carrying missionary Robert Moffat and trader Sam Edwards, came rumbling over the pass and into the land of King Mzilikazi and his fierce Matabele warriors – who had themselves only arrived from South Africa some 16 years before.

A Verreaux's eagle sits out on the rocks above us, its nest clearly visible on a cliff face streaked with yellow lichen. Tracks have been made in the cement below the memorial: Boet's feet have walked next to the hoof prints of two oxen, Roman and Witvoet, and those of a horse called Joe. The original road took a sharp turn around the back of the memorial, and Julius shows us the scratch marks left there by passing wagons.

From there we drive to the family cemetery, its entrance

framed by the axles of Max and Jessie's original wagon. There are graves and alcoves in the wall where, amongst those of other family members, lie the ashes of Chappie Rosenfels, Ernest and Betty's oldest son, who was killed during the Bush War when he went to the assistance of a wounded comrade; and Ian, son of Max Snr and Mary Rosenfels, killed on their farm during a spell of R and R when he joined the police reserve on a follow up.

It's a hot, dry day. We can hear the sound of crickets, the rustle of dead leaves. Ernest and Julius have lived amongst these hills all their lives, but now the roots that their family have put down over a century ago are exposed, and their foothold in this land is increasingly insecure. History has come and gone, sweeping away the rule of the Matabele and now the white man. Julius is nearly 80; Ernest is 81. For all the tragedies and anxieties they have suffered, they have led full and fascinating lives, and they can be proud of the contribution that they and their family have made to the land of their birth.

'I've had a good innings,' Ernest remarked, running his hands over the smooth wood of a small table he had just completed.

And so he has.

THE PACE OF THE OX

What do we know (and what do we care) of
    Time and his Silver scythe?
Since there is always time to spare so long as a
    man's alive:
The world may come, and the world may go,
    and the world may whistle by,
But the Pace of the Ox is steady (and slow), and
    life is a lullaby.

What do we know of the city's scorn, the hum of
    the world amaze,
Hot-foot haste, and the fevered dawn, and
    forgotten yesterdays?
Men may strain and women may strive in busier
    lands to-day,
But the Pace of the Ox is the pace to thrive in
    the land of veld and vlei.

Crimson dawn in the Eastern sky, purple glow in
    the West,
Thus it is that the days go by, bringing their
    meed of rest –
The future's hidden behind a veil, and the past is
    still the past –
But the Pace of the Ox is the sliding scale that
    measures our work at last.

The song of the ships is far to hear, the hum of
    the world is dead,

And lotus life in a drowsy year our benison
    instead;
Why should we push the world along, live in a
    whirl of flame,
When the Pace of the Ox is steady and strong
    and the end is just the same?

Henry Cullen Gouldsbury

Chapter Twenty-Seven – Wings

November 2006 was the month that Badger stepped out of the protective circle of family and friends and into his own perilous world. I wasn't there to see it. At aged 91, my father had suffered a stroke from which it seemed unlikely he would recover. I left for Australia, and in doing so, unwittingly released Badge from the maternal bonds that had been holding him back from true independence.

Early one morning, he left for Marshlands, and now Rich takes up the story:

He stayed there for the day and we found him close to the

Sandown boundary on the Shashani River. He came a lot of the way home, either in front or following the vehicle with one of us running alongside, but when he reached the Stone Hills boundary, he turned and headed straight back again.

It's very hard to face, but Badger does not want to come home. He needs his freedom, and that's the reality. I only hope he can sidestep all the human dangers and not get caught up in dog hunts or with people who like to shoot small carnivores. There is no hunting on Marshlands at the moment, but he'll probably go even further afield.

Using the receiver, Khanye located Badger the following afternoon, deep in the hills around half a kilometre away from the Marshlands hunting lodge. Rich drove as close as he could and called him.

He came, in his own good time, having obviously only just woken up after a wild night, in every sense. He was very pleased to see us and curled up in my lap, giving me a secret Badger moment. He looked as though he hadn't eaten properly since he left home two days before, so it must have been other badgers that lured him there. Perhaps he recognises my status as Stone Hills' dominant 'badger', but since we have such a good rapport, he would rather move away than challenge me.

Rich opened the back door of the vehicle's canopy and threw in some small pieces of meat, but Badge wasn't falling for that one. He put his feet on the tailgate, grabbed the meat and ran off with it. Only when Rich himself climbed into the back was Badger persuaded to join him. And as he clambered over Rich's legs to reach the meat in the far corner, Khanye closed the doors.

Apart from when he had arrived as a tiny cub, Badge had never travelled in a vehicle. At first he panicked and tried to get out, but very briefly. Then he seemed to resign himself to the fact that both he and I were captives, and he settled down to contemplate his position. He didn't try to scratch at the door or windows, or bite at the rubber as I would have expected. He just looked a little disturbed, though definitely accepting.

Khanye started the engine, and turned it off quickly. Badge did not react. He then allowed the vehicle to roll backwards and down a hill very slowly. Badger just sat with head lowered, listening and thinking. The next step was to drive, at walking pace, along the road to let him get the feel of the movement. He didn't like that. He stood on my lap and put his front paws around my neck, hugging me tightly with his head pressed up against me.

Exactly like a child wanting comfort and protection from the big bad world.

The next morning he was back to normal, and making up for a couple of hungry days. He didn't need to travel far to find food. Termites, toads, tortoises and terrapins – each one required a different technique, which Badger had mastered all on his own. He even found a way to get his claws into the rock-solid balls rolled by the industrious dung beetle, which they bury as sustenance for the growing larvae inside.

Khanye had always maintained that when Badger arrived on Stone Hills, the snakes fled in terror. We used to laugh about it, but the fact was that most snakes he tackled had one thought in mind – to get as far away from him in the shortest possible time. Take, for example, the very large spitting cobra he dug up from under an acacia bush: it slithered off rapidly towards a thicket, head up and hood extended, with Badger in cautious pursuit. As it began climbing into the low branches of a bush, he stretched up to sniff at its tail. This was an insult the snake couldn't ignore – twice it lunged at him, but it seemed to be unwilling to make contact or even to spit, which would have been its normal defensive reaction. Badger tried to climb after it, but the bush couldn't hold his weight and down he fell with a resounding thump. Meanwhile, the cobra slid into a tree and headed for the very top ('If it had wings, it couldn't have got any higher,' said Rich) where Badger couldn't possibly follow – its fear, apparently, matched only by our cub's nonchalance.

'Press on regardless' – that was my father's motto, and it was one that suited Badge's attitude perfectly. When I arrived at the hospital, Dad was already talking about what we would do when he came home. It had happened time and again over the past couple of years. His body would start to fail him but then, once again, his will would triumph. He was tough. Born in 1915, he was, like his own father, a professional soldier: the sort of Englishman who formed the backbone of a proud country. His craft was one of the first to land on Gold Beach in Normandy on D-Day, the 6th of June 1944. Having run the gamut of the German guns and making it safely to the wall on the other side, he went back to the sea under heavy fire to rescue his comrades, receiving a bullet through his helmet, both sleeves and both trouser legs. On the 13th of June, Dad was in a wood, hunkered down alone in a shallow depression at extremely close range to the enemy, with flamethrowers falling all around him. The only way of inflicting maximum damage was to give his own exact position to the guns lined up behind him, and this he did, knowing full well that he couldn't possibly get out of it alive.

But he survived, and for that act of suicidal bravery, he was awarded the Military Cross.

Only a few years before he died, I found a small leather-bound notebook, its pages damaged by water. I recognised Dad's neat columns of figures, faded as they were, and took it to him.

'Good Lord,' he said, carefully separating the pages with a great smile on his face. 'I'd forgotten all about that. When we were waiting in the boats for the order to land, we played endless games of poker, and I was keeping the score. I won a lot of money, but it didn't do me much good. Every other player was killed on the beach the next day.'

When he began to slip away, the nurses moved him into a private room. I was holding his hand in those last moments, believing him to be in a coma, when suddenly his blue eyes opened and he looked straight into mine.

'It's okay, Dad.' I told him. 'You don't need to hold on any longer, it's time to go.'

He died a few minutes later, but somehow I was certain that his spirit had already left him. What a privilege it was to have been with him on that final journey.

I have never felt comfortable with a supposedly merciful god who one day helps you find your car keys, and the next wipes out your whole family in an earthquake. Africans believe that the spirit of the deceased family member lives on, not as some ephemeral visitor but as a real presence in the home, protecting and advising as he did in life. I found that thought immensely comforting, so I had some of Dad's ashes transferred into a little urn that I could keep on my bedside table at home.

Some years before we had scattered Rich's mother's ashes on the top of Dibe Hill.

'She'll keep the wovvets away,' Mafira had predicted. Now we'd have two strong spirits looking out for us.

When I called Rich a few days later, I timed it so that I'd catch him on his way out with Badge in the early morning. Sure enough, he was already at the back door laden with cameras. He put them down and ran to the mobile telephone under the aerial by the window, and to his great surprise, there was Badge whining on the other side of the glass, with his head through the grass fence and his paws on the ledge.

'Guess who's here,' said Rich.

'Badge!'

'Of course. And I think he wants a word with you.'

And with that, Rich opened the window and put the phone to Badge's ear.

'Hello, Badgie, my darling,' I said.

I couldn't understand his reply, but I guess it was equally as loving, for he started crooning at me – making a low, throaty noise that we had never heard before. And when we had finished our conversation, he jumped down off the ledge, and joined Rich and Khanye for his walk. Prior to that, he had never been up on the window ledge. And what made it all the more amazing, was that he was there, waiting and whining, even *before* the phone rang. Coincidence? We don't think so.

So despite all his adventures, I had not been forgotten. And I was interested to learn from the Beggs that it's the sassy female cubs who leave home for good when they are between one and two years old, perhaps because they are at that time already sexually mature. The boys on the other hand (little wimps), tend to stick closer to Mum for a few months after independence. One little chap missed his mother so much after a couple of months on his own that he rejoined her, and stayed around till he was over two years old.

313

Meanwhile, Badger was still making the headlines, as Khanye liked to put it. He was trotting home in front of the vehicle one night, having spent another day at Marshlands, when he suddenly veered off into the grass. By the time Rich and Khanye found him, he had already dug up a beehive from the side of a small termite mound and was feasting on a large comb full of larvae. He was fluffed up to double his normal size, a ploy to keep the angry bees away from his skin. And he wasn't wasting any time: the aim is to get in, tuck in and get out as quickly as possible. Badgers can take a great deal of punishment, but even they have their limits. In some cases where badgers have become trapped in a hive, they have been found stung to death.

Having demolished the combs full of larvae, Badge dug into another part of the termitaria, and finally found one dripping with honey. He carried it about a metre away from the hive and settled down to eat. By this time, the bees were swarming towards the video light, but when Rich used the small beam of his head torch he was able to get in close to Badger and continue filming quite comfortably. Whenever bees flew into the light, he switched it off and they buzzed aimlessly away.

Badge had an easy time of it: bees are almost blind at night, so he escaped with very few stings. Most of them were concentrated on his back, which gives credence to Rich's theory that the bees are attracted to the white fur, which happens to cover the thickest and almost impenetrable part of the badger's skin.

Despite frequently muscling in on leopard kills, Badge had up to then never actually met one – as far as we knew. That changed on the morning that Khanye and Badge visited Skeleton Koppie, where, years before, the scouts had found human bones and a skull buried in a rocky crevice. Badge trotted off to the left, and Khanye went right, intending to meet up with him on the other side. And at the moment Badger came into view, so did an enormous leopard. Khanye stood absolutely still as it passed by, no more than 10 metres away. But then, sensing something, it looked back, saw him and raced into the koppie, jumping straight over the rock under which our clever little Badger was hiding.

Now that he had conquered his fear of travelling in the Hilux, he turned his attention to the Toyota pick-up, the vehicle that he had so desperately tried to break into when David hid there after the cobra incident. He wouldn't come home from Marshlands again one night, so Rich tried to lift him into the back. But that wasn't interesting enough for Badger, and he debussed soon after the vehicle started. No, he wanted to be in the front, with all that lovely plastic just begging to be ripped apart. Rich opened the door and he climbed in, slowly and suspiciously, stretching himself so that his body was inside the cab, but a leg still sticking out of the window. Eventually, Rich managed to shut it, and Badge travelled home on the back of the seats, taking turns to drape himself over Rich and Khanye's shoulders.

Although he still loved and trusted us, his relationship with his family was changing, as Rich wrote:

I wanted to get photographs of him, so I followed him to his play area, where he had once hidden my shoe. Initially, it was fine but then he quickly became rough, more so than he has ever been with me. He was telling me that this was his domain, and that it really was time that we distance ourselves.

I'm convinced that the second phase of his development is now kicking in. His mother is far away; he has no reinforcement of her presence from smells that would be around when he comes back at night. He's trying to relocate and establish himself, but we keep getting in the way by bringing him home.

Then a few days later, things changed again:

Badger's attitude and affection are about back to normal, as they were before his departure for Marshlands, where he picks up skin infections, fleas, smelly breath and bad behaviour. What else can one expect from that part of town?

Khanye arrived before me for the evening walk at Three Badger Hill, where Badger had holed up for the day, but then the most intense electric storm I can remember blew in from the south-west, bringing with it a short heavy shower.

We couldn't find Badge, but Khanye picked up a faint signal coming from the direction of home. We drove back and there he was sitting in the garage, very wet and cold. I got hold of a towel and called him. He jumped into my lap and sat still, quite happy that I should dry him off, and even when he was smothered completely in the towel, he behaved as if this was something that happened every day. He probably realised, intelligent animal that he is, that his hunting would be curtailed because of the storm and that a big meal and dry bed awaited him at home. I'd also like to think that because he had not seen me at the start of the walk, he came all the way back to catch up with me (wishful thinking, I know) ...

The next day, Rich took Badge one of my shirts to see how

he would react:

He vocalised and became very excited and wanted it immediately. I hope this will remind him that his mother has not abandoned him completely.

Meanwhile, I was getting ready to come home, and coincidentally Rich had to make an unexpected trip to Johannesburg. We decided that we would meet up the night I landed, then I'd fly home the following morning, and Rich would drive back a few days later.

He went walking with Badge the morning before he left:

At 8am Badger went to ground in a cave with a passage right through it. The light shining from the other side made a good photo, as he lay on his back and fiddled with a stick. He then came out to play with it and be close to me. He had decided to spend the day there, but he still wanted to delay my departure. I had to go into Bulawayo for the rest of the day and got back too late for the evening walk. But I waited for him to come home with Khanye, and we played before he went to bed.

I left the following day with a very heavy heart.

Chapter Twenty-Eight – Beyond The Wild Wood

Only one thing could ever deflect Badger from a hunt: the smell of another badger, particularly if it was close to home. We were watching him one evening strutting fluffily along the road, tail high and nose pressed to the ground on the spoor of an intruder.

'Uh-oh,' said Khanye. 'Someone has been here without a permit.'

That's how we all were with Badger; he didn't have to speak to make it absolutely clear what he was thinking, and we couldn't help but put words in his mouth.

When he killed his second leguaan, way down in the Pundamuka hills, late at night, Khanye tried to bring him home, but Badge was loathe to leave. Finally, he decided on a compromise. He escorted Khanye halfway back, and then with a look that said, quite clearly, 'Okay, you can bugger off now,' he turned around and headed straight back to his meal.

The other scouts used to ask Khanye if he felt lonely when he walked with Badger.

'Never!' he said. 'Because he always makes me laugh.'

Between the three of us, we followed Badger for around 3 500 hours – through icy winter nights, sweltering days and wild electric storms. As soon as he'd been old enough to go walking, we realised that we would need one of the staff to step in on the occasions that we could not accompany him. Khanye was the only volunteer, and he approached his new project with a mixture of curiosity and outright terror. In African lore, he told us, it's far more dangerous to meet a honey badger in the bush than a leopard, or even a lion.

It took him a good few months to feel comfortable with his charge, but by then, like the rest of us, he was hooked. He was even proud of the war wounds on his arms inflicted by Badger at play, though I noticed that when his fingers were in Badge's mouth he always grasped the loose skin at the back of Badge's neck – just in case.

His painful discovery that he was allergic to bee stings would have made anybody else quit the job immediately. Not Khanye. His only concession to the risk of anaphylactic shock was the packet of antihistamines he carried his pocket, which fortunately he never had to use.

What made his devotion to Badger even more interesting was that up to then he had never had a close relationship with any animal, even a dog. His father was employed at Hwange National Park, as Khanye himself was after school, and the keeping of domestic stock in any National Park was not permitted.

Like any gifted naturalist, he is fully in tune with every one of his five senses, alert to all those small clues that point to the bigger picture. He found some scattered remnants of the farm workers' lunch by the river one evening along with fresh badger tracks.

'Mm,' I said, 'sadza with mouse relish – Badger's best.'

'Oh yes,' he replied. 'And it's wild sadza, always nicer if you hunt it yourself.'

We couldn't always find Badge with the receiver – he could be down a hole or behind a rock, and there would be no signal. But more often than not, Khanye would be able to second-guess him.

'Let's try at the phone shop,' he'd say, a little clearing amongst the Lost Watch Hills much favoured by networking badgers. And sure enough, there he would be, sniffing around, growling and pasting his own newsletter on the ground in so much detail that he must have rubbed his bottom raw.

To Badger – David, Nigel and Khanye were all his knockabout mates; to be treated as equals, with affection, but not a great deal of respect. So, when Rich took off to South Africa, and Mother was safely out of the way, it was time to cut loose and go in search of the nearest party.

First stop was a beehive at Dunu, already plundered by two other badgers. Badge ate a comb that they had left, then tracked them onto Good Luck, Julius Rosenfels' farm on our southern boundary, where he spent the day – for the first time. That evening Khanye found him back on Stone Hills, still tracking the other badgers, and he followed, sometimes walking, sometimes at a run, till Badge eventually caught up with what looked like a mother and her male cub, just slightly larger than Badge, at the foot of one of the Boboza Hills. All three were rattling and growling at each other, but by then it was too dark to film. When they saw Khanye, the two strangers ran up the hill with Badger after them. Then, a few minutes later, down he came again, straight for the protection of Khanye's legs, with the male in furious pursuit.

'The female didn't join in,' said Khanye. 'And I heard her making some strange noises. I think she was telling her son to please leave that young man alone.'

Up and down they went, three times, till Badge gave up and trotted off, still issuing threats and rattling horribly. Despite all the commotion, he had no injuries, so it looked as though the two badgers hadn't made contact.

Three days later, Khanye followed his signal to Marshlands, once again close to the hunting camp, around 8 kilometres from home.

The signal was strong, but kept changing direction, he wrote. I climbed up a little hill and saw him chasing a beautiful female badger, very white on the back.

At first I thought I should get him away, but then I saw that they were playing. Their mouths were open, and they were laughing, running around after each other. The female was somersaulting and Badger was nipping her feet, just as he used to do with Nandi. So I stood in one place and watched them for about an hour, till she came to within a couple of metres, saw me for the first time, and began growling. A bit worrying! She ran away and climbed up another hill. I tried to call Badge but he went after her.

The next day, Badger had moved further north, onto Sandown Farm, and Khanye located his hole.

When I arrived back there in the afternoon, he was in the Honeymoon Room and I could hear that the female was with him. He came out briefly to take some meat, but he was walking as though his ribs were sore, and there was a bite on the side of his face.

Tactfully, Khanye left them to it.

The pair had moved to another hole by the following morning. Khanye found them at around 9am, and left them for the day, confident that they would stay put till that evening. By then, Badger was hungry. He followed Khanye to the vehicle, but slowly, and the wound on his face was bigger, having most likely been inflicted by another competing male. After a large meal, he went back to his lady.

27th of November:
I departed for Sandown early, arriving well before 6.30am. I climbed a few hills until I got a strong signal, and then ran to meet a happy Badger ...

At 6.30am, Rich and I were just getting out of bed at a friend's house in Johannesburg. I'd arrived late the previous evening, and had slept only a little. My plane to Bulawayo was due to leave at 11.30am.

We were having breakfast when Rich's mobile phone rang. He listened for a few seconds.

'Oh God,' he said. And then: 'Where? How bad is it?'

I grabbed hold of his arm. 'Badger?' As if I didn't already know. He nodded.

322

Rupert was calling from Bulawayo. Khanye had phoned to tell him that Badge had been severely mauled – exactly what we had always feared would happen. We stared at each other wordlessly across the table. Khanye wasn't prone to exaggeration: Badger would need help and quickly, but it was going to be hours before I reached home. Rich had already asked Rupert to pick me up at the airport; now he agreed to stay on with me to assist.

I was at the check-in desk early, but there was no one in attendance, only a sign reading: Flight SA8111 to Bulawayo delayed until 1.30pm. I pushed my trolley to a row of seats by the window and sat there, staring at the blur of cars and people passing by, but seeing nothing.

Two more hours. That meant that I would arrive in Bulawayo at 2.30pm, another half an hour to clear customs, and a one and a half hour journey home. We would pass Sandown Farm on our way, but we couldn't drive in straight to Badger. We'd have to go home first to collect up the veterinary stuff, tarpaulins, blankets, water – anything that might help. At the earliest, we'd be with Badger at around 6.30pm: 12 hours after Khanye had found him, and perhaps many hours since he'd been attacked.

By the time the flight was called, I had convinced myself that he was going to be okay. The Beggs' research in the Kalahari had suggested that adult males were generally tolerant of young males and that truly aggressive encounters were rare. And anyway, badgers were bombproof, weren't they? With their loose skins and bones of steel, how could anything really hurt him? Whatever his wounds were, we would nurse him until he recovered.

I managed to keep that shaky optimism alive until we reached the Sandown turnoff, close enough to contact Khanye by radio.

'It's serious,' he confirmed. 'You must get here quickly.'

From then on, everything seemed to move in slow motion – my mind raced ahead, but my legs felt as though they were made of lead. Even when we drove through the Sandown gate at dusk, the track seemed to twist and turn forever until the moment that Rupert stopped the car at the top of a rocky slope, and I saw Khanye in his khaki overalls, maybe a hundred metres away, his arm raised.

I flew out of the car and down the hill, empty-handed, leaving Rupert to bring everything with him. Badger was on his feet, slowly lurching toward me. His body was horribly swollen, his paws so torn that he could hardly walk.

I sat in front of him with my arms outstretched. 'Come, Badgie, my darling. Come, my boy. I'm here now,' and somehow he managed to crawl into my lap, crying as he had never cried before.

Khanye and I tried to roll him gently onto a tarpaulin; my hand was close to his mouth, and in an instantaneous reaction to pain, he bit into my index finger: the first real (and totally unintended) bite he had ever given me. Then Rupert came in from behind and injected a tranquilliser into his back leg. Badger did not react, and seven minutes later he was deeply asleep. We carried him to the vehicle, drove back to town and woke the vet up. She injected him with an antibiotic and put vaseline into his wounds that were by then infested with fly eggs and maggots.

When we got him home, back to his own room, Rupert and I knelt by him for hours, wiping the wounds clean with cotton buds and antiseptic. Although he was still comatose, every time we moved him he growled and snapped in pain. We tried to keep him warm, but when I took his temperature, the indicator didn't move. All body heat was gone.

Rupert went to bed at 2am, and I switched off the light and lay next to Badge. He was still comatose, breathing noisily but steadily. Then his breathing changed – it became shallower and harsher, with long gaps between each breath, just as Dad's had done in his last few moments of life. And at 3am it stopped, and Badger lay still.

It was the 28th of November 2006 – our 19th wedding anniversary.

Rich was already in Durban, seeing his producer about the film on Badger's life.

There was nothing to say. We cried together, and held onto the phone for an hour, often in complete silence, as if by staying connected, we could somehow stop Badger from leaving us.

I don't want to labour this tragedy, but Khanye had stayed by his side all day, and his story needs to be told:

I found him under a bush lying on his side. I called him and he only raised his head, looked at me, and dropped it again. He called back to tell me his agony, a low crying. I tried to take him to the car, but he couldn't move. Other badgers had attacked him badly: he had terrible wounds to his face and his feet; two claws were missing. I had to stay and watch him in pain for the whole day, but his cries would make me sometimes go somewhere else, so as not to feel guilty because I could not help him. I gave him water and poured it on his side and his face to cool him, and he was happy about that. But nothing could stop the flies. He kept moving slowly from bush to bush to try and get away from them, and I would move with him, using a tarp to shade his body.

I watched the sun go down forever on my friend, who in the good old days would run around, full of hope, tail up and nose down. I despaired because in our culture, the sun goes down with trouble. Witches and evil spirits operate in darkness, and one has less chance of surviving than during the day, when they are asleep.

Half an hour before I even heard the vehicle, Badger got to his feet and began climbing the slope. He was hardly managing to walk, but he was crying because he knew that Mrs Peek was coming. When they met, his cries were even louder and more prolonged. He was injected by Rupert and taken to town to the vet. That was the last time I saw him alive.

The next morning, when I was getting prepared to see a sick Badger, Mrs Peek sent me the heartbreaking news that he was dead.

For a long time, Khanye sat next to Badger's body. His final words are more beautiful than I could ever write:

I went into the room to see his body – and there lay a teacher, a hero, a prophet, a wise animal to people like me who spent so much time with him. He showed me many things, some of which, if I tell people, they think I am a liar. But I will tell the truth, and whoever will not believe, it's up to him or her. God knows, I saw it.

Chapter Twenty-Nine –
Not The End . . .

When I draw the bedroom curtains the next morning, two majestic kudu bulls are looking over the fence at me, their great spiralled horns silhouetted against the glow of the pre-dawn sky. If they were truly wild, they would run away, but we've known these two since they were born, and they often browse on the trees around the house.

Shortly before I left for Australia, Nandi had very nearly died from a twisted gut, but now she is waiting for me at the door, stretching and yawning with a smile that goes all the way from her mouth to the tip of her tail. Our miracle dog, David calls her, still painfully thin but on the way to a full recovery.

A loud bang on the window announces the arrival of Archibald and Gwendolyn, the two yellow-billed hornbills. After knocking themselves silly a couple of times, they sit chuckling at me through the glass with their heads cocked to one side. The white-browed robin is waiting for his mealworms: I can hear his melodious whistles enticing me to the kitchen – so different from the strident calls of the Australian birds in my mother's garden.

Badger has been the focus of our lives on Stone Hills for two summers and two winters, but today the world is waking up without him.

Everywhere I look, there are little reminders: the holes in the carpet, the ragged bits of tortoise shell on the mantelpiece, and worst of all, the empty enclosure that stares back at me from outside the bedroom window.

Dad's little urn is on my desk: I'm keeping him close so we can have a chat every so often. We're going to keep him very busy in the months to come, but I didn't know that then.

Two deaths within a month of each other: they are the same in their finality, and yet so very different. Dad was a child in Dorset between the two world wars, an age of relative innocence, or so it seems today. During the summer holidays, his happiest times were spent travelling on old Tom Riley's horse-drawn cart, delivering parcels around the district. He fought fiercely for his country, but at heart Dad was a gentle man who above all, loved his home, his family and his dogs. When the end came, it was truly his time, and his spirit left him peacefully. But for Badge, his life had only just begun. And where had we been when he needed us so badly?

'Regrets come home in waves of pain and there is no cure,' said Rich.

If only he had delayed his trip to South Africa.

If only my plane had left on time and we had managed to get him to the vet earlier.

If only ... we might have saved him.

But the fact is that at least half of all honey badger cubs don't make it to independence. To us, being so solicitous of *all* human life, it seems like carnage – a terrible waste of the mother badger's huge investment of time, risk and energy. And yet this is how nature selects the best and the fittest for the continuation of the species. There is no other way.

Rich took Badger into our vet, Gerard Stevenage, for a post-mortem. None of his bones were broken, and his internal organs were all intact. But his skin and his nose had been torn from his skull, both his front legs bitten and totally bruised, and his chest cavity was full of blood. He had probably died from continual haemorrhaging. So it wouldn't have mattered if Rich had been there, or if my plane had been on time, and all the other if-onlys had come to pass – Badger's attacker had made sure to put him out of action forever.

We buried him under the weeping schotia tree outside our bedroom window. It will be flowering again soon, in deep red clusters dripping with the sweet nectar that is irresistible to both insects and birds. Poombi is under a Cape fig close by, planted both for her and in memory of Abel Ncube, the man who truly knew how to talk (and listen) to the animals in his care.

I was sitting on the veranda that evening, watching the wildebeest come down to drink, when one of the barn owls Rich had recently released flew up onto a wooden crossbeam under the thatch, and sat there preening, quite at ease. Another owl called in the distance and it responded with a soft wavering screech, then flew off silently into the gathering

329

dusk. It struck me anew how little we know of other lives besides our own. We see a wildebeest, an owl, a honey badger; we note it and we move on, our curiosity satisfied – and yet each creature is its own complete story: the passage of its life marked by childhood, adolescence, maturity and death, just as ours are, and accompanied by all the same emotions. Only those who have completely distanced themselves from the rest of the animal kingdom can truly believe that fear, affection, jealousy and sorrow are confined to our species alone.

To us, Badger was the teenager on the powerful motorbike, certain of his own invincibility. And like a teenager, he did things his way and in his time, no matter how much we tried to change his mind.

When he first came to us, no one knew if a honey badger cub could become independent without his mother's tuition. And given the length of time he stays with her and the strength of their bond, it seemed unlikely. But even in those early months, I had a dream for him: that one day we'd see him as an adult running alone through the grass towards the house, on his way to pay us a visit. It was a vision that seemed almost impossible for our sickly, traumatised cub.

Well, the dream came to fruition, although far too briefly. Badger reached independence, and apart from relying on us for protection and support, which of course was essential, he did it all on his own. What an incredible achievement.

Our home was a safe and a comfortable refuge, but at a mere six months old, Badge began taking himself off into the bush and finding his own place to hole up for the day. With no one to show him the ropes, he learned how to climb trees (and fall out of them); how to stun lizards with rocks; how to catch mice hiding in a warren of holes, and nip the tails off scorpions. This was impressive enough. But spitting cobras and African beehives are a challenge even for an experienced badger. The Beggs once saw a mother killing a puff adder with her cub close by. When he tried to approach, she growled a warning and sent him scuttling away. How could our cub learn to deal with such dangerous prey without his mother's guidance?

But learn he did, and even though some of Badge's techniques were rather novel, like his habit of grabbing the snake's tail first instead of its head, as wild badgers do – they worked.

We knew from the experience with Khanye that he had learned that leopards were to be avoided. And he always kept well away from humans that he didn't know and trust.

Perhaps without his mother, the lessons were harder and there was further to fall, but he got there, right on time, driven by willpower, determination and formidable intelligence. Of course, he was programmed to be a badger, and impelled by instinct, just as we are as human beings if only we would acknowledge it. He knew what he had to do, but he had to get there all on his own.

The joy for us was that we could be part of that process, not as active participants, but as onlookers and protectors. And what's more, Badger wanted us there in that role; he welcomed us into his life and gave us his trust and love.

Even if he had been raised in the wild, the odds would have been heavily against him. Out of the 15 cubs the Beggs studied in the Kalahari, three out of five males died before they reached maturity, though none of them through violent interactions with adult males.

There's no doubt that Badger's lack of experience with others of his kind was a serious disadvantage. But, having said that, we didn't know what he got up to during his days and nights alone. He certainly couldn't have avoided meeting other badgers, especially on his frequent excursions into Marshlands. From the injuries to his face that Khanye noticed when Badge was down the hole with the female, it looked as though he had annoyed someone, but not seriously enough to warrant a proper beating. Real aggression between males is rare, but it happens, particularly when there is competition over a female in season. Maybe, at the end, Badger just picked the wrong guy to tangle with, and it cost him his life.

We received letters of sympathy from all over the world – from people who had never met Badger but had fallen in love with him anyway. And then there was the one from Colleen and Keith Begg, the only people who have ever studied honey badgers in depth. It was a message that continues to give us both comfort and hope.

'What can I say,' wrote Colleen, 'except bugger the science – he was part of your family and ours and I just cried on receiving your email. We shed so many tears for wild badgers we knew in the Kalahari (despite it not being 'allowed') and Badge was even more special than them. Everything must seem so empty without him to structure your day and make you laugh. Why can't they ever die of old age?! I guess it's just not part of their make up – better to burn up than to fade away.

'Just remember, though, that the subordinate males often end up fathering a cub because of early sneak matings (50 per cent of the time), so there is a good chance that Badge might have got his genes in there somewhere. And at least he had a chance to mate. In fact, he managed to have all the experiences that a badger should have in his life … thanks to you.'

So there it was. Badge was with a female in the Honeymoon Room for two days. From his early injuries, it looked as though he had encountered opposition, but there was every chance that he had hung on long enough to have fathered her cub. Just imagine that.

We had known from the start that Badger would be lucky to make it to maturity, but even with hindsight, we wouldn't have done it any differently. His mother had been killed by a hunter when he was six weeks old. If we had not taken him in, the safari operator had decided to hand him over to the local zoo, where no doubt he would still be alive today. Alive, alone and in a cage, he might have lived for 30 years – never to have climbed a tree, dug up a mouse, chased a cobra or met a lady. A badger's home range is huge – in the Kalahari it's around 600 to 800 square kilometers. Sometimes they'll travel around 30 kilometres in a night with that springy rolling trot, up for anything that comes their way.

All Badger's instincts were leading him out into his own world, and he might just have made it. Some do, but many don't. Burn up or fade away? We think we know which Badger would have chosen.

Epilogue ... But Another Beginning

At 6am on the chilly morning of the 9th of April 2010, a passing motorist on the road to Ventersdorp, South Africa, stopped to look at the carcass of a honey badger lying in the road. It was a female, and she had been hit by a vehicle sometime during the previous night.

The motorist was about to get back in his car, when he heard a slight sound in the grass. There he found a tiny cub, hungry and almost frozen. He bundled him up in his jacket, turned up the heating, and drove as fast as he could to FreeMe – a rehabilitation and release centre for indigenous wildlife in the Rietfontein Nature Reserve in the northern suburbs of Johannesburg.

He handed the cub over to Jean and Frances, a couple of volunteers, who immediately warmed and hydrated the badly traumatised cub. Later that day, he was examined by a local vet, who confirmed that apart from a few abrasions, he was uninjured.

Manager Nicci Wright, who has been working at the centre for the past 12 years, took him over, and for three months she cuddled, comforted, fed and played with the growing cub. Someone lent her our book *Wild Honey*, the story of Badger's first year, and she wrote to us: 'I may possibly have been the only person on the planet reading the book with a baby honey badger sucking my fingertip!'

The cub thrived under her expert care, and Nicci began taking him for walks twice a day, exactly as we had done with our little Badge – slowly introducing him to the natural world.

'He began to invite play with a backwards bouncing movement, while huffing through an open mouth, almost laughing,' she reported. Just the same.

FreeMe runs only on donations, but manages to treat around a staggering 10 000 orphaned, abandoned or injured animals every year, ranging from a baby shrew to an adult eland bull. Nicci talks about oil spills, collapse of bird roosts, poisonings, and other disasters: wherever animals need to be rescued, FreeMe is on the front line. Their aim is to release every creature in their care back into its natural habitat, often wildlife reserves and conservancies. But Nicci despaired at trying to find somewhere suitable for her vulnerable little badger, whose home range would extend over many hundreds of square kilometers. Not only that, but he would need to be in the care of knowledgeable and compassionate people for as long as it took for him to become independent. It seemed an impossible task.

Then, a miracle. Through her network of contacts, she was put in touch with Gus van Dyk, Director of Conservation at Tswalu, South Africa's largest privately owned game reserve in the Kalahari region. Gus didn't hesitate: he offered Tswalu as a release site with as much support and monitoring as would be required.

'On June the fifth,' wrote Nicci, 'Dylan Smith, Wildlife Projects Manager, picked us up and we drove to the Kalahari. The cub was an excellent passenger, sleeping and eating most of the way, and at times sucking on my finger. The next morning, he awoke calling me, and we went for our first walk on the red sands that were to be his home. Seeing him in this habitat luxuriating in the soft sand and digging until he was exhausted, was an incredible joy and relief. Dylan responded so well to Badger and intuitively understood how to interact with him.

'He was so relaxed with both Dylan and his partner Theresa, that the handing over process went remarkably smoothly and much quicker than I'd anticipated. I flew home feeling empty but absolutely content that the cub had found the right place with exactly the right people. They've called him Badger.

'At the time of writing, he continues to thrive, walking into the desert three or four times a day with Theresa and Dylan. They hide natural food items for him, and he finds some of his own too with his incredible olfactory powers. He's begun learning to climb the gnarled desert trees and to explore the (hopefully!) disused burrows he comes across.

'His weight is now 5 kilograms and his appetite voracious

and varied. The daily walks are introducing him to what will be his home range in ever widening circles from Dylan's house. Hopefully, he will know where home is if he needs support in the future.

'For now though, Badger is about five months old and the long, slow release process which will unfold naturally could take up to 18 months to two years, the time when sub-adult badgers leave their mothers in the wild.

'I am planning to visit Badger soon and observe how well he's growing into his new home. I can't wait ...'

Acknowledgements

In a sense, I'd like to have called this 'the last book in the Stone Hills trilogy', because trilogy is a nice word, and I have a rather pleasing picture of the three books displayed together in a neat little box – ideal for Christmas and birthdays, and all that.

But it's not going to happen, because as long we are here (and even if we are not), Stone Hills has many more stories to tell. This little corner of Africa weaves a powerful kind of magic over all those who visit, or simply read about it, judging from the many messages of interest and concern we receive from people all over the world. Somehow, these ageless hills seem to be at the centre of the earth as it ought to be – wild and yet comforting: a place where, at last, you feel you belong.

Stone Hills would not be what it is today without the contribution of so many people, and though we cannot name them all – we know, and we thank you.

The energy and commitment of our staff, particularly game scouts Mafira Chanyungyna, Jabulani Khanye and Richard Mabhena, never flags, and we are ever grateful for their optimism and unquenchable good humour.

The indomitable Mrs Danai Dube, headmistress of Marula Junior School, helps us to put the conservation message across to the children, and rallies staff and pupils alike with her strength and leadership.

My oldest friend, Hennie Walton, with her partner Pete Evans, somehow finds the time to organise gymkhanas, talk to schools and colleges, and badger friends and family in the UK to raise money for the children at Marula. No wonder she is loved by everyone.

Pierre de Jaager taught the children and local people to farm in harmony with nature – lessons that we hope will stay with them for the rest of their lives. And Bert Bouwer gave generously of his time and expertise to enable the school to develop its vegetable garden.

We are grateful to all those who contributed to this book:

First, a message from Slug to Worm, with love. Keep walking, we're not over the hill yet.

Barbie Murray, for her unshakeable friendship. Stone Hills is waiting.

The Rosenfels family – especially Rosa York for her beautiful account of life in the early days, and to Ernest and Julius.

Brian Jones from Moholoholo Wildlife Rehabilitation Centre and Fraser Henderson for their fascinating and hilarious accounts and photographs of the inimitable Stoffel.

Theresa and Gary Warth, Janine and James Varden and Lisa Hywood, for the story of Kimba and their tireless work for Zimbabwe's wild animals.

Steve and Anna Tolan for their inspiration and the mirror trick.

Thomas Bulpin and family for T V Bulpin's story of *Shidzidzi* and the elephant from *The Ivory Trail*.

The Marillier family, Father Noel Scott, and the Stakesby-Lewises – who shared their experiences as jailbirds.

The Goodwin family, for their courage and friendship.

The girls from Werribee Zoo, Melbourne, Rachel Lowry and Katie Pahlow, who lit a fire under teachers and pupils alike and inspired them to learn about wildlife.

Tikki Hywood Trust's Kusanganisa education project for its support and assistance at the school.

Maureen Harrison and her friendly ghosts.

Jonathan Scott, for his encouragement, generosity and instinctive empathy with our love of the land and its wildlife.

Wayne Grant – who freely admits that he was 100 per cent wrong when he called badgers 'foul-tempered things', having been converted by some very close encounters with them in the wild.

Rodney (Nimrod Smith), snake catcher and champion buffalo jockey, whose exploits always seem to find a way into our books (although our accounts tend to differ widely).

Richard and Marion Trotter, for the facts on Winchester House and for those unforgettable dinners.

Moira Fitzpatrick, who gave us information on the *Parabuthid* scorpions.

Kerry and Iain Kay, for their story of extraordinary courage.

Don Parry, who made the remarks about the habits of the alpha male and has appeared (anonymously) in our other books.

Dr Don Broadley, for his inexhaustible knowledge, and his identification of frogs who say 'Ow!'

The Penguin (SA) team and editor Jane Bowman, for their enthusiasm and expertise.

Thanks to Nicci Wright of FreeMe in Johannesburg, we managed to end this book on a positive note. Her orphaned baby badger is now in the care of Dylan and Theresa Smith of Tswalu Game Reserve in the Kalahari and from what we hear, is making great progress in returning to the wild world where all badgers ought to be.

Our eternal gratitude to Badger's friends: Mike Bromwich – his rescuer; Dave and Marina Jackson, who loved him so dearly and laughed and cried with us; Jabulani Khanye – Badger's friend, playmate, biographer and ultimately the one who saw him through his last, heartbreaking adventure; and Keith and Colleen Begg, who taught us so much about badgers, shared their insights, and gave us their friendship and support.

A special tribute from Rich: In memory of my mother, Pat, who first introduced me to photography and encouraged me in all my interests; and my father, Dick, who passed on to me his great respect and understanding of wildlife and the environment, and his love of books.

And lastly, to our Badger and all the wild animals of Stone Hills – who have shared their secrets, accepted us into their lives and in many cases, given us their love and trust.

There could be no greater gift.

Stone Hills

References

BBC Worldwide Ltd. *The Nation's Favourite Poems*, London, BBC Worldwide Ltd, 1999

Books of Zimbabwe, Bulawayo, Rhodesiana Reprint Library and African Hunting Reprint Series

Bristow, A. *The Sex Life of Plants*, USA, Reference International Publishers, 1978

Bulpin, T V. *To the Banks of the Zambezi*, Johannesburg, Thomas Nelson and Sons, 1965

Bulpin, T V. *The Ivory Trail*, South Africa, Books of Africa, 1967

Burchell, W J. *Travels in the Interior of Southern Africa*, London, Longman, Hurst and Co., 1822

Cattrick, A. *Spoor of Blood*, Cape Town, Howard Timmins, 1959

Gouldsbury, C. *Rhodesian Rhymes (volume 6)*, Rhodesia, Rhodesiana Reprint Library, 1969

Grahame, K. *The Wind in the Willows Collection*, London, Grandreams Ltd, 1991

Grant, W M. *Into the Thorns*, Zimbabwe, African Hunter, 2007

Kingdon, J. *The Kingdon Field Guide to African Mammals*, San Diego, Academic Press, 1997

Leopold, A. *A Sand County Almanac*, New York, Oxford University Press, 1949

Linden, E. *The Octopus and the Orangutan*, New York, Penguin Books, 2002

McLynn, F. *Hearts of Darkness*, London, Pimlico, 1992

Rosenfels, L. 'They Lived a Full Life at Marula' in *Down Memory Lane with Some Early Rhodesian Women 1897-1923*, Harare, Books of Zimbabwe, 1979

Selous, F C. *A Hunter's Wanderings in Africa*, London, Richard Bentley & Son, 1881

Selous, F C. *Sunshine and Storm in Rhodesia*, Bulawayo, Books of Rhodesia, 1968

Taylor, S. *The Mighty Nimrod*, London, Collins, 1989